THE BEST OF
2.13.61
PUBLICATIONS

THE BEST OF
2.13.61
PUBLICATIONS

EDITED BY HENRY ROLLINS

2.13.61
P.O. BOX 1910 · LOS ANGELES ·
CALIFORNIA · 90078 · USA

CONTENTS

INTRODUCTION

I STARTED **2-13-61** PUBLICATIONS at some point in 1983. My aim was to put out one fold-and-staple book of my own work. I had very little money, and not much writing. I saved funds any way I could, and after awhile I had enough to put together the book. I had no typewriter so I wrote everything out long hand. I was living in the back yard of the house that Raymond Pettibon was living in, so I asked him to let me use some of his great artwork for the cover. The book was to be called *20*, as there were twenty pieces in the book.

During the process of pasting up the print master of my first ever book, which was nothing but a low rent fanzine, I was told by a friend that I had to have a company name or I wouldn't be allowed to sell the book. Seeing that this was going to be my only book, I called the "company" 2-13-61 Publications, after my birthday. It was a joke basically.

So, I folded and stapled the first print run of 500 and sold them here and there for two dollars each. Probably gave away more than I sold. I saved the money I made from the first run and made another run. During this time I started becoming ambitious about my pursuit; in other words, my young man's ego swelling enough to think that it was time for me to get real and publish a paperback of my work, seeing that I was a real deal writer and all.

I put together more of my writing and had it typeset. A woman working for the typesetter, Laura Cloud, helped with collating and binding the book. She would later help me with other books over the next few years until she cracked up in a haze of cocaine, wine and prescription anti-depressants. Anyway, this slim paperback was called *Two Thirteen Sixty One*.

Others followed: *End to End* and *Polio Flesh* which were repackaged as *High Adventures in the Great Outdoors* and then later as the first several pages of *The First Five*.

In 1990 I contacted Nick Cave's publisher in the UK and asked him if I could license Nick's lyric and prose book, *King Ink*. At the time the book was trickling in as an overpriced import, and I figured that the fans would appreciate a domestic version at a fraction of the cost. Simon over at Black Spring said yes and all of a sudden we had another artist on the label.

When I say "we," I mean to say that I hired a couple of guys to run the place; the place was now a very small office crammed with boxes of books and t-shirts. Our first computer was a Mac because they were handing out credit... we had no money but all of a sudden we had a computer and a printer. We liked how that worked.

Books by other writers followed, such as Don Bajema and Bill Shields. We moved the offices a couple more times.

One of the great things about the early stages of this company's development that some of you might remember was our info. line. The staff, which at this point consisted of Stan Fairbank, Gary I and Joe Cole, turned the info. line messages into extravaganzas of epic proportions. They would tape a local gay hotline called the Load Line and also use bites from people who had left angry messages on the office machine and fly these sound bytes into the info. line message. Several tapes survive and they are hilarious. Years have passed since then and while things are a bit more orderly around here these days, they're also a lot more efficient which is better for the long term.

One thing I think that is important to mention is the concept behind the company. It's not as if we're just throwing these books out there to see what sells. I have always hoped to turn people onto something that they have never encountered before. I am fascinated by the American voice in literature. Especially the ones who are out of the mainstream. People like Hubert Selby, Jr., Nelson Algren and John Fante. I wanted to provide an outlet for a few writers who weren't like others. I have always gravitated to people who wrote in order to deal with the situations that they found themselves in, not necessarily someone who was schooled to be a writer. A guy like Bill Shields probably never thought he was going to write and have his work published when he was in the jungles of Vietnam. He wrote to keep from killing himself. There's a vitality and a strength there that is undeniable. One thing I have learned after over a decade in the book business is that there are easier roads to take than the one we are taking, but "easy" means no books by Alan Vega or Ian Shoales— and that is unacceptable.

We put this "Best Of" together as an invitation to you to check out what we have devoted so many years to. It is my hope that the work interests you and you investigate these writers further. We are playing outside of the mainstream and taking the shots that come with that route. Financially, it's not the smartest thing to do but as far as doing the right thing, we're knocking it out of the park. We have some great projects up the road, and I hope that you will stay with us as we go.

Thank you.

Your long-suffering publisher,
Henry Rollins

HENRY
ROLLINS

SHORT PIECES

⚡

VULTURE

⚡

OF A SUMMER

⚡

MY LAST LOVE LETTER

SHORT PIECES

You
Walking alone, anywhere
Looking up at the stars and thinking
Not looking at the stars like they would
Not thinking the things they would think about
Not like any of those bastards...
Those idiots
They're not like you
Nothing like you
This fuckin' world man...
Always trying
Look at those stars
The poets will write it to pieces
Like it was some fucking dream
Dehumanized and no one can tell you a damn thing
Sidewalk under your feet
Looking at the stars
Thinking your thoughts
Fuck what any one of them think
They fill you with so much wasted time
You're cool
And the stars are all yours

∗ ∗ ∗

Funny thing about charisma
Ha ha

~ ~ ~

She's beautiful
She never judges me
She understands me completely
She heals my wounds
I could look into her eyes for days
I think of her
Every time
I fuck you

~ ~ ~

The guy yells
MTV!
Yo, MTV!
I seen you man!
I sit up on my hind legs and say thank you

~ ~ ~

Staring at forever through the cigarette smoke
The young black man walked onto the bandstand
Rarely took his eyes off the ground
Inhaled the rank air
And exhaled
The shack he was raised in
The threats and the fear
The taunts and the slurs
Through their heads and into the street
Blew a beautiful new animal through the bell of a horn
Defined and re-invented itself with every turn

No one got it but the young man
His eyes burning hot into the unpolished wood
Be Bop

Open your arms to hold me
Open your eyes to see me
Open your mouth to kiss me
Open
Open everything
You come over here
I'll go over there
We'll run around
We'll braid our secrets
We'll always know
We'll never tell

VULTURE

WHEN I WAS VERY YOUNG, my mother took me to Jamaica. We stayed in a small fishing village with a family my mother knew. We slept in a spare bedroom. We stayed there for a few weeks and I made friends with the boys in the neighborhood who were very nice to me.

One day me and the boys went down towards the bay to throw rocks at lizards and to look for dead blowfish that had washed up overnight. On the way there we saw a small dog walking crookedly like it had been hit by a car or was overcome by the heat. I remember looking up and seeing vultures circling the dog.

A while later we were returning with a few dead lizards that we were going to put in the backyard by an ant hill to watch the ants reduce the lizards to skeletons. The dog was not very far from where we had seen him the first time. The dog had been gutted and cleaned out. I remember seeing the dog's windpipe sticking out of its neck. The eyes were gone.

Years later I would daydream about vultures. I am walking alone across an arid, desolate stretch of nowhere. I see vultures big as I am circling over me. I slow down my pace and act like I am disoriented and diminished. The vultures swoop closer and eventually two of them land and boldly walk next to me, their eyes are level with mine. At this point I run at one and grab it by its neck and smash its skull with my fist and stomp its ribcage until it dies in front of the other one. I am able to catch the second vulture by its wing as it tries to take off and I kill it too. It screeches loudly, infuriated that I am bringing it to Death's embrace while the others watch, stunned, from above.

I always have hated vultures, hyenas and the small fish that swim underneath the bellies of sharks. I hate them because I deal with them in human form all the time. I live in an environment where either you command respect, fear, or a mix of the two—or you don't exist. When you slip, the vultures circle and close in. They like to detail the downward spiral of the fallen as they rip at the eyes and fight for mouthfuls of intestines. They moralize, shake their heads and wear masks of profound knowledge. They collect their check and wait for the next one to fall. History is mutilated by these weaklings all the time.

I have felt their presence for years. Every year I deny them their due and they're getting angry at my seemingly indestructible constitution.

When I was younger, I knew the day would come when they would circle and show their teeth. I knew that when that day came, I would have to be walking dead. Unstoppable. Devoid of anything to lose. The eyeless killer who crosses borders undetected. King of the frozen wasteland. Horror's favorite son. I had seen them take out others and knew that at some point they would eventually come for me, thinking I had grown weak.

I prepared for this time. Looking at it now, it seems that almost my entire life was devoted, in part, to their arrival. Now they are here in droves and I am ready. What brought them? Perhaps I have been around too long and it threatens them. Those who live vicariously are very astute, their senses are perhaps sharper than those of a predator. They lie constantly and must mask their weakness. They are masters of cowardice.

They come close out of malice. They come close out of jealousy and hatred. They come smiling and snarling. This is the moment I have been waiting for. Little do they know this is the part that I will enjoy the most.

I make sure I wear little in winter. I like to walk out into freezing weather knowing that I don't have nearly enough clothing on to keep me warm. I say out loud, "It sure is cold out," and I laugh. Within a few minutes of walking, I am freezing. Soon enough I am past that and I feel myself becoming stronger. I imagine that every day is hours spent on the Blacksmith's anvil. Every freezing inhalation is a blow of his hammer, tempering me into a harder metal. I love the feeling of my freezing skin pulling tight over my knuckles and the cracking sound it makes. I feel safe when I am wet from freezing rain. My entire being smiles when I am riding a wave of pain. I feel secure when I am actively extending my pain threshold. It is an investment towards the future.

I live in a small room with few possessions. I have no close friends, only acquaintances. People's names go in one ear and out the other. I don't fall in love. I dream of trees of iron that bend in the wind but do not break. I dream of beatings by police that make me laugh until I lose consciousness.

Come closer, I have been waiting for you. I guarantee you it's not going to go like you planned. I'll make your history books scream and puke blood. You work on your hair. I work on my guts. You worry about what people think of you and are afraid of what you really want. You fear. You live off the blood of others. You will never taste mine.

Your weakness repels me and inspires me to go on. It would be wonderful to be able to live off human flesh. It would be joyous to drag you out of a restaurant and beat you to death, clean you on a car hood and carry the choice cuts home. Your woman and I would eat your flesh. We would laugh and lick your blood off each other's mouths and then fuck.

OF A SUMMER

I WANTED A PLACE TO WRITE. I needed a place to go where I could be understood. An invisible ocean or a distant, undiscovered planet. I have stopped trying to be understood by people. I'd rather look at the moon and walk through beautiful, hot nights and hear the songs of the insects. I'd rather smell the trees and feel the furnace air surround my body. People have a way of bringing it down and painting it all in one color. This is my uninhabited desert. My sunless flaw in the earth's surface in which I can breathe without hesitation.

I am thinking about a summer night in Washington DC. I am thinking about the nights that I will walk through this summer. I have always thought that there is something in the night that I am supposed to find. I don't know what it is but I have been looking for it for almost twenty years. I think of nights in that town even when I am in cities far away.

Last summer, I was sitting on the street in Norway. I was looking at the moon while sitting on a curb. I kept thinking that this was a night on earth. In that moment, I wanted no friends, no brotherhood, no link to mankind. I wanted to walk all night through barren Norwegian countryside.

It's the plague of language that threatens to destroy me at all times. So many nights I wished to be able to stop thinking with words, with language. I wanted to think with the sound of the night, with the sound of Coltrane's horn. Better than words, better than thinking, where words collide and compete and thoughts and images fight to survive and memory strains to pull me back to times that hurt hurt hurt.

All the way here in Los Angeles, the dead city, the city buried under the silent screams of dead Indians and pollution, distant, clean summer nights call to me. Death calls to me on ink black summer nights. After I die, the summers will go on without me but they will not be the same because no one will be around to appreciate them as I have all these years. The summer nights will be lonely after I have gone.

I see white sheets, or maybe they're white sails. They are bil-
lowing silently against a pale moon. I am thinking about the way the
phone would ring at night in the place I lived in many years ago. In
the middle of the night the phone would come alive with people call-
ing and using only their first names. They would tell me their prob-
lems and I would listen. Unhappy stories. Stories about lovers who
cheated. The drugs they were trying to get away from. The pain. I
was alone in my room with nothing to my name except my rage and
my life.

In the next room, my roommate was slowly and quietly killing
herself.

I never knew the full extent of Laura's unhappiness. I do
remember that it grew and grew with each passing month. Men
would come and go and she would hurt and hurt more. She used to
drink wine alone in her room, cry and pull her gun out and lay it on
the table next to her small bed. She would take drugs and call what
friends she had left, one after the other, and tell them lies about how
great she was and of all the things she was doing. It was the same
story every call. She would do this for hours. I could hear it through
the walls of my room. She never stopped talking. I knew that she was
driving the people she called out of their minds. You could almost
hear their agony on the other end of the line. I miss her sometimes.
One of the funniest people I have ever met. She was so funny that
you knew it was hurting her. Everything was hurting her. She was
the most in pain person I have ever met.

Hot coffee at night. Walking on streets that are still cooling
from the sun's punishment. Catching a warm breeze. Wind at
night feels different than wind by day. I am lonely all the time but
I don't miss anyone. I don't know what it is that I am searching
for when I walk for hours down streets of cities at night. I go all
over the world. I need movement. It's the only time I feel like I
am living. Sitting alone in the darkness. No one in sight. No one
knowing where you are. This is the silent perfection that I dwell
in as much as possible. The sounds of the rotting city around me

and my breathing. I am lonely all the time. I am hungry all the time for the night. I am hungry all the time for the sound of music at night.

> Night with heavy feet
> Stands in front of me
> Its face, a questioning mask
> Why do you look at me so?
> Is it because you think I have betrayed you?
> Is it because you think I have left you
> For the dizzying madness of the day?
> Have you forgotten that we share the secret language?
> That we are one in our invisible truth?
> Have you not seen me wander through you?
> Staggering tragically by in search of revelation?
> Did you not see my face
> Pressed up against the hotel window
> Watching cars roar by
> After you had darkened the streets of Tokyo?
> Yes, you have seen me as you will always see me
> You will see me on hot summer streets
> You are the only home I have

I sometimes think I have messed my life up. I think about this all the time. I have doubts even though it hurts to say that it's true. I have no idea how I would have done anything differently. I think of this all the time and can't come up with anything.

It hurts me to have regrets. It hurts to have a vacancy in me that I have no idea how to fill. There have been women who I wanted but that was a long time ago and I don't think of them anymore. They were cool, I think. They all survived me just fine I imagine so there's no need to think of them anymore.

I get optimistic here in this darkened room with the music filling the air. I get to thinking that maybe this summer is going to be the summer when things change. Something will happen and I will get some answers. What's the question? What do I need to make me feel like I want to live? I hate to say that I don't feel good. I know full well that I have nothing to complain about.

How can I not feel some excitement with the summer drums beating in the distance? My hot box season on its way to me. So what of it? I will go find hot night streets to walk down and I will find them empty of what I need. I will ask the same questions over and over again. I don't mind because I am used to this riddle that never reveals its answer to me. I am used to the frustration and the emptiness. I feel at one with the dark places. I'm going to get there anyway so might as well get to where it's at in a hurry.

I can see some of the places I want to go this summer. I want to go to the streets of my youth, walk there and see if they tell me anything. I want to walk the streets of American cities and see if there's anything to be found.

I don't feel a need to love people. I want to love the night. I want to love darkness and the magic that happens on Earth when the sun is gone. I want to love music and solitude. Oceans and deserts, cities and empty streets. Patches of earth that have been left devastated by disaster. Miles of land where everything has been rendered extinct or moved on. Leave this part of the world to me. People are too painful with their beauty and their desperation.

If you're going to go your own way, don't expect anyone to come with you. If you are an artist and you do exactly what you want and not many people appreciate it, that's just the way it is when you are going for your own. If you are a warrior of the soul in the present climate, then you will always be met with mediocrity and resistance. Do you care? Why should you? Why waste your time being frustrated when you don't seem to "measure up" to the smirking cowards that line the highways? What did you expect? A parade? Open arms? Maybe you should take a step back and reevaluate yourself. Perhaps this is not the life for you. Perhaps you are not strong enough to live this way. It is only a few who can walk the line and thrive. I am not talking about casualties who are limping through it, looking like hell. I am talking about those who are filled with joy when they see obstacles and pain on the horizon.

In my mind I am a warrior. In this night I am steel wrapped in flesh and I only live to confound and out do myself. Not a great deal else interests me at this point. For me, it has all boiled down to this. I look ahead and I see just this life.

The temples have been ransacked yet people say they are beautiful. The cities have been overrun and are mere shells of what they were and people say that things are great. Cowards are in charge, they tell you to trust them as they lie and laugh. They know they have pulled yet another one over on the unsuspecting. Tobacco and alcohol companies spend millions to addict and slowly annihilate generation after generation. I am told that I am an anachronism. The last of the species. That may be. Doesn't matter. I was never one for company. One is the only number that matters. The rest is at best, momentarily amusing. Chances are, these words separate the two of us.

Years ago I sat in a hot room and I thought to myself that times are hard and hard words were in order. When I thought that, I felt alone and slightly insane that no one seemed to be as disgusted with the way things were. I didn't feel like being branded as some nut, but I said what I felt and took the shots leveled at me.

It is many years later and I am sitting in a larger room thinking these thoughts. I have changed over time and no longer feel the need to say out loud all the things that I feel. I am content to know what I know and get by as best I can and be very careful what I say to anyone anywhere.

I am filling with disgust again. My recoil reflex is back and kicking like it was all those years ago. I listen to contemporary music and see the corny "artists" collecting their prizes and I think it's all over. The corporations have things right where they want them and most of the consumers went for it. I can't say I blame them. It was packaged well and sold to them shrewdly. The dealer has sharpened his claws and mastered his craft.

I have seen a few people I know fall away from drugs or too many years of inspiration met with apathy. They finally wore themselves out beating on the stone wall they thought was the door. All they wanted was to give all and they were left to die as the fakes imitated them to the top and went into the hills laughing and shrugging their shoulders at how easy it all was.

Do I care to strike out at what I see as weak and vile? Should I care that culture is dying and we're dancing in the shadows of its fallen body? Or should I sit in this room and think these thoughts silently? Who is there to tell the story to? A slack faced youth high on the same poison they took the Indians out with? For myself, I have an understanding. I have an understanding that they won. This is what I believe to be true and fighting this down will only slowly diminish me. Years ago I would have willingly thrown my shoulder against that solid rock wall, knowing that my good will would some day surely knock the door down. Now I know better. It's all yours. So many will think they are doing what they want with their lives but they will be actually living in a constant state of compromise. They were so easily overrun.

Wind and rain. Heat and cold. Seasons that pull the paint off houses and break roads to bits. The brutal elements are the only things that tell me I am alive. Their words are wordless and hold nothing for me. Their emotions and needs are draining traps that avoid real life at all costs. They tell me that I am dysfunctional and am in need of close and meaningful relationships. I tell them that I would rather notch passing winters on my arm with a knife. I would rather lose fingers to frostbite and go insane in boiling, sleepless nights. Give me rotting jungle. Frozen wasteland. Arid desert. Weather that ravages. You are watching television and arguing about the score. I am laughing and putting black grease paint on my face. You are gaining weight and letting yourself go. I am laughing and slipping silently into the treeline. I am done with being disgusted with you. I take my orders from the cold that breaks thermometers. I listen when the furnace of summer calls. The elements. I am yours. Break me. Inject into me a new language that melts me and forges me into the new steel. Help me find the beauty that lurks in the steaming cracks of the broken spines of trails I walk night after night.

MY LAST LOVE LETTER

I am sorry that I am mean when I talk to you on the phone. That I shatter your good intentions with cruelty. I can't explain how easy it comes to me. Abuse seems to be my specialty. I like to get it as well as give it. When I get abused, all I can do is nod. It makes sense. When I say that you're a stupid piece of shit who bores me and I want to put a plastic bag over your head and bash your skull in, I mean it, but I don't mean to hurt your feelings. No, really.

I am sorry that I cannot control the things that I say, but I want to shoot myself in the mouth so much these days that anyone who comes near me gets some. When I think of you I can see no worth in my life at all. Wake up in the morning so I can be insulted by the existence of legions of men in baseball caps turned backwards. It's all too much sometimes. I know what you'll say when you hear this.

I am the dog who threw up on your rug. Hit me. I still don't know what I did wrong.

What you think is a two second trip through the mind of an insect. Remember that one? That's what I said to you the other night when you called and told me that I need to have more friends and that you were going to help me find some.

A few days ago, I was breaking things with a sledgehammer I had found. I broke things until I broke the handle of the hammer. I saw my life in the stroke that split the wood in my hand. I have been smashing myself to bits. I am a blunt instrument like the hammer and unknowing like the rock that it hits.

I was a wolf in a trap once. I chewed off my leg to get out of the trap and did it in less time than I thought. It hurt but freedom hurts. Here's the good part—I chewed off the wrong leg. I barely dragged myself out of that one. Remember when I said that to you as a joke and you told me to shut up and I told you I wanted to crush your body with a baseball bat to the point of non-recognition in the parking lot of a shopping mall?

I meant it, but I didn't mean to hurt your feelings. No, really.

You remember that party you took me to a few weeks ago when the host, your friend, asked me if I could please leave? You were so embarrassed. What was it that bummed him out so much, the part where I said that I could take his woman away and kill him with my hands? I walked to a hotel and called a cab. You didn't call me for awhile.

Isn't there a law against brutal thoughts? I spend time with overpaid smiles who bask in a recently acquired comfort they see as their birthright. Don't expect nice things to come from me. I hurt myself more than anyone else. There's always a warning on my label. I telegraph all my punches. I am easy to knock out. If you don't see it coming from a long way off, then you get what you deserve. Like a lot of people, I don't care about the truth anymore. All it did was waste my time.

Like I said at the beginning of the letter, I am sorry to have hurt your feelings. You'll be fine soon enough. I only hurt when I mix with people. Otherwise I can live inside my coma and go for days.

Sometimes I wish that I was not how I am so I could adopt a child. I think of children in orphanages and it kills me. People are mean. Here I am. Want me to evolve? What does that entail? That I ignore 99% of what I see and fall in step?

I saw you caught in a trap. You didn't have the courage to chew your leg off to get free. I chewed your leg off for you. Wrong leg. I know that must have hurt. No, really.

HUBERT
SELBY JR.

IT NEVER RAINS WHEN THE CROCUS SING

⚡

THE HEALING

IT NEVER RAINS WHEN THE CROCUS SING

The locust's song swells... hangs for a moment in the still night air...
then drifts to silence; the leaves of the dark trees immobile.
Silence...

Silence...

that wondrous rest between notes
filled with their memory, and expectation...

the quiet magical in its
presence, so all embracing, impossible to ignore...

Yet only a pause, a time of gathering until the locust once again
fill the night, and the silence, with their sharp, vibrating crescendo...
the night, and the trees, once more filled with their song; the trees
sturdy, solid, yet in harmony with the quivering humming of the
song, their leaves breathing into the stillness of the night air.

Night. Quiet, comfortable, languorous and faintly seductive in
its peacefulness. Soft, almost indiscernible shadows caressing the
leaves, the massive tree trunks emerging from their own shadows.
The sound of distant traffic unable to disturb the soft, summer air.

Yes silent stillness can be so crushing while sitting alone.

Night. Night with its expectant coolness. But where is the
breeze? There had been a promise of rain, but it is well known it
never rains when the locust sing. Such is the old tale. Yet she sits on
the porch, windows open, listening to the locust, waiting for the rain
that will bring the coolness she is hoping for, the rain she hopes will
come with a breeze gentle and sweet, a breeze so kind it will allow
her to keep the windows open and cool her bedroom. Those win-
dows were open too and she prayed it would only be a slight, cooling
breeze so the rain will fall straight and not blow in the windows. She
knew she took a chance on water spotting her parquet bordered
floors for heaven knows she would never be able to get up there in
time to close them if it were a sudden, summer downpour. Please
God, let it be gentle. You know how long it takes me to wobble to

the stairs with my walker, how long it takes me to crawl up them. Let it be gentle like a baby's smile... yes... like my great grandchildren, O what sweet little Angels. I love them so much, moving her leg with her hands, settling the ankle on the padded footstool, then adjusting herself slightly in her chair, leaning just a wee bit closer to the open windows, they're such precious little lambs.

A distant, deep throated sound from a tugboat in the harbor drifts soothingly to the porch, gently laying itself on her ears. O, such a sweet yet plaintive sound, lonely yet reassuring that even in the night life is going on, the boat cutting through the dark waters... seen only by its small lights, otherwise invisible, unseen... unseen... would otherwise pass through the night unnoticed.

O yes, such lovely nights riding the ferry, just a few blocks from her house, to Staten Island, holding tightly to the hand of her son as they enjoyed the cool breeze on a hot summer's night, O, if only I could have had more than one child, but I guess it wasn't meant to be. My son so far away, yet always in my heart... my dear, precious son. But I do have my littlest Angels. (Hello geat gammah. Hello, my precious little Angel...)

Well, I have lived longer than anyone else in the family. Mother was 81 when she died... upstairs. I held her hand... yes, I held her hand and sang her favorite song, Macooshla. Her had was gnarled and misshapen and she clung to me, O so hard she clutched my hand and then... then it opened, slowly, and it was the hand I remember brushing my hair, tucking me in bed and gently touching my cheek as she kissed me good night. I wonder, do You think these old twisted hands will open? I wonder.

But they don't hurt anymore, praise God. But they are so ugly. But You don't think they are do You? I truly am so grateful for all Your Blessings. Though I do wish I could walk without staggering and falling. But when I go to the clinic and see those children with heavy braces on their legs, and in wheelchairs O those poor precious little lambs. I would gladly take their pain if it would help. The poor little angels...

She looks into the night at the textured trunk of the tree in front of the house, and listens to the locust... then becomes aware that she is trying to breathe in time to their song, then laughs, O Adalin, you are such a dilly. Don't You think I'm a dilly?... O, what would I do without You? I can't even open the windows without Your help... but You always help. O, I am so grateful. I get so tired and weary, unable to do all the things I used to do... can't even walk to the stores, or scrub the floor... but I'm grateful to have a roof over my head. There are so many poor souls with no place to put their head, no place to sleep and rest...

And all those poor souls starving and being tortured all over the world, O dear God, the things we do to each other, such inhumanity to man, mothers watching their children being shot or slowly starving to death, O dear God, watching your own child dying, O how I weep for them.

Her finger tips rubbing the leaf of a philodendron, a plant so old she can't remember how long she has had it... 40 years, perhaps 45... who knows, but like so many other plants on the window sill of her little sanctuary they are old and dear companions. Her eyes watch her finger tips, aware of the cool, smooth softness of the leaf... The garden is such a mess. I just can't get to it. Just overgrown with weeds. But the forsythia and the crocus bloom every spring. Sometimes the crocus force their way through the last crust of snow. O, such a Blessing.

Leaning toward the open window a little more as once again the locust buzz, but it is the tapping of rain she hears, falling gently with a summer-rain fragrance, and yes, it does seem to bring a breath of coolness. She puts the back of her hand against the screen... no, no rain coming in, just continuing to tap its way through the leaves of the trees to the ground below. A lovely, sweet sound. And still the locust sing. She laughs and chuckles, remembering telling her son when they spoke yesterday about the locust singing while it was raining and saying, But it's not supposed to rain when the crocus sing. They had laughed and now she shook her head, O Adalin, you're such a dilly, leaning closer to the window, feeling the freshness of the air on her cheek...

Then leaned on her walker and wiggled her way to the edge of the chair and tugged herself up, leaning forward on the walker, catching her breath and waiting for the pain to pass. She spreads her legs for balance, then closes the windows, time to go to bed. She stood as straight as possible while leaning on the walker, then hunched over it and started pushing it to the stairs, a few inches at a time, leaning heavily on it as she moved first one foot forward, then the other, O dear God I get so weary, continuing to push her way to the stairs, one slow, arduous step at a time. She placed the walker against the post then slowly lowered herself until she was kneeling on the second step, then crawled up the stairs, leaning forward as far as possible, struggling one knee on the next step, then the other, over and over, one knee, then the other, the pain in her arms causing her to wince, stopping several times to rest, hand hanging, then looking up to see how much further she had to climb, counting each step, O, dear God, help me up these stairs. When she reached the top she pulled herself up on the railing, then using the cane she kept there, slowly hobbled the few feet to her bedroom. She made her way to the chair by the bed, then shifting her weight between the cane and the chair, she undressed and sat on the side of the bed and worked her nightgown over her head. She sat for a moment looking out the window at the tree, almost hypnotized by the rain on leaves, rain on leaves, rain on leaves, then lowered herself to the bed, hoping that tonight, perhaps, she would fall asleep before the sun came up.

(Wait for your Angel gamma.) Seems like it was only yesterday... and now he has children of his own. O, they grow up so fast... Where does the time go?

She sighed and thanked God for all her Blessings, one after another, after another, an almost endless expression of gratitude... yet she was weary... O so weary... just barely able to take care of herself... yet wanting to live. She knew she could let go of this life. God had told her so, but she wanted to see her great grandchildren. She loved them so, her precious little Angels...

The locust and the rain seemed to compete for her attention, first one, then the other. She lay on her back and chuckled, It never rains when the crocus sing... O Adalin, you're such a dilly.

THE HEALING

THE MAN GOT UP FROM THE COUCH and sat beside his wife who was reading. A soft light came thru the shadowed windows of the porch and he watched her for a moment, smiling at the way the light reflected on the short hair in the mole on her cheek. If he could have chuckled aloud he would have. How funny that he should be amused by that hair. The woman moved slightly while continuing to read. She hadn't moved much, but now her ear was highlighted and he remembered she wore earrings when she went to church on Sundays. He wondered if he had been aware of that before...

Did you always wear earrings to church Flo?

Of course I did. Didn't you know that?

I'm not sure. Maybe.

The woman moved another fraction of an inch. The man leaned forward, wanting to touch her cheek. You look very pretty in the light.

She lowered the book and looked up at the ceiling, noticing a leaf move out of the corner of her eye. You haven't told me that for... I don't know... for... what suddenly brought that up?

I don't know, just felt it I guess. Sort of strong.

It must have been extremely strong, overpowering. You haven't said anything like that since our honeymoon more than 50 years ago.

I'm sorry. You're mad at me but I don't want to make you mad.

I should think not—slamming the book shut—you did enough of that while you were alive.

The man cringed, but continued smiling. I know I did Flo and I'm truly sorry. From the bottom of my heart sorry.

What's the point of all this Stan? I'm 80 years old and you made my life a living hell for more than 50 years... and the last 10 I never knew if you would kill me when you came home so drunk you couldn't stand, blood always dripping from a bang on your head but you wouldn't listen to me, O no, you had to have your way and just keep drinking no matter what happened it was always your way while I sat here night after night, year after year never knowing if you were alive or dead, terrified when the phone rang because they would tell me you're dead and terrified you would come home alive and kill me in your rotten drunken rage. O, I really don't want to talk about this, you ruined my life, you and the drink. O, how I hate drink and that temper of yours, that evil Childers temper and you gave it to your son, our only child, and he has your evil temper and almost killed me once while in a drunken stupor but at least he stopped drinking but you would never listen to me. I always tried to help you, to show you you were just as good as anyone else but would you listen? O God no, you had to go get drunk at the least little thing and I'm left to pick up the pieces and even when our son was dying you didn't stop drinking long enough to even visit him, my god Stan, how could you do that, it's inhuman, he was still just a child, only 18 when they sent him back from Germany, and 4 years in the hospital and you visited him once even with all those operations you were only there once-squeezing the book so the veins in her hands bulged and pulsed-and you say you're sorry well I'm—

Flo, I'm not trying to hurt you I—

—Hurt me?! Hurt me?! How can you possibly hurt me any more than you have? If you cut my throat and dismembered my body you couldn't possibly hurt me any more than you have and what about our son? When he came out of the operating room each time I was there with him and stayed with him until he was out of danger while you drank with your friends and just had a good time in those rotten gin mills of yours, don't want to hurt me? I don't know why god didn't just let me die for all the heartache I suffered with you and we knew after Lawrence was born that we couldn't have any more children and you wouldn't let me adopt another one, you knew I wanted children, I told you that before we got married, I told you I wanted at least 3 children but you always have to have your way, you and the rotten drink, and I never did have any more children to raise and died everyday for years while Lawrence was so sick and he turned out to be a rotten drunk just like his father for god's sake. Stan why don't you leave me alone, why do you continue to torment me? Haven't I suffered enough because of you? Haven't you gotten your pound of flesh, and then some, from me? What in god's name do you want from me? Didn't you torture me enough when you were alive, do you need to haunt me now that you're dead? Can't you simply lay in your grave and just be dead, I need the rest, don't you understand, I can't take any more, it's been peaceful since you died-and you died drunk, you know that? are you aware that you were drunk when you died in the Smithson's house? You couldn't even die in your own home but someone elses and you had to be drunk—

Please Flo, let's talk about—

Don't please Flo me, you disgraced me as well as tortured me, didn't I keep a nice enough home? was there something wrong with it and no matter what you did I was always here-

I know that Flo, please let me—

There's nothing you can tell me, now or ever—

But Flo, we've gone over this before can't we—

No we can't, my heart is broken, I kept up our home and if it wasn't for me we never would have had a penny, you would have drunk up every penny we ever had. I scrimped and saved so we could have a nice home and this is a nice home, free and clear, but you only came home to sleep off a drunk and then stagger out to your drunken friends and raged at me and called me every foul name you could think of even in front of our child and my family and now you suddenly come around here sounding all sweet and lovey and expect me to just forgive you for all those horrible years, more than 50 godforsaken years and how come you're suddenly so gentle when you were always such a violent foul mouthed drunken bum, what is it you want from me Stan because it doesn't make any difference—

I wanted to talk Flo—

—your life is over and I found some peace at last... you know I go out now, ever since you died I've been going to plays and concerts and I even go away during the summer to different places for weeks at a time: Connecticut, the Poconos, and I go on trips with the church and the library... a whole lifetime with nothing but waiting for a drunken madman to come home and I'm finally finding some peace so don't for god's sake bother me with...

Please don't cry Flo. I can't stand to see you so upset and sad.

The man watched the tears form then flow from her eyes, one at a time, glistening in the faint light from the windows and the lamp. There was a profound sadness and recognition flowing through his being and if he had a body it would have been twisted and knotted. He wanted desperately to reach out and brush away the tears and absorb her sadness and pain but all he could do was look at the woman sitting ramrod stiff in the chair, her hair gray and thinning, loose flesh hanging from her upper arms, a woman he had lived with for more than 50 years, a woman suddenly silenced by grief, each tear that staggered down her cheek screaming with anguish as her arthritic hands screamed with pain. A woman 80 years old. A woman he loved. A woman who never looked more beautiful in her life. A woman he never really knew, just as he never knew himself. The man had sat quietly, almost mute, during her previous tirade because he knew that was the most important thing he could do for her at this time, that it would be impossible for him to do what it was he had to do if he didn't allow her the privilege and necessity of venting her anger and rage...

and
he also knew she was right. He visited Lawrence once. Only once. All those years...

O god, how he tortured himself. Their only child. He loved the boy so much... so desperately. Even after death he tortured himself. How could he do that? His son. His boy, yet he visited him only once. Once. Once in four years. Endless, crippling years. That simple fact tortured him more than anything else in his life. How many times did he wake up screaming? How many nightmares? Hideous, crippling nightmares? Endless. He wanted so desperately to hold his boy in his arms, to take his pain. How many times a day did he pray he would die so his boy could live? And his boy did live. No thanks to him. And he did die. Over and over again he died. Yet he was powerless to change his actions. Booze was all there was. It didn't dull the pain, but, in fact seemed to increase it at times. God, how many times did he sit with a drink, crying, looking into the glass hoping to find some light. But never did. But he did get to pass out. Only the oblivion of booze made it possible for him to survive that torment. The bestial ravages of guilt. He did go with her once, but almost screamed with terror. To this very moment he had no idea how he survived those hours. His son was always big and strong, and now he was pale, thin, propped up in bed gasping for air. Just a boy. Only a boy and his life was disappearing in front of him. He knew he was watching him die. And he knew, in his heart of hearts, in the marrow of his bones, in his very soul, that he was responsible. He was murdering his son. He didn't understand how, but he knew, absolutely, it was true. This boy he tried to reach out to through the years. Tried so hard to be a father to, yet never seeming to succeed. He just didn't know how to be a father. To be a husband. To be anything. Only a drunk and a bringer of pain. He always knew he was not only a useless human being, but the most loathsome creature that ever crawled on this world. He stood there that day watching the life leave his son's body. Watching his eyes cloud with every breath... and sink deeper into his skull. He wanted so desperately to just fall on his knees and ask his son's forgiveness, Lawrence, Lawrence I'm sorry. I'm so sorry. I didn't mean to do it—feeling like he was drowning in his own tears, all the demons of hell screaming in his head yet he could do nothing but stand there and stare, stare at the disappearing life... then run to the bar when they go home.

The man wondered if he would ever forget that day. Those endless years... He thought not. But at least the suffering was gone. Now.

Since his death he had made discoveries about himself and knew what he had to do, but was still uncertain of how to do it, or what to say, even though he was now free of the body. He was never able to use words adequately, but she always could, Florence was really wonderful like that. She could explain things so people understood what she was talking about. But take him out of an engine room and he was overwhelmed, terrified and could only grin and sputter a stupid chuckle and pray he'd be able to get a drink soon. But it was important the he learn how to use words, it was important that he learn how to alleviate at least some of the pain he had caused her. He wasn't even sure why he was here at this moment because he still didn't know what to say, but he only knew he had to be here, now, and that somehow the words would come... they had to. His sense of time was so different now that he didn't know what to make of it. He somehow didn't see the 80 years she had been alive but only the vitality and indomitable energy the woman still possessed. He wasn't even certain he knew just how long he had been dead, but he thought it was a few years, years in which he wrestled with his history and came to realize and understand enough that he knew, absolutely, that he loved this woman and had always loved her, and that seemed to be the important thing, he was certain all things would come from that understanding. What she had said was true... all of it. It was true she would tell him he was as good as anyone else, but he knew that she didn't know what she was talking about. But how could he get her to see that he now understood the things that were always so foreign to him? He watched her breath and in time she released the book she had been squeezing, and her hands opened and rested on her lap. The tears ceased and she wiped her eyes and cheeks with a tissue and her body shivered ever so slightly and she started to relax and he watched the tension flow from her body, knowing... remembering how his body always felt so twisted with tension when he wasn't drinking, but he never knew anyone else felt like that, and now he could see it in her body and he almost wept with joy to see something within her that was within him, something to bind them, something that united them, something he could understand about her from his own tortured insides. A sense of love and affection welled up within him and gently flowed through and from him, he could see it flow to this woman he loved and help ease her pain.

There's something important I have to tell you Flo.

Her shoulder moved almost imperceptibly. Her eyes blinked. The resistance was gone, only grief remained, sagging her body slightly.

The man watched the feeling of futility flow through her, another point of identification between them he had never seen before, yet the old energy was still there, seeming to be waiting for something to stir it up, to reanimate it.

There's something important I have to tell you.

The woman simply blinked in recognition, too weary to reply, feeling so overwhelmed by the grief and resentment she wasn't certain she even cared to hear anymore, but unable to dismiss the man.

I learned I really love you—she blinked and moved her head back slightly—I truly do Flo... and always did and always will.

He watched the information move through her body, bouncing off barriers, being rejected and redirected as parts of her fought to believe and assimilate the simple yet unbelievable statement.

Again, he had no idea of time but spoke when it seemed right. It surprised me too. I didn't know.

Her eyes looked in his direction but she remained silent.

I couldn't believe I could love you and do the things I did. I don't know if I can explain it, but its something like you used to talk about I guess, sort of that church stuff about life after death, that's about as close as I can explain it.

Her body moved slightly and he leaned forward, not having a body makes a big difference, I don't know how all this works, but I just don't feel the same. I don't seem to think like before. Maybe I don't think, not like I used to anyway.

She stirred a little more and leaned against the back of the chair.

The man continued to speak slowly, surprised at what he heard himself saying, yet it all seemed to make sense. I was always overwhelmed with feelings and over here it's different, and I got help getting free of the guilty feelings.

Guilty feelings?

The woman's voice surprised her as much as it did him, the words seeming to come involuntarily from her, You felt guilty?

Yes Flo, I did. It just seemed to eat me up.

She looked puzzled, I never thought you felt guilty.

Well, I really didn't know what it was either. I just knew I was responsible for all the problems, all the trouble, and I couldn't do anything about it. I just couldn't seem to stop doing what I was doing and I just kept causing trouble. Even as a very little boy I thought everything was my fault.

The woman continued to stare and frowned, You felt guilty and I always wondered what I had done to cause you to treat me the way you did. I just could not understand what I had done.

And I couldn't understand why I was doing it.

He could see the tension start to leave her body and her severe expression started softening. He watched the change occurring, not certain what was happening, but then slowly, gradually, he realized that she was seeing something of her in him, just as he had a few minutes before, and he now had another point of identification, one he knew they both shared.

You honestly felt guilty for the things you did?

It ate me up alive Flo. Over and over I thought of killing myself but couldn't do it. I tried to change, but I didn't know what to do.

The woman shook her head sadly, her voice low, soft and bewildered, You wouldn't stop drinking. It was only when you were drinking.

Yes Flo, I know. But I couldn't stop. It's hard to explain, or even believe now, but things used to happen in my body when I didn't drink and I'd just go crazy... And then I'd be drinking.

She was looking at her arthritic hands, her voice sad, And then you would go crazy.

I'm sorry Flo. If I could have done it different...

He could see her spirit continue to absorb the information and her body became increasingly relaxed, and there was a certain sense, an aura of recognition and acceptance, and she seemed to be surrendering more and more to the essence of what he was saying. Lawrence used to tell me to leave you.

Most people would have Flo.

But I couldn't do it. What would have happened to you?

I probably would have died in the gutter, on the Bowery.

That's what I told him. At least you always knew you had a home to come back to.

And I always came home.

She lifted her head and looked at the couch across the porch he always laid on, her eyes blinking, something significant obviously happening behind her eyes... That's true, isn't it, you always did come home.

Yes Flo, I did. And you always let me in.

You might have killed me if I didn't.

That's true.

And you almost did when I did.

That's true.

And sometimes you would lose your key and pound on the door and kick it in the middle of the night... her voice trailed off and she shook her head with sadness... O Stan, it was all so horrible, I just could not understand what I had done.

There wasn't anything Flo. And I know now there was nothing I could do either. I was totally baffled.

The woman shook her head gently as she silently wept for all the lost, tortuous years... And so was I Stan. I was totally baffled too. I would pray and pray and sometimes I would doubt God. I couldn't understand why it was all happening.

I had the same battle in my heart Flo. I couldn't understand why all this was happening. What had I done to become such a monster?

There was a silence, a comforting silence, as the meaning of what had been said continued to resonate within them as a familiar song, each hearing the tune in their own way while singing it to each other.

I just want to do whatever I can to relieve your pain Flo. I know it may sound pointless, but maybe it's not. Just tell me what I can do Flo... Please...

The silence was comforting. He watched her as she closed her eyes for a moment, her head moving as if in time to music. In her mind she heard the old hymn, THE OLD RUGGED CROSS, and could feel her face relaxing in a smile... She opened her eyes and blinked them a few times to focus her vision, I tried so hard to help you see you weren't bad.

Yes, Flo, I know. But I couldn't hear you.

I feel tired... worn out.

I know.

If only all this could have happened...

He watched her shrug and dismiss the futility of the thought.

She sighed, Then I did not do anything wrong.

No Flo. Nothing wrong.

And you always loved me.

Yes Flo. Just as you always loved me.

O, I hated you sometimes Stan.

Yes.

But I always loved you... didn't I?

Yes. You always did.

And you always did find your way home, even when you didn't know where you were... O, it all seems like such a waste, all those years...

Maybe not Flo. Maybe we can let go of the pain... and the scars. Maybe it's never too late.

Do you really think so Stan?

Yes, I do Flo. I don't know how, but I think so.

You really believe that Stan, don't you? You really do.

I don't understand it, but I guess love takes care of that.

And the memories? Can it take care of those too?

Yes. That's where the scars are and they go too... if we let them.

The man watched the woman's face soften as she already started experiencing the healing of the pain and scars, her eyes becoming more alive with light from some place within her, her folded flesh glowing and everything about her softening. She gently rubbed her arthritically gnarled hands as she looked up at the ceiling, her body relaxing and glowing...

And we didn't do anything wrong...

She sighed and her smile continued to broaden until all of her being was smiling and rejoicing and light seemed to leap from her eyes and her hands opened, resting on her lap, her fingers straightening, light dancing around them, the man remembering when first he held them so many years ago and they felt so light and delicate he was terrified the roughness of his hands might injure them or scratch them or something, and was sure she would yank her hands away but she didn't, but allowed him to hold them and it felt like their softness and strength were cleansing his in some way, the life that came from them flowing through him and stirring his heart and he tried to utter the words he felt there, but his fear, and paralyzing sense of inadequacy closed his throat and all he could do was look at her and feel the smoothness of her hands, a smoothness he had felt as a boy when he rubbed the bloom of an Iris between his fingers for many wonderful minutes and now the wonder of that moment filled him again as he watched her hands glowing with the old light and he could see their young smoothness and promise...

That's right Flo, we didn't do anything wrong.

JEFFREY LEE PIERCE

FROM THE BOOK

GO TELL THE MOUNTAIN

1980 - 1981

"THERE IS NOTHING AS UNREAL AS LIFE."

This is what I thought as I lay in a Japanese hospital with my head ringing and blood caked in my hair. Looking for the answer in my social worker's eyes, I wonder what Miss Kotoda thought at that moment. I know what I thought.

Fifteen years previous to the Kobe earthquake, a band called The Creeping Ritual was rehearsing and drinking. Drinking and rehearsing in a cheap studio on Selma Avenue, Hollywood, CA 1980. The band had been formed for two reasons: 1) My sister's boyfriend, Nestor Aquino, had left a drum kit at our house. 2) Kid Congo Powers, a.k.a. Brian Tristan, had bought an amp and a guitar which he did not know how to play. Other contributing factors were a universal hatred of rockabilly fashion and a recent performance by The Damned. As Tristan said, after viewing the concert, "I really needed that."

We all really needed it. Roots revivalism was taking Hollywood by storm and boring some of us catatonic. This, along with the arrival of The Cramps in L.A., had convinced us there was plenty of American culture out there that needed to be destroyed. I highlighted this period by smashing a one hundred dollar Ersel Hickey single on Sunset Boulevard and shouting, "Fuck rockabilly!" According to Phast Phreddie, I then promptly hid in the brush beside the Cinerama Dome at the sound of police helicopters, convinced that I was a Viet Cong cadre escaping "the Americans."

Phast Phreddie had held a "Charlie Parker Drink To The Death Party" that night. The party was attended by Top Jimmy, X, Lenny Kaye, Darby Crash and Lorna Doom. Phast Phreddie was such a good host; he even invited all of the Japanese massage parlor girls from the Oriental Massage Parlor next door. This helped save Lorna Doom from the constant advances of a house full of drunken men.

I have never met a nice Chinese girl — even in Hong Kong

(many years later), or in China (a few years after that), or even in San
Francisco, which is where they all come from anyway. Where are
they? I played so many Chinese restaurants that I even knew a
Cantonese folk song. It was taught to me by the waitress downstairs
at Madame Wong's. I don't remember it now. I do remember her
name. It was Mei.

Girls influence my music. Hanging around with Rosemary
Patronette influenced "Sex Beat." The Slash secretary, Robyn Weiss,
was the subject of "She's Like Heroin To Me." The list goes on and
on. However, it was during this Chinese Restaurant Tour '80 that I
met the girl that set me off writing songs.

She was standing in front of the Hong Kong Cafe, while I was
chillin' out by the plaza fountain. She wore a yellow plastic raincoat,
designed like a short, leather thigh-length coat. Very fashionable.
She also carried a yellow film can. Her hair was jet black. Bright yel-
low high-heels. I thought, "At last! A hip young Chinese girl!" I
walked up and invited her into the club. I was sure I had scored at
last. She was from Tacoma, Washington. Her name was Linda
Hayashi. She was, in fact, Japanese. And so began another disastrous
relationship with a Japanese girl. Its most sensitive moment docu-
mented in "Promise Me," the most sad of the early songs. I still think
about her when I sit alone at the Club Manhattan in Osaka. And my
big Chinese wedding? The blaring horns? The clan sitting in forma-
tion? The wedding veil? Uniformed party members discreetly giving
their approval? Forget it... The sun rises in Osaka Bay now. And it
always will, I guess.

Despite my romantic fantasies, the most common subject
remained low-life Amerika. It appears in the early songs. I was filled
with anger, hatred and sexuality. Dejected, disbelieving and disap-
pointed. In a sense, a punk. Although, out of uniform.

I was in the early stages of forming a band which had not yet
played out. A friend, Don Waller, said something that still echoes in
my ear.

"Tell them what they don't want to hear."

So, as a rule, all of the lyrics of the early Gun Club dealt with unpopular subjects, namely: Sex, Murder, Drugs, Insanity, Desperation, Loneliness, Suicide and just plain Bad Vibes. There is also a fair amount of Self-Destructive Serial Killer and Racist War Criminal mentality portrayed. Much of this was based on people I had either encountered or read about.

My wanderings through the East Coast and Deep South around 1978 and 1979 had brought me face to face with the drifters and the loners that make up the wandering American underclass. They were people going nowhere, on the hustle, and preying upon anyone who showed them any interest. Cheap bus station hotels and vagabond bars were the stage for this performance. A habitat of lost souls, staring down a vista of Lost Highways, always sneaking out of town on the next Dog — the Greyhound, that is. Some were veterans of foreign wars. Some were running from a bad divorce. Some were drug addicts. Most were alcoholics. Some of them were probably murderers. I drifted for a spell, too. (*Some people say I still am — only on a bigger scale.*) That's how I learned my lesson.

In those days, Hollywood was always good to return to, and soon, my barely listenable band was invited to play its first concert by Keith Morris with his band, The Circle Jerks. It was in a Chinese restaurant. In fact, our second gig was in a Chinese Restaurant. And the third, too. We were the CHINESE RESTAURANT BAND NO. 1.

There was so much to do then, so much music to destroy. We trashed "Slippin' Into Darkness," "Inner City Blues," and "Disco Inferno," but we saved our special hatred for blues and rockabilly. "Willie Brown" by Mack Self was given the comedy treatment. Its flipside, "Mad At You," was played in a Sex Pistols manner. "Preachin' Blues" by Robert Johnson died a special death and so we concentrated more on blues parody, since "blues" was the newest L.A. obsession. (I confess that I liked it, too. When I first heard "Smokestack Lightning" in a car behind the Licorice Pizza Record Store, I immediately ran across the street and forced Lorna Doom to listen to it. She was not impressed. The Germs already had a blues song, it was called "Shutdown.")

The other major influences then were voodoo culture (courtesy of Exene Cervenka), fear of parasitic invasion (courtesy of *Alien* by Ridley Scott), and The Germs. I, in fact, saw *Alien* with Gary (Ryan), The Germs' roadie (who later lived with Lorna in N.Y.) and future member of Joan Jett's Blackhearts. Kid was also there and the discussion often jumped between the film and The Other Newest One Germs' thing. Darby hadn't realized that he had written a blues song.

We discussed this when we both found ourselves in jail for a night. I got picked up, drunk at an X gig; Darby was picked up later from the same gig. We sat up all night talking shit and Darby shouted down some cowboy who took a piss on the floor of the cell. That cowboy could have torn Darby Crash to pieces, but he didn't care. I liked that part of him. When the police put Darby in the cell, he ridiculed and teased them. He was a true member of the gang.

Later that night, the police released me and I had to telephone Joan Jett at 7 AM to come and get Darby out. He was being held because of his warrants. I had to memorize her number in jail. I saw him a few days later, so it must have worked out. Although I'm sure the LAPD gave him a bad time. They're such motherfucking fascist assholes. Anybody who would want to be a cop, military officer, immigration inspector or customs official should be shot on sight for betraying their human citizenship. The LAPD rate high on the non-human totem pole and should be sent to re-education camps or liquidated on all levels.

It was around this time the line-up changed. The Gun Club, as we were now called (courtesy of Keith Morris), lost its bass and drums when original members, Brad Dunning and Don Snowden, quit to take real jobs. Our last gig was with The Bags at the Hong Kong Cafe. After the show, Rob Ritter complimented Kid and me on the set and offered to join the band. He said that he could probably get The Bags drummer, Terry Graham, as well. Kid and I were astonished. Rob and Terry were big pop stars to us. Despite our fear of inferiority, we set up rehearsals. I ran downstairs and across the plaza to Madame Wong's to tell Mei all about it. She didn't care; she didn't like rock music. She said we should play the Cantonese folk song I learned.

At rehearsal, Kid and I were almost afraid to speak, and when Terry and Rob left, we wondered if they liked it. I guess they did. We debuted this line-up in early summer 1980 at Madame Wong's West — Mrs. Wong's new restaurant. In attendance were Phil and Dave Alvin, Lux Interior and Ivy Rorschach, who really liked us. Kid dropped some acid and complained that the strings were turning into rope. Mrs. Wong stiffed us twenty-five bucks and said, "You boys stay on the East Side."

So, our next gig was Club 88, I think, somewhere on the West Side (I never do what I am told). We also played a UCLA sorority house. At this show, I exited the stage by crawling out the window and dropping to the street below. We did a different Chinese Restaurant called The Golden Gate. Went back to Chinatown and did the Hong Kong Cafe again. I was covered in festival banners and thought, "If we ever play in San Francisco, we are going to make it big time!"

However, it was about this time that the party ended. The Hong Kong Cafe closed down. Madame Wong's was angry with us. The Golden Gate never even got started, and there were no more gigs to play for the Gun Club in Los Angeles.

I was becoming more and more exposed to Cajun music when I ran into Lux and Ivy, who were having a terrible time on tour with the Buzzcocks. There were also problems with Bryan Gregory, but I thought nothing of it. On my return, I composed a waltz called "Opelousas Love Magic" and sang it in French, so taken was I with Cajun music. We played this song twice, but never recorded it. I was talking with Phil Alvin, my guitar teacher, about this and he said we should all go see Clifton Chenier at his annual dance and gumbo dinner in Watts that month. So I phoned John Doe and Exene and God knows who else. Dave Alvin phoned Rosemary and Chris D., and we all got rip-roaring drunk and danced to Clifton Chenier. The only white people in the place. I still remember Chenier staring at us in disbelief. All of us, front of the stage — black clothes, rosaries, teased hair, dancing along as if it were The Damned.

The Gun Club went back to rehearsing when we were offered a show at the Culver City Arena which was really just another bar. An auspicious meeting in my life took place at the Whisky around this time. Very tired, but almost intuitively, I got into my car and drove down to the Whisky to see a show I was not even interested in — the Modettes and the B-Girls. I wondered if Debbie Harry liked this sort of thing. I had befriended Debbie back in 1977 and often drove her around Los Angeles, thriftshopping and dropping her off at airports. Lying on her couch at the Tropicana, throwing food at each other while Chris Stein stared catatonically at the TV. Debbie was one of the few white women to enjoy an influence over me. And a big influence at that. I always trusted her and still do.

Somehow, I had lost track of her during her rise to fame. The last time I'd seen her was on Broadway and 54th in early 1979. Since then, she had become a mega-pop star in every sense. Strangely, I walked up the steps of the Whisky as if guided by radar and spotted a small bleach-blonde girl stepping nervously beside the backstage door. It was her. She was in town doing an album called *Auto American* and oh yes, she had not forgotten me. She, in fact, planned to come down to Culver City and check the gig out. Although this never happened, we would soon be seeing a lot of each other by 1982. She gave me a number and raced backstage behind the B-Girls when they left the stage.

Before the Culver City gig, Rob Ritter, who went through periodic depressions, quit the band. He said that we were stagnating. We probably were. We hadn't played in two months. He was replaced for a short while by Anna Statman and we played some benefit with X, The Blasters and The Go-Go's. I think it was a benefit for Bill Bateman, The Blasters' drummer, who owed a hotel some money after he destroyed his room. He might have been arrested and nobody wanted him to go to jail. We had all been punks and we all hated cops. I still do. The LAPD Drunken Off-Duty Sheriffs once beat my father so bad that he looked like a frog. Then they came over to our house and told him that if he tried to sue, his wife and kids would have far more difficult lives. My father dropped his complaint. This was in the mid-'70s and long before Rodney King. It's just

LAPD tradition.

Lux and Ivy were at our Culver City show and Kid broke the news that he was joining The Cramps. They loved his looks and his style. He was still playing guitar in Open E as I had taught him. He didn't know the name of the chords; he played by numbers. A song like "Sex Beat" would be taught to the bass and guitar as follows:

"F1... Johnny's got a light in his eyes... A5... E0... Shirley's got a light on her lips... G3."

Sort of like bingo.

"For The Love Of Ivy," a song written by Kid and me from a book he found called *1001 Insults*, sounded even more like bingo.

"E0... I was all dressed up like an Elvis from Hell! E G3 E A5!"

Later the song incorporated some insults, racial slurs and Leadbelly to give it a more down-home-with-the-KKK feeling. Eventually by the time the chorus kicked in, all this angst would be directed at Ivy, whom Kid and I both worshipped. I once started kissing her at Club 88 while we were both drunk at an X show. Then Lux came and said, "Break it up, guys." I never forgot. I told Kid and he was so jealous.

Yes, but now, it looked like only Kid would be enjoying her attention. I really didn't mind his leaving. We had little to offer and The Cramps were hugely successful. Also, I thought I had made my statement, although it remained unrecorded. Our last show together was also in Culver City. Rob Ritter ended up playing again when Anna Statman, who had been hiding behind the P.A. column throughout the show, left the stage to pee and handed the bass to Rob in the audience. He walked up and finished the set.

Rob and Terry wanted to continue with the band, but I couldn't imagine it without Kid, so we split up for awhile. Don Bolles was not surprised to see Kid go to The Cramps.

"You gotta watch those mulattos," he warned. Probably thinking of Pat Smear.

Off I went to work at May Company. I thought of joining the Merchant Marines for awhile. I didn't want to play music, but I wrote for *Slash* magazine and still saw a lot of everybody. I told

Exene that I had feelings of impending doom. She did too. Only this time, it was adultery with Lorna Doom. Actually it was far worse. Ronald Reagan was elected president of the United States. We simply could not believe it. Doom had really arrived.

That winter, the Hong Kong Cafe reopened, simply to shut down again. The last show was on New Year's Eve 1980. The Circle Jerks played. Somebody broke the glass in the front entrance and the Chinese finally got sick of us. Later that night, as I left a late party, John Doe and Keith Morris set a dried out Christmas tree on fire in the middle of Cahuenga Boulevard. The flames rose at least forty feet high. What a sight.

January saw the revival of the Gun Club. Before our first breakup in 1980, we had managed to cause a lot of talk. Rob Ritter in particular was very enthused to try it again. I was ambivalent. Working at May Co., destroying shop window displays with my Mexican friend, Adolphe. We were assistants to the store carpenter and when we didn't repair things, we destroyed old displays with unrestrained violence. It often frightened the customers on the other side of the walls who complained about "terrible noises." After work, I would dress entirely in black and go down to Club 88 or wherever, get drunk, and end up sleeping in my car, a green 1966 Mustang.

At this time, there was also a rumble at the *Slash* office. I wrote under the name "Ranking Jeffrey Lea," usually about reggae, R & B, or New York groups such as James Chance & the Contortions. I also reviewed The Urinals, The Germs, X, and The Cramps, as well as Black Flag at Polliwog Park.

Black Flag at Polliwog Park was an interesting turning point for me. I was invited to a picnic by Dianne Chai of The Alley Cats, whom I desperately had a crush on. I still remember her braless in the summer sun of Redondo Beach while I tried so hard to sit cross-legged in the park grass without my manhood bulging down my leg. Trying to remain polite (her boyfriend was there), and avert my eyes from her perfectly proportioned breasts.

She said that some weeks the park amphitheater presented musical entertainment for the picnicking families and that on this day was a band she liked. The band came onstage and I recognized the singer who I often saw hanging out in Hollywood at various punk gigs. It was Keith Morris. Later it was Keith who gave us the name "The Gun Club." The gig was incredibly wild. Families throwing all of the picnic food at the band which only got them more excited. Keith shouted abuse. Greg Ginn barely plugged into his amp. Chuck Dukowski all over the stage sliding on baloney, cheese, Wonder Bread, jam, peanut butter or whatever. It was great punk rock at a time when I thought I had seen it all. I wrote them up immediately for *Slash* and later went down to Hermosa Beach to watch them rehearse, which was nearly as wild, and hung out at the old abandoned church which everyone lived in. There I discovered Red Cross and The Descendents, whom I also wrote about. That was 1979, I think.

By 1981, *Slash* was nearing its end. Bob Biggs had formed Slash Records—his first release being a Germs single in 1978. They later released the Germs album, *G.I.*, and X's first album, *Los Angeles*, in 1980. The label was in full swing now and the magazine had become somewhat of a burden. The real catalyst was Claude Bessy, the editor whose desire was to return to Europe (he was French). Also, his girlfriend Philomena wanted to go home to England. They had befriended The Fall and had many connections in Manchester and London. (Years later, I would run into Claude again in Manchester, London and Barcelona. We would swap videos and wine in my crypt-like London flat while Asian women stared on in disbelief.) Claude also had been planning to write a novel. One of our last projects together was a feature and interview with Bob Marley. There was a large party for Claude at Bob Biggs' house in Laurel Canyon. I think John Belushi was there hanging around with Fear, his favorite band. I once again got smashed with Robyn Weiss and I don't remember who drove home. Claude was gone. He is still sadly missed in L.A. The magazine folded and I reformed the Gun Club into a full-time outfit.

I had met a guitarist in a parking lot named Ward Dotson. He was kind of shy and a big Cramps fan. We gave him a tape of earlier gigs from 1980 and asked him to tune to open E, like Kid Congo, and play some slide on the solos. Rob, Terry and I already knew most of the songs and we soon did our first reformed gig at the Country Club in Reseda, opening for X in front of about a thousand people. It must have seemed as unreal to Ward as it did to me, neither of us having played to an audience that large. I was a bit afraid, since the only other large audience I had sung for was during the filming of *The Decline Of Western Civilization* at the Fleetwood in Redondo Beach, where we were booed and spat on.

Later that Spring, we became darlings of The Cramps and supported several of their Roxy shows, one of which featured Kid accidentally setting his hair on fire — it was saturated with hairspray — and myself being dragged off the balcony into the audience where I was defended by a vicious Lois Graham with high heel in hand. We also played the Roxy supporting X. I got so friendly with the Roxy's owner Mario, that I still visit him today.

Around this time, there was a party at Cathy's. Cathy was a Chinese actress who lived on Highland Avenue. When Bob Biggs made some rather lewd comments about his secretary, Robyn — my heartthrob — I challenged him to a duel. This brief fracas was quickly broken up and I left with my honor frustrated. It was, however, an important event. Two months later, I saw Bob lifting crates of records at the new office on Martel Avenue. We buried the hatchet and he expressed interest in any demos or recordings that we would produce in the months ahead.

Little did he know that my fellow Latino, Tito Larriva, had already arrived on the scene. Recording for the Plugz' Fatima label, we already had six tracks for our debut EP. IRS Records had been doing good business with EP's and Fatima followed suit. I also enjoyed the comfort of an all Mexican label, since I was raised by a Mexican mother in El Monte and had spent my entire life in her family environment. I was even briefly in a gang at Valle Lindo Junior High School. I understood Spanish and spoke a little. Tito's label consisted of The Plugz, The Brat and The Gun Club. Indeed, even now, I still find Anglo-Americans strange and foreign. I have a penchant for black haired girls and can deliver a fearsome street rap. It's all a part of my Mexican upbringing. The girlfriends of my youth were all either Mexican, Korean, Japanese or Black. My first kiss was with a girl named Sandra Gutierrez, and my first tit game was with a girl named Darcy Kimura. Miss Kimura's pearly little breast in my palm is still a memory I cherish. The Mexican girls were often inaccessible — property of the cholos. But the Asian girls were excellent students, and often lonely and as inexperienced as I was. So I continued to see Miss Kimura until high school split us apart (she went to Rosemead; I went to Mountain View).

Later in my life, that comfort was always still there. Among Latinos or Asians, I always felt quite at home. I even experienced some militancy when my family moved to the San Fernando Valley, being unable to get along with the wealthy Anglo kids. I was always reading Eldridge Cleaver or Huey Newton, supporting the Viet Cong, who were then my idols. Needless to say, I didn't have many friends.

Fatima looked like a good home to me, until the news hit. Fatima didn't have any money. Then, Chris Desjardins came to the rescue. Bob Biggs had heard the Fatima recording, but held no opinion. My only white girl heartthrob, Robyn, tormented Bob daily by blasting Tito's production at full volume in his office's anteroom until Bob began to like it. Chris phoned and called me to a meeting with him, Tito and Bob to discuss finishing the project that would become *Fire Of Love*. Robyn sat at her desk outside, smiling, knowing full well that her guerrilla tactics in the office had secured the deal. I recall that after hearing Tito's recordings, she said, "I'm gonna drive Biggs crazy with this tape until he decides to release it." And so he did. What a girl that Robyn Weiss was.

At the meeting, it was decided that Chris D. would oversee the completion of the album and deliver five more tracks. We stayed up all night on speed at Quad Tech on Western Avenue, where The Germs had also recorded, and finished mixing at 7 AM. I went over to Rob Ritter's apartment and fell asleep on his couch. Neither Tito nor Chris answered the phone until very late. Rob, however, woke up at his usual time and realized that we had lost the bass in the mix. We complained to Biggs. They said that it could be fixed in the mastering. It never really was.

While we awaited its release, we did some shows with Fear and Wall Of Voodoo at the Whisky. Lee Ving and I had a small amplifier climbing contest. I made it to the top of a PA column, but Lee topped me by climbing the same PA and hanging off the speaker cables on the roof. What fun! A young Flea was at one of these shows and almost bit his tongue in half by pulling a stage dive as a joke during one of our slower songs. By Halloween that year, Kid and I were a regular couple. He showed up dressed in green skin at our show at some all female college. We played a rousing version of "Dancing By Myself" while I hid underneath the stage riser shouting, "You'll never get me out of here! Leave me alone!" The next night was Halloween and Rosemary Patronette drove me out to the Valley where The Cramps were playing. Kid was with us. We were dressed as Rita Moreno and Marilyn Monroe from Hell. Kid and I were always looking for some excuse to put on women's clothes. Phil Alvin was backstage complaining to Lux Interior about how horny he was.

Lux simply pointed to us and said, "There's plenty of girls around, Phil. Look at those two lovelies there."

Phil then walked up to me and said, "If I didn't know that was you, Jeffrey, I swear I'd fuck you."

"I'm not a cheap girl," I replied. "Ask Rita, not me, you dreadful man." At which point I turned a flattened, rouged cheek and slammed the door behind.

A week or so later, we played an interesting set with Big Mama Thornton, who drank loads of gin and mothered me all night.

"Just be careful," said Brendan Mullen. "Remember what she did to Johnny Ace."

We played "Run Through The Jungle" for Brendan's birthday and I had to make up all of the words since I never understood John Fogerty's. Most of them I plucked from "M & O Blues" by Willie Brown. This was meant to be a one-time thing, but our second album's producer, Chris Stein, insisted on recording it for *Miami*.

The record was out and receiving ecstatic reviews. The biggest shock was the response from the East Coast and San Francisco. We were never hometown favorites. We received lukewarm reactions from both Chris Morris and Robert Hillburn. The *New York Times*, however, loved us and talk of going to New York City began. Our first date outside of L.A. was quickly approaching. It would be in San Francisco!! THE WORLD'S BIGGEST CHINATOWN! I danced in anticipation of what restaurant we would play. Maybe all of them! Maybe we would never come back! I would learn Chinese and stay there forever. Get married and start a Gun Club Chinese Take Out and Delivery. Make it BIG TIME! My records available from Gerard Street to Shanghai on cheap cassettes behind the cashier of every Asian market from San Jose to Guangzhou. Number One Biggest Gweilo Capitalist Reactionary Western Restaurant Band this side of the Great Wall. I remembered my Cantonese folk song. I bought a plane ticket and packed my dress. It was @#!@ to Los Angeles. Chinatown, I go. Bye bye. I be big Gweilo singa. New high heels, I have.

LOS ANGELES, 1988

"It is not death you fear, it is oblivion."
— From *Lord Jim* by Joseph Conrad

I HAD BEEN HURTING ON TOUR and now it was over. Kid and I returned to L.A. for the first time in two years. We watched the cable stations at my mother's house and were amazed at how many channels the Americans have. We had gotten used to three or four channels in Britain. The strange thing is that they are all filled with ignorant nonsense. We turned it off in horror. I went in for a medical check since I was having trouble with internal pain. The verdict from the serious faced doctor was a surprise at 29 years old. Cirrhosis of the liver, malnutrition, and hypothrombosis due to repeated bouts of hepatitis and alcoholism.

The girls were looking more yellow than usual when I left London. The doctor also stated that I should file for disability and quit music forever. He also said that such a disease had a high mortality rate even amongst those who give up drinking.

My first impression was to go out and get drunk, which I did. I got so drunk, I was arrested and thrown into jail. The same holding tank I had once shared with Darby Crash. I wished I could call Joan Jett to bail me out this time, but I just waited it out. My cellmate was a Black Vietnam veteran. There were lots of them in jail. He convinced the L.A.P.D. to let me go somehow. I never phoned anyone or told anyone. I just walked home and went to sleep.

Dried out for once, I stopped lushing it up. The doctor was prescribing me valium anyway, and I had a nasty valium habit when I returned to London. I countered the withdrawal with massive doses of Heroin, and then countered Heroin withdrawal with alcohol. What a routine.

When Romi and Kayoko returned from Japan, I was a little shaky from alcohol withdrawal. However, there was some stability at last. The girls were home. I felt so much regret for drunkenly messing around with their minds and sexuality. I wanted to confess and beg Romi's forgiveness, but Kayoko would never permit that, and I needed them both there. If Kayoko could forgive and forget, then so should I honor her by never breaking my promise. Well, what Romi doesn't know won't hurt her. It seemed like hundreds of years ago anyway. Things were back to normal, except I wasn't quite there. I was lost somewhere in deep thought. Inactive and unexcited. Preoccupied with death and lost in a world memory.

I spent lots of time dwelling on childhood. Particularly the late 60's and early 70's. Many images came flooding back of burnt-out hippies, head shops, divorces, suicides, wars and riots. The Black Panthers' headquarters near my father's work. My cousin, Roger Dale, all fucked-up and home from Vietnam with his tattoos and sinister chin beard. Going to see the Los Angeles Rams at the Coliseum with my father and uncle. "Hold On, I'm Coming" by Sam

And Dave blaring over the radio through the traffic and the smog. Mexican gangs patrolling my street. Zig-Zag Man patches on my navy cut bell-bottoms. Later on, baggy pants, chinos and pendletons. Darcy Kimura hiding in the closet with me from my mother. Holding her little tit underneath her shirt while watching the sun rays through oak tree branches. Both of us lying there listening to "Get Together" by The Youngbloods. I remember I was sad because the school zoning laws did not permit her to go to the same high school as me. When I got home, Ray Macias had stolen me a bottle of Colt 45 and we drank it together listening to "Red House." Ray thought I should have "the blues." You see, even hoodlums have a heart.

There was one more tour to do, however. It was America. Our first since four years before. Our tour manager, Benny Brongers, ran it like a pro. It was the first and last tour that reached the professional organization and performances of the European ones. (You see, America had never really seen us at our best.)

Mother Juno had earlier reached the top of the CMJ list and we also did shows with Henry Rollins, The Goo Goo Dolls or Pussy Galore opening. Robin Guthrie and Richard Thomas visited us in New Jersey. I was sick most of the time and didn't socialize much. I just wanted it to end. In Santa Cruz, I thought I was dying. In Detroit, I went for a walk outside the club and returned by way of the rear entrance. In the alley, a large Black man walked up and pointed a 20-gauge shotgun at me. He was the club security. Detroit had actually gotten worse than before. It was always dangerous, but it had a lot of soul. Seems like crack finished the good vibe. Bands regularly got robbed and security needed shotguns.

When the fucking thing was over, Romi, my mother and I lit out for Hawaii. I was too weak to do anything. Romi adopted a family of wild cats that lived along the beach. She spent all her time tanning or feeding cats, while I watched the waves and wind. I wondered what Singapore must be like. I feared I would never know. I always wanted to visit Southeast Asia and adventure like Lord Jim. Shop in tiny oriental alleys. Get in barroom brawls. Lost in the jungle. Lead an insurrection. Get beaten with rattan cane. It was my greatest wish.

However, this didn't seem possible at the time and it depressed me. Yes, I had not been a model human being, but I didn't think I deserved to be stranded on Death Row. I felt ripped-off. I blamed God personally, and whatever traces of Christian belief I may have had quickly drained away into nihilism.

I had begun to go to AA meetings, but when my friends asked what was my "higher power," I simply said, "Ain't you?" Maybe more of a punk than before, I had no positive views of anything. Certainly not Jesus or any other formal organization. I hated holding hands and repeating "The Lord's Prayer." It filled me with loathing. My mother with her rosaries and weeping, "Oh God!" After all, this God had burned me in the street, taken my money and never came back. Christianity had done nothing I could see except barbecue Indians, start wars, and create a race of hypocrites. Bible in one hand and a shotgun in the other. Racist, cruel, vindictive, and secretly filled with hate.

"He was a good Christian man."—often heard remark in Texas.

If anybody ever said that about me, I would haunt them. Christians are a race of lunatics abiding by the words of a Jewish chronicle, edited by Romans, and dictated by six generations, none of which actually knew the Messiah. It was presented for the amusement of the educated Romans, but the fanatics in the tunnels took it literally. That's like believing in *Uncle Tom's Cabin* as a guide to Black American origins. I will admit the Bible is good "poetry," but so is *The Epic Of Gilgamesh* or *The Koran*. In fact, The Koran is even better poetry. Philosophy is the point of it all, and Jean Jacques Rousseau or Confucius are far better and less contradictory than Mr. Jesus H. Christ. Even Zoroaster is more interesting, although probably totally insane.

The Bible strictly belongs in the cinema with other Hollywood screenplays. Only good stuff in there is "Sodom & Gomorrah" or Ezekiel's psychedelic visions, although I do love the giant scorpion bit by St. Paul. Oh, if only Passolini were alive to put it on the screen. This time without George C. Scott. They could skip the Noah bit anyway, since the *Gilgamesh* tells it even better. Only the Torah bits work anyway. The First Testament has Solomon sleeping with Black women. Its more fun. The Second Testament fails everywhere. The Romans killed him, not the Jews. (Yes, it was whitey who killed Jesus.) If you were a Roman provincial Governor, you would have killed him too. To prevent an insurrection.

Although anyone who believes this stuff deserves to kneel or become a snake handler. I must admit there is one very true line in the Bible. It's at the very end in St. Paul (I forget which verse) "…and the yellow race shall inherit the earth…"—St. Paul AD 65. St. Paul could weave a wild story of bullshit that even old sailors and conquistadors could admire, but something struck him at the end. Perhaps it was complete irony of western civilization or maybe even his God. Maybe he was banging some Chinese bitch that he picked up on the Silk Road, but he never told more truth than that. He wandered off into Northern Turkey and disappeared. Nobody knows when he died, but I'll bet he followed the Silk Pussy Road all the way to Manchuria thinking to himself, "My God! Women who don't grow hair on their asses or even their legs! Always young looking too! Well, the Romans was gonna crucify my ass anyway. I'm gettin' a shack in downtown Peking. Never believed a word of that Jewish bullshit anyway."

Yes, but I'll never forget the giant scorpion bit. St. Paul was up there with the best of the rest in the world of surrealism.

"Great giant scorpions arose from the blackness. Many men sought death, but death could not be found."

And that's not even mentioning the seven devils and earthquakes and floods. All the same, the sting of those damn giant scorpions must have really hurt. And the Four Horsemen of the *Apocalypse Now* must have been ugly motherfuckers. After having visions like that, I would also retire in the Orient.

As you can imagine, I dropped out of AA. They kept having meetings at churches. They drank so much coffee and smoked so many cigarettes, it was fucking up my serenity. Wired-up foul breathed ex-drunks all repeating the same shit. I hated school, so I quit. I didn't start drinking again, but instead, I reckoned my serenity was home with the girls. While they chattered on incessantly in Japanese an overwhelming calm would come over me. I could read and relax and actually stay out of the bar. I was beginning to write songs again. One of which was "Emily's Changed," and the other one, "Flowing." I wrote them sitting in front of the window watching the trees on Elsham Road in warm summer heat. Windows open. Romi and Kayoko sewing dresses on the floor. I was comfortable just like that. Concentrating alone, but not alone.

As imagined, I ran into difficulties. I never slept well since going on the wagon and complained to the doctor in London. He prescribed a sedative that I suspect was valium based and by August, I was drinking again. It started in New York, at the Cherry Tree Lounge on Lexington Ave. Richard Thomas was in N.Y. too and had moved from Sonic Youth's loft to the Iriquois Hotel. I moved in with him. While I was alone one night, I threw up blood, and followed London's advice, going straight to the hospital. I was so embarrassed at being sick, I put down Debbie Harry as my next-of-kin. I know Debbie would never betray me. This was so I could keep it all a secret. I was in two days and out on the street on the third. Debbie didn't want to visit, because it was Lennox Hill Hospital, where Chris Stein had also been seriously ill. She did, however, stay in touch with me while I was on the inside and checked with my doctor regularly.

Once out of the hospital, I caught a flight to L.A. It seems rumour did not catch up with me, but my bills did. Blue Cross, upon hearing of my condition, dropped me and commented I was in the highest risk category. Uninsurable. Certain death. I wonder if these constant medical judgments didn't influence me, because in L.A. I didn't give a fuck anymore. Peter Case tried to take me to meetings. He even enticed me by telling me of a pretty Korean girl who would be at that night's meeting. I went. It was Lucy Kim. She had really changed. Nervous as usual, but without drugs. She looked much older. I wondered what she must have gone through.

I was still coughing up cigarette smoke from the meeting when

I got an exciting phone call. It seemed Haruko Minakami was in town. She went to go see Coverdale/Page and then came and stayed for two days. I really liked her. We danced all day and went swimming. I got smashed and fell in the pool. Hung around Sunset Blvd. I probably asked her to fuck me too, but I don't remember. I was so drunk. I went to sleep for two days afterwards, then ran across LAX and JFK to get home to London.

I arrived back in London and passed out again. When I woke up, the 60's had come back to get me. I opened my bedroom window and a huge demonstration was parading down my street. It was Moslems who wanted Salmon Rushdie killed. A week later there was a riot over the new Poll Tax (Flat Tax for you Americans) which made it very easy in Britain for rich people to get out of having to pay for social programs like the N.H.S. and better public schools. Maggie Thatcher introduced it under the influence of her close personal friend, Ronald Reagan. It set tax rates in accordance to districts so that the wealthy boroughs paid less Poll Tax than the poor ones. At a flat tax rate, the rich could easily afford it, but the poor could not. It would also lead to less public funding for social welfare and near abolishment of socialized medicine. Maggie was a cunning bitch alright. Ronnie and Maggie would have made a perfect Czar and Czarina. Mr. & Mrs. Whitedevil. The working class British were not all fooled however. Scotland refused to pay at all. There were over a million offenders in the first year. Scotland Yard flatly stated that they couldn't put everyone in jail. When they got us, we just paid. I tried to write it off on my U.S. taxes, but was denied. I had to accept double taxation. I vowed to escape them, but you never can. I asked Kayoko to set up an account in Luxembourg, but our money was just confetti to those banks.

Now I had to escape the 60's. Everywhere I went, I was hearing Hendrix or the Velvets being rediscovered. We fled to Greece.

ART

FEIN

FROM THE BOOK

THE L.A. MUSICAL HISTORY TOUR

CAPITOL RECORDS

1750 N. Vine
Hollywood

The "stack of records" building opened in 1955, thirteen years after the label's founding. It has been home to many hits. Just look at the lobby—the walls are festooned with gold records by The Beatles, Frank Sinatra, Glen Campbell, Helen Reddy, The Band, The Kingston Trio, Peggy Lee, Steve Miller, Pink Floyd, Les Paul and Mary Ford, Nat King Cole, Bob Seger, Duran Duran, The Beach Boys, Dean Martin and many others. Its still-operational recording studios reverberate with the history of music that has rocked the world. Today Capitol continues as a player in the tempest-tossed record business, making it easily the longest running Hollywood record company (more than 55 years). The light atop the Capitol Tower "needle" blinks H-O-L-L-Y-W-O-O-D in Morse Code. In December, the pole is draped with lights making an illuminated Christmas tree.

CARPENTERS APARTMENTS

We've Only Just Begun –
8345 5th St., Downey
Close To You–
8356 5th St., Downey

When Karen and Richard Carpenter hit it big in the seventies, they invested in the old neighborhood, building these across-the-street from each other apartments buildings and naming them after their two biggest hits. The song-naming penchant continues: Richard houses a collection of vintage cars in a building named "Yesterday Once More" in Downey. (Downey is a suburb ten miles south of downtown L.A. that has produced famous musicians over three decades. In the sixties The Chantay's did "Pipeline" on the now-defunct Downey label; the Carpenters emerged in the seventies; The Blasters broke through from Downey in the eighties and Downey is just a stone's throw (well, if Hercules threw it) from Hawthorne, where The Beach Boys grew up—See WENZEL'S.)

THE CASTLE

(former location)
4320 Cedarhurst Circle
Los Feliz

In 1966, Arthur Lee and his band Love lived in this rambling manse which was not the location of the first album's "rock" photos. (That stone formation, in a well-hidden Laurel Canyon location, has been demolished.) The song, "The Castle," appears on Love's *Da Capo* album, and a fanatical Love appreciation magazine, *The Castle*, is published in England.

CAT & FIDDLE

6530 Sunset Blvd.
Hollywood

British musician Kim Gardner (Creation, Byrds, Ashton, Gardner & Dyke) owns this British bistro in the heart of Hollywood with his wife Paula. It is not just a pub with dart boards and pints—though it is that—but a respected restaurant with English & American fare, on a large outdoor patio. Many British musicians (Gardner's old bandmate Ron Wood, for one) and sports figures make this a home away from home

when they visit L.A. There is no set live-music policy though Jazz on Sundays and open-mike Mondays seem in palce, but it is always interesting—for example, in mid-1997 Carlos Guitarlos debuted the Top Jimmyless Rhythm Pigs here.

CATHAY DE GRANDE

(former location)
Selma & Argyle
Hollywood

The Cathay de Grande was a Chinese restaurant turned punk nightclub that reigned during that music's heyday in the late seventies and early eighties. Blues (Roy Brown, Memphis Slim), punk (Black Flag), roots (The Blasters,

Rose Maddox), and pop (The Go-Go's, The Knack) bands played in its danger-ously crowded basement until the club closed in 1985. (It reopened briefly as the All American Tavern later that year.) The Van Halen song "Top Jimmy" was written about the club's blues-belting mainstay, who, with his band the Rhythm Pigs, held sway here on Monday nights. (Top Jimmy got his name by working at Top Taco, across from A&M Records.) The Cathay's sign can be seen in the film *Eating Raoul* when Paul Bland is riding atop a truck at night.

THE CATHOUSE

(former location)
836 North Highland
Hollywood

This club, described by founder Riki Rachtman as "a rock and roll haven for decadents," was a slice of heavy metal heaven. Hard rockers in leather with big hair used to come here to meet girls in various states of dress and undress. This Tuesdays-only club operated for about four years and closed in the early 1990s.

THE CAVERN CLUB

(former location)
alley behind 6419 Hollywood Blvd.
Hollywood

The swinging "mod" scene burst forth anew in 1985 at this colorful but short-lived club. It started here in the old KFWB radio building as a sixties club called Rave-Up that was run by "King of Clubs" Larry Lazar. When Bomp Records maven Greg Shaw took over from Lazar shortly after its inception (Lazar moved on to other projects) he renamed it The Cavern, and installed deejay Audrey Moorehead (who later co-hosted the "It's Happening" TV show with Domenic Priore). The apparition of sixties-clad-and-coiffed teenagers dancing anew to "beat" records caught the fancy of the media and The Cavern was covered by People, Time, "Entertainment Tonight," and other news outlets. The Cavern closed after less than a year.

THE CENTRAL
(former location)
8852 Sunset Blvd.
West Hollywood

From 1969 to 1981 it was Filthy McNasty's nightclub (the old Filthy McNasty's awning can be seen in the upper-left corner of The Sweet's 1975 *Desolation Boulevard* album cover—See FM STATION). Prior to that it was The Melody Room. For many years The Central was a dependable work-horse bar for bands on the way up, and also a well-known jam club—Eric Burdon and John Belushi used to sit in, and many big stars did guest stints. Chuck E. Weiss and the Goddam Liars held forth every Monday to packed houses for more than six years, drawing a diverse swatch of show business revelers and savvy civilians. The Central was made up to be the London Fog for the Oliver Stone Doors movie, but this was not the location of that club—it was up the street, west of the Whisky (See BETWEEN CLARK AND HILLDALE). In 1993, actor Johnny Depp opened The Viper Room in this space (See THE VIPER ROOM).

CENTURY CITY
Santa Monica Blvd.
Avenue of the Stars
Los Angeles

Tom Petty sang "Don't Wanna Live In Century City" as a protest against the coldness of this Brasilia-like city, built on the former back lot of the 20th Century-Fox film studios (hence "Century" City, see?). This slab of pseudo-Manhattan is known for its tall buildings full of lawyers—perhaps that's why Petty thought it lacked warmth. (Petty's song was reportedly inspired by a visit with his idol, ex-Byrd Roger McGuinn, who once lived here.)

CHADNEY'S RESTAURANT
3000 W. Olive
Burbank

Not rock-historical on its own (its adjacency to NBC-TV doesn't concern us, this is a music book), it has been a regular gig site for two prominent LA session men, Earl Palmer and Emil Richards,

who have performed here weekly for much of the 1980s and 1990s. Palmer is a jazz-based drummer whose rhythms have powered countless hit rock & roll records, starting in 1949 in his native New Orleans with Fats Domino's "The Fat Man." He played on most New Orleans hits of the early and mid 1950s, including virtually all by Fats, Little Richard, and Professor Longhair. In 1957 he moved to Los Angeles and became (permanently it seems) one of our town's most important percussionists, playing on records ranging from "La Bamba" and "You've Lost That Lovin' Feelin'" to 'class' acts like Sinatra and Diana Ross. Percussionist Emil Richards played on countless records in the 1960s and was an original member of Phil Spector's "Recking Crew."

RAY CHARLES' OFFICE (RPM PRODUCTIONS)

2107 W. Washington Blvd.
Los Angeles

Ray Charles runs his businesses from this office building, which also contains recording studios where he has made records since 1963. He has not done much outside production lately, but during the 1960s Charles recorded artists like Louis Jordan and Billy Preston here for his Tangerine label. Stevie Wonder, Glen Campbell, and Quincy Jones have recorded with Ray as well. (Don't show up here. Send a tape.)

CHATEAU MARMONT

8221 Sunset Blvd.
West Hollywood

A manor in the old-style manner, this space has long been a beacon to movie stars and also to rockers: Bob Dylan, Iggy Pop, Mick Jagger, Gram Parsons, Ringo Starr, and the Jefferson Airplane have been tenants. Barry Mann & Cynthia Weill wrote "You've Lost That Lovin' Feelin'" in the Chateau, and first played it for Phil Spector over a Chateau phone. Jim Morrison took his friend Danny Sugerman here to see drug-wracked Tim Hardin. (Later, when Morrison lived here, he hurt his back trying to swing from the roof into his window hanging onto a drain pipe.) John Lennon and Yoko

Ono sometimes stayed in the nearby bungalows, Led Zeppelin rented them for orgies and, of course, in 1982 John Belushi died in one. In 1990, actor Bud Cort, a former tenant, co-directed a documentary film about the Chateau for German television. The rooms are old-worldy, and the lobby is too—the Chateau is the height of good taste and discretion.

"CHERISH" BIRTHPLACE
721 N. Alfred
West Hollywood

Association founding member Terry Kirkman was living in this apartment in 1965 when he had a decision to make: whether to watch the 11:00 news or write a song. He opted for the latter, and in a half hour composed "Cherish," ("The word had interested me for a long, long time," said Kirkman) which became the band's biggest record. (Two Association recordings rank in the 50 most-played songs of all time: "Cherish," and the Addrisi bothers' composition "Never My Love.")

CINNAMON CINDER
(former location)
11345 Ventura Blvd.
Studio City

This big teenage night club of the sixties was run by enterprising radio personality Bob Eubanks, who rose to TV fame as the host of "The Newlywed Game." In 1964 Eubanks presented The Beatles at the Hollywood Bowl, and it was here that The Beatles held their press conference before the show. Three Dog Night singer Danny Hutton remembers, as a teenager, being personally ejected by Eubanks when he was hanging around without the price of admission. The house band, The Pastel Six, scored a national hit with "Cinnamon Cinder," written for them (the club predates the song) by Russ Regan (See WENZEL'S). There was also a Cinnamon Cinder in Long Beach. The site next became the Magic Mushroom (Firesign Theater did some memorable KPPC broadcasts from here); then the Point After sports bar; and then a country-music club called V.I.S. (purportedly Very Important Shitkicker), run by Dick Clark.

CIRO'S

(former location)
8433 Sunset Blvd.
West Hollywood

Now a legend in its own right as The Comedy Store, this building originally held Ciro's, a high-life club for the rich and famous from 1939 to its closing in 1957. In the early 1960s it reopened as the Crazy Horse, a twist club, featuring Donnie Brooks ("Mission Bell") as the house band. Next it reopened as Ciro's, and featured hot new acts like Sonny and Cher (part of their 1967 movie *Good Times* was shot here), The Lovin' Spoonful, and The Byrds (their first album's back cover shows them onstage here with Bob Dylan). By 1966 the name had changed to It's Boss, and the club held sway over teenyboppers with a regular menu of hot acts: Love, Tom Jones, Dino, Desi and Billy—and a fifteen-year-old age minimum(!) After the Sunset Strip fracas in late 1966, It's Boss reopened on February 22, 1967, with more mature music—Marvin Gaye was the first headliner, followed by Brook Benton, and The Fifth Dimension. It rode out the sixties with a variety of acts, including that of the temporary home of the psychedelic club Kaleidoscope (See AQUARIUS). From 1970 to 1976 Art Laboe ran his Oldies But Goodies club—the first of its kind in America (See ORIGINAL SOUND RECORDS) —here, and then the club was taken over by Sammy (later Mitzi) Shore's Comedy Store.

CLUB 88

(former location)
11784 Pico Blvd.
West Los Angeles

This was the west side equivalent of Hollywood's Cathay de Grande in the 1980s, the former strip-show house showcased rising bands, including The Go-Go's, The Bangles, The Blasters, and X. (Much of the X footage in Penelope Spheeris's punk documentary *The Decline of Western Civilization* was shot here.)

CLUB LINGERIE

6507 Sunset Blvd.

Hollywood

As Club Lingerie it has hosted The Plasmatics, The Replacements, Joe Turner, The Cramps, Sleepy La Beef, Foster and Lloyd—a diverse bag. During the seventies this was Souled Out, a soul nightclub. Many performers hung out here, including Tina Turner, Etta James, Kris Kristofferson, Bloodstone and Stevie Wonder (Motown had its office right across the street). During the 1960s it was The Red Velvet. Though The Kinks, Sonny and Cher, and The Turtles appeared here, The Red Velvet generally drew an older rock crowd for bands like The Righteous Brothers, The Bobby Fuller Four, and The Knickerbockers (the house band, whose "Lies" hit number twenty on the Billboard charts in 1966). As a result, it was summarily dismissed on Zappa's "freak" map as "HQ for the plastic & pompadour set." (Perhaps prophetically as a new "pompadour set" emerged in the 1980s at the club's "Rockabilly Wednesdays.") Going still further back, Eddie Cochran played here in 1959. And record producer Kim Fowley remembers coming to the KRLA Teen Night Club here in 1960 and seeing Eugene Church, Bobby Day and John and Judy (a brother-sister act from which John Maus and Scott Engel of The Walker Brothers emerged).

EDDIE COCHRAN GRAVE

Forest Lawn Cemetery

Cypress

Eddie Cochran's grave is little noted at the Cypress branch of the famed Forest Lawn cemetery chain, Karen Carpenter's nearby crypt well overshadows it. The beautiful relief-engraved headstone lies flat and attracts little attention—quite a contrast to what Cochran album annotator Lenny Kaye called "his mad dash through life." As a teenager in Bell Gardens, a factory city in south L.A., Eddie was constantly writing and singing. Like Buddy Holly, his earliest effort was in a country duo, with Hank Cochran (no relation). He recorded for small labels and appeared at record hops and school assemblies with deejay Art

Laboe. Liberty Records in Hollywood signed Eddie in 1956, and a string of hits followed, including "Summertime Blues," "C'mon Everybody," and "Something Else." He also appeared in two seminal rock movies, *Untamed Youth* and *The Girl Can't Help It* (to which he was added at the last minute after the film company's negotiations with Elvis Presley fell through). Cochran led a rocker's lifestyle. He rode a motorcycle, and hung with Gene Vincent, Buddy Holly, Ricky Nelson, and Johnny and Dorsey Burnette (See GENE VINCENT, RICKY NELSON, BURNETTE BROTHERS). His popularity in England was enormous—he was one of the few American rockers to tour there. On his U.K. tour in the spring of 1960 he traveled town-to-town like a Caesar in a triumphant motorcade flanked by his girlfriend, Sharon Sheeley (See SHARON SHEELEY), and fellow rocker Gene Vincent. But that was his final tour. On April 17, 1960, he, Sheeley, and Vincent were heading to Heathrow airport for their return flight to America when their taxicab skidded on a rain-slick road and crashed, killing Cochran and seriously injuring Sheeley and Vincent. Cochran's memory is still cherished in England and France (many rockers there sport his likeness in tattoos). The English film Radio On (1979) features Sting as a gas station attendant who works near the crash site and dedicates his life to Cochran.

COCOANUT GROVE
Ambassador Hotel
3400 Wilshire Blvd.
Los Angeles

Look quick—this venerable old nightclub, and the hotel that surrounds it, is scheduled for demolition (though as of 1998 its fate is still far from settled). The wrecker's ball will end a story that started in 1921, when The Ambassador opened as one of the classiest hotels in the world. Along with the splendid hostelry came the Cocoanut Grove, whose tropical-palm motif set the stage for elegant movie star parties. Even when times changed, the Ambassador moved with them and remained a top-notch venue throughout the 1960s (though it's most remembered, alas, for the killing of Robert Kennedy here in 1968). The Cocoanut Grove changed too. For a while it was the Now Grove with Sammy Davis, Jr. and it booked rock acts as well. On April 16, 1967, The Kaleidoscope temporarily set up shop here, calling itself the Banana Grove and presenting a bill that consisted of The Grateful Dead, Jefferson Airplane, and Canned Heat. Rock acts continued to appear sporadically through the 1970s—Ike and Tina Turner, Etta James, Waylon Jennings, Bonnie Raitt, The Boomtown Rats—but ultimately it just didn't work, and the Cocoanut Grove became inactive in the 1980s. It continues to be used for movies and videos. The televised Roy Orbison tribute with Bruce Springsteen and Elvis Costello was done here on October 30, 1987. (The Lovin' Spoonful do a song, "Coconut Grove," on their *Hums of the Lovin' Spoonful* album, but it's about a place in Florida).

NAT KING COLE
former home
401 South Muirfield
Hollywood
(Do Not Disturb Occupants)
When Nat King Cole moved into this luxurious home in the elegant Hancock Park area of L.A. in 1947, the residents revolted against "coloreds" moving in. Daughter Natalie Cole says she can remember seeing the word "nigger" burnt into their lawn. Cole weathered this storm by going door to door and introducing himself to his neighbors. (It is said that a neighbor told him he was wary of "undesirables," and Cole said, "If I see any, I'll call you.") He died here in 1965. It is no longer the Cole family residence.

HIGHLAND GROUNDS
742 N. Highland Ave.
Hollywood
A definitive nineties venue (it opened Jan 1, 1990), this quaint restaurant/beer & wine bar/ coffeehouse features acoustic performers of all stripes: folkies, hicks, glam bands, whatever. For instance: Beck and Lisa Loeb; Chuck E. Weiss held a weekly slot here for a couple of years; and Randy California did his last performance here. Owner Rich Brenner is proud of the club's "strong sense of community" — and who can argue with that?

THE HOLLYWOOD BOWL

2301 N. Highland Ave.
Hollywood

Built in 1929, it's seen the best rock acts, from the 1960 Dick Clark/Art Laboe show with Frankie Avalon, Freddy Cannon, et al., to The Beatles, Bob Dylan, Donovan, Santana, Elton John, Janis Joplin and many others. Hendrix opened for The Monkees here in 1967. A Doors performance was recorded live here in 1968 and released on video. This beautiful outdoor arena seats 18,000. Today, it concentrates mainly on classical music, as well as on an annual jazz festival. (As with the Greek Theater, beware of "stacked parking" in the lot.)

THE HOLLYWOOD HAWAIIAN HOTEL

(former location)
Yucca & Grace
Hollywood

These rooms held a lot of musicians. In his 1977 song "Desperadoes Under the Eaves," Warren Zevon sings about sitting here listening to the air conditioner hum. Joe Selvin's book, *Ricky Nelson: Idol for a Generation*, recounts Ricky and songwriter Sharon Sheeley going to the Hollywood Hawaiian in 1958 to pick up The Everly Brothers, who were staying there. (It all ties in—before going solo, Zevon played piano with The Everly Brothers.) Pink Floyd stayed here in the late sixties, as did The Kinks. In 1970, when Jeremy Spencer of Fleetwood Mac left to mail a letter and never came back, he left from this hotel.

HOLLYWOOD PACIFIC BUILDING

6425 Hollywood Blvd.
Hollywood

In the early 1960s, this place held the offices of Sam Cooke's SAR Records and Lew Chudd's Imperial Records until Imperial's sale to Liberty in 1963 and Cooke's death in 1964.

THE HOLLYWOOD PALLADIUM

6215 Sunset Blvd.
Hollywood

Opened in 1940, this 5000-capacity (not seated) venue has been host to a giant selection of music, from Frank Sinatra in the forties, to The Teenage Fair in the early sixties, to The Rolling Stones, The Grateful Dead, The Who, David Bowie, The Ramones, The Clash, the 1973 Surf Revival, Chuck Berry (the 1973 concert where he kicked Keith Richard off the stage, discussed in the Chuck Berry bio-movie *Hail Hail Rock and Roll*), the Blues Brothers movie concert scene, the Grammy awards, Mexican dances...everything. In photos of the Palladium from the sixties and seventies you see Lawrence Welk's name atop the marquee, as he owned the place and broadcast his TV show from here.

HOLLYWOOD ROOSEVELT HOTEL

7000 Hollywood Blvd.
Hollywood

Opened with great fanfare in 1927 (the first Academy Awards ceremony was held here), this place grew shaky by the 1970s, but in the mid-1980s underwent a tremendous overhaul that made it one of the first "magnet" buildings of the "New Hollywood." The attached Cinegrill restaurant/ nightclub has been presenting cabaret acts since its reopening in 1987. Some rock stars stay here, and The Everly Brothers are said to be investors, which could account for their Walk of Fame star being right on this corner. Also famed for a once-only punk show featuring The Go-Gos, The Germs, The Mau-Maus and Hal Negro & The Satintones.

HOLLYWOOD SIGN

Mt. Lee
Hollywood Hills

Erected in 1923 for the Hollywoodland housing development, it's smiled down on Hollywood ever since. (Occasionally it didn't smile, like when an unsuccessful actor or actress would try to use it as a permanent ticket out of show business.) The sign fell into decrepitude in the 1970s, and demolition was considered until a group of Hollywood do-gooders donated $27,000 each for its restoration in 1978. Musical contributors were Alice Cooper, who donated the last "O" on behalf of his friend Groucho Marx, and crooner Andy Williams, who donated the "W."

HOUSE OF BLUES

8439 Sunset Blvd.
West Hollywood

Since it opened in late 1994, this club has not just dominated the upper end of the L.A. club scene, it has become it. High priced club acts (Tom Jones), auditorium fillers (Eric Clapton), local bands (the Sprague Bros.) and more all play this 1100-capacity instant-landmark, leaving all other clubs behind. Owned overtly by Dan

Ackroyd and supported by a cabal of Hollywood high-rollers who pay to keep the blues alive (blues acts do play here, there's a gospel lunch every Sunday, and they sponsor workshops in Watts), it must be saluted for filling this city's need for a large nightclub with a blues/roots emphasis. Of course there are those who complain that the club with such a name is not an 'authentic' Mississippi Blues Shack (though part of it is), but most people simply shrug like Joe E. Brown in *Some Like It Hot* and say "Nobody's perfect!" Don't miss the spectacular Elvis Presley Birthday Bash held here every January 8th.

HOUSE OF FREBERG LIMITED (BUT NOT VERY)

(former location)
89720 Sunset
West Hollywood

Satirist Stan Freberg had his headquarters here during the 1960s, producing ads and occasional music parodies. The humorist grew up in Pasadena and cut all his great Capitol records in Hollywood. His monumental *Stan Freberg Presents the History of the United States of America* was released in 1990 on CD with extra cuts. Volume 2 of this record was released in 1996 and was a runaway hit for Rhino Records. This building was once a Hollywood designer's studio and now houses a fancy restaurant.

THE ICE HOUSE

24 North Mentor
Pasadena

The popular folk club of the fifties, sixties and seventies is now a comedy club (with music thrown in too), still nestled down an alleyway off Colorado Blvd. People who've played here include Peter Tork (pre-Monkees), Roy Brown, Steve Martin, The Association, The Standells, Bob Lind, Ian Whitcomb, Hearts and Flowers, The Yellow Balloon and many other folk, country and blues-oriented acts.

BILLY IDOL CRASH SITE

Gordon & Fountain
Hollywood

February 6, 1990, Billy Idol, celebrating both the completion of his new album, Charmed Life, and the imminent arrival of his parents from England, took an 8 a.m. spin on his motorcycle. For no apparent reason he spilled the bike at this intersection and suffered a broken arm and broken leg.

IRV'S BURGERS

8289 Sunset
West Hollywood
This was the location for the inner foldout of Linda Ronstadt's *Living in the U.S.A.* (1978). The same photo could not be taken today because the garage next door has erected a fence.

THE IVAR THEATER

1605 Ivar
Hollywood
Recently a strip-show house, The Ivar was a legit theater when Lord Buckley recorded a live album there on February 12, 1959, and when The Grateful Dead played there on February 25, 1966. (The Tom Waits song, "Emotional Weather Report," makes reference to "a ticket taker's smile" at The Ivar.) Strip shows have only recently ceased.

JACK'S SUGAR SHACK

1707 Vine St.
Hollywood
After a couple of years bouncing around various locations in the early 1990s, Jack settled his tropical decor club here, a few feet from Hollywood & Vine. Roots-rock and country and blues are always on tap. Don't miss Ronnie Mack's long-lived widely-loved Barn Dance here Tuesday nights — it's free, and jammed with stars both known and not.

BILLY JAMES
FORMER RESIDENCE

8404 Kirkwood
Laurel Canyon
(Do Not Disturb Occupants)
When Columbia A&R man Billy James moved to Elektra Records in

1967, he moved into this Laurel Canyon home. His house was a gathering place for musicians, including Jackson Browne, who lived downstairs in the laundry room for about a year. (James, when at Columbia, wrote the liner notes to the first Byrds album, and signed The Doors—whose option Columbia later dropped due to lack of interest.) From 1969 to 1971, James also co-owned The Black Rabbit Inn at 8727 Melrose, a mellow show-biz boîte that was partly bankrolled by Elmer Bernstein, Jack Nicholson and The Doors, among others.

JOAN JETT FORMER RESIDENCE

1025 San Vicente Blvd.
West Hollywood
(Do Not Disturb Occupants)

Rocker Joan Jett lived in this apartment in 1977, when she first moved to Hollywood. Not surprisingly, it is close to The Whisky (it would be in the club's shadow if the sun shone from the north). Jett began her musical career in the all-girl hard rock group The Runaways in 1975. In 1978 she produced the first Germs album. She began her own band, Joan Jett and The Blackhearts in 1979, through an ad in Music Connection magazine. Their fame grew steadily, from small gigs around L.A. to international success in 1982 with "I Love Rock & Roll".

BENNY JONES'S HOUSE

(former location)
3438 W. 118th Pl.
Inglewood

In early 1962, musician Gary Usher ("Driven Insane", Titan, 1960) came to visit his uncle Benny at his house on the Inglewood/Hawthorne border. Like everyone for several square blocks, he heard rock & roll blasting from the Wilson family garage on nearby 119th St., and walked over to see what was going on. He struck up a friendship with the band, The Beach Boys, then collaborated with bandleader Brian, writing two of the Beach Boys' biggest hits, "409" and "In My Room." Usher went on to create studio bands like the Hondells and the Super Stocks, produced three Byrds' albums (*Younger Than Yesterday, Sweetheart Of The Rodeo, Notorious Byrd Bros.*), and become head of A&R for RCA Records, among other things. He died May 25, 1990 of lung cancer at age 51

JANIS JOPLIN DEATH SITE
Landmark Hotel
(now the Highland Gardens)
7047 Franklin Ave.
Hollywood

Once Janis Joplin took the stage at The Monterey Pop Festival in 1967 she was on a one-way rocket to the top— only to die alone at age twenty-seven, in room 105 of this Hollywood hotel from an overdose of heroin. A lot has been written about the pain Joplin endured. Roundly rejected in her hometown of Port Arthur, Texas (she was voted "Ugliest Man on Campus" in a college poll) in 1966 she fled to San Francisco to seek a new life, and found it with the band Big Brother and The Holding Company. They grew with San Francisco's burgeoning music scene, and she was catapulted to the top, becoming the single most celebrated singer of that town and that era. Wealth, fame and world acclaim followed, yet she remained the wild, sad, hippie girl with a pint of Southern Comfort always at hand. Her death here at the Landmark Hotel on October 3, 1970 from an overdose of pure heroin (reportedly mistaken for diluted) was a shock to fans throughout the world. Her latest album *Pearl* (1971), had shown a new maturity that seemed to promise even better days. "Me and Bobby McGee" from that album was her first number one hit, averring "freedom's just another word for nothing left to lose."

JOSHUA TREE
NATIONAL FOREST
Cap Rock
Joshua Tree

When Gram Parsons' body (See GRAM PARSONS DEATH SITE) disappeared from the L.A. airport September 20, 1973, police suspected devil-worship

or worse, but the reason for the theft was friendship. Depressed at band-mate Clarence White's funeral a few weeks earlier, Parsons told road manager Phil Kaufman that he didn't want a funeral if he died, he wanted his body to be burned in the desert. Kaufman, and partner Michael Martin, took the body from the airport (where it was to be flown

to New Orleans for burial) in a hearse (which made their ruse believable to airport authorities) and drove to Cap Rock in Joshua Tree. (Kaufman says Cap Rock was not a favorite spot of Parsons, it was chosen because they were too drunk to drive any further and afforded ample getaway space.) They doused Parson's body in gasoline and lit it, causing at first a fireball, then bubbling and "melting" of the body. The perpetrators fled, and the remains were once again routed to New Orleans where they were buried.

JUMBO'S CLOWN ROOM
5153 Hollywood Blvd.
Hollywood
This is the strip club where Courtney Love allegedly danced topless when she first moved to L.A.

PHIL KAUFMAN
FORMER RESIDENCE
Chandler St, W. of Ethel
North Hollywood
(Do Not Disturb Occupants)
After the arrest of road manager Phil Kaufman, and partner Michael Martin, for stealing Gram Parsons' body from the airport and immolating it at Cap Rock (See JOSHUA TREE NATIONAL FOREST), a

concert was held in the back yard here to raise money for him. (The criminal charge was reduced to misdemeanor theft, and settled with a fine). Barry Hansen, radio's Dr. Demento, remembers that there was a small crowd for Kaufman's Koffin Kaper Koncert, with acts ranging from Barry 'Boris' Pickett ("Monster Mash") to The Modern Lovers. The show raised a few bucks for Kaufman (rodeo tailor "Nudie" Cohen dropped by and donated $500), and he resumed his career as, to cop the title of his autobiography, a Road Mangler Deluxe. Among the more noted residents of Kaufman's guest house were Gram Parsons and various members of the Manson family (before their "notoriety"). But perhaps Kaufman's attitude was encapsulated best on his personalized license plate which read PH KAUF (someone took offense and the DMV revoked it.)

E L L Y N
MAYBE

FROM THE BOOK

THE COWARDICE OF AMNESIA

DO YOU FEAR ME

Do you fear me cause I wear
    a purple friendship bracelet?
Do you fear having me as a friend?
Are you afraid to introduce me
    to your grandparents?
The only perfect thing about me
    is my perfect lack of confidence.
Does that freak you out?
I'm fat.
How does that sit with you?
I wear political pins.
Does that bother you?
I'm a bookworm.
Does that depress you?
Are you terrified
    cause I've been bas mitzvahed?
Are you scared
    cause I think spiders are sacred?
I'm left handed. oooooooooooooo No comment.
Do you worry about me cause I'm a virgin?
Cause I'm loud and sometimes embarrassing,
    are you wary of spending time with me?
I know where the feminist bookstores are
    in a whole bunch of states.
Does that make you tremble?
People think I'm younger
    and older than I am.
Does that reflect badly on you somehow?

I don't always comb my hair.
Can you hear it coming?
Is it my ugliness or beauty that
frightens you the most?
Are you afraid of me cause I'm human?

I HAVE NEVER FALLEN IN LOVE WITH ANYONE WHO FELT COMFORTABLE IN AMERICA

I have never fallen in love
    with anyone who felt
    comfortable in America

people who wear the 60's
    on their eyebrows like a birthmark

who wear turn of the century Russia
    like a boat with a hull made of flame

people who wear Montreal
    like an almanac
    that is a forbidden book
    floating on their adam's apple

people who wear a T.V
    under their arms
    like a deodorant
    trying to decide
    where the antenna belongs

people who can recite 80 poems
    but can't remember
    their driver's license
    have my respect

people who can sing 100 bottles
    of sandpaintings on the wall
    backwards
    in the time it takes
    to pour the shotglass
    that pulls its trigger slowly

people who talk to dogs
    and trees
    and are afraid
    to ask the time
    and yet somehow know
    are beloved

people who wear anthems they make
    with paisley and parsley
    and mesh together a bell
    that rings through the soundproof sky
    the government is trying to sanction

people whose fingers tell stories
    of peace and love and thunderclouds
    overcome by a dish of lightning
    with a side of stars

people who don't listen
    at the most popular
    time of day
    to the most popular
    radio station
    because they'd rather be wishing

people who have cars
      so full of bumperstickers
      the engine is only incidental

the people
      who miss card catalogs

the people who miss
      cream rising to the top
the people who yearn for deja-vu

the people who love Leonard Cohen's voice
Leonard Cohen

these are the ones I sing to
      in my overbitten sleep.

A DAY IN THE LIFE OF A
WORKING POOR XYLOPHONE MAKER

the psychedelic alarm clock that knows
      all of the songs by the byrds,
      the monkees, and various barnyard animals
      is broken so I wake up when I wake up
      and try to call time to find out
      what it is, man.

but the collection agency took my phone away
      so I put on some bellbottoms
      and trust the sun like a compass
      and try to estimate the time.
L.A. is smog urchin of the science fiction
      nightmares so my eyes begin to sweat
      like bruce springsteen's forehead
      in a bandana after a concert in wyoming.

I still don't know what time it is
      but I remember my upstairs neighbor
      has a grandfather clock so I walk upstairs
      and realize she's run off
      with my boyfriend, tire
      an automobile mechanic who only fixes
      deadhead vans.

they left a hologram for the slum landlord
I read it as best as I could with the help
      of a tiny tim strobe light

"dear slum landlord who charged a buck extra
      for rent every time we played truckin'
      who drew a salvador dali mustache
      on the poster of janis joplin
      we're leaving this land to start
      a new life defending tubas
      from the threat of harmonicas."
tire used to think the feminine nombre
      of el salvador was la salvador
      and that they were separate countries
      but agreed on i before e except after c.

ciao there are edible tambourines in the oven
meanwhile the oven was involved
      in a court case charging brillo pads
      with unnecessary cruelty.

so 1984
I went hungry and went to work at
      vegetarian records and benevolent videos.
my job is at a record store that
      ironically doesn't sell records.
we sell software, hard contact lenses,
      guitars that gently weep,
      hysterical mandolins, drums that chant,
      day-glo patio furniture, compact discs
      and there's a 12 inch singles dating club
      for classical and rock fans who like bach
      and bachman turner overdrive and know the
      difference between g sharp enough to
      cut glass and g dull.

my record store has only one employee
me
it has 85 bosses
there's a boss for a-l jazz / m-z punk
a boss for the tofu licorice aisle
a boss for customer bitching
a boss for my bitching
a boss for time clock grievances
a boss for sex harassments
a boss for posters of 70's disco icons
     turned talk show hosts.
a great deal of worker-employer tension
     is created by the dress code congress
on monday I wear scottish kilts
on tuesday I wear a see through blouse
     with a polka-dot bra that I burn
     just before my shift
wednesday I wear platform heels
     and dress up like a subway
thursday I wear maps in my hair
     and guitar picks in my teeth
friday I dress in a miniskirt
     made of spinach
saturday I keep the sabbath and at least
     seven out of the ten commandments
sunday I dress like a minimall,
     which means I wear a yogurt hat
     and my shirt is made out
     of 7/11 bags and there
     is the inevitable laundromat tag
     around my neck like a steady ring.

I work there to make ends meet
      my ends don't even meet, get close,
      get married or nothing
      my ends aren't even acquainted
      on a first name basis.
I am paid the minimum wage
      and lots of money is taken
      out of my paper airplane paycheck
      cause george bush thinks the minimum wage
      is too high and subversives like me
      might spend money buying groceries.
i've had weeks where toothpaste on crackers
      was both meal and hygiene.
this while aaron spelling builds his
      800,000 square foot home for two.
the murder of robin hood remains unsolved.

being the only employee has its moments
the league of athletics for
      macrobiotic record stores
      disqualified me saying there is no way
      I can be shortstop, pitcher,
      cotton candy hawker and left fielder
I said yes yes more more
i'm a liberal
      and I saw tom waits playing babe ruth
      playing w.c. fields in a movie once
it can be done.

needless to say my team made
      the solitaire finals.

people tell me i'm modest but I have a
        thriving xylophone making thing going.
in some circles i'm known as the
        les paul of the xylophone.
granted I haven't sold any
        but not cause they're atonal.
the true reason was a jealous accordion
        player with a john wayne fetish saw me
        picketing his star on hollyhype boulevard
        screaming
        "custer died for your sins"
        and "pow wow power."
a xylophone maker has to follow her heart.
I recognize woodstock nation.
anarchist nation.
sovereign nations.
and I recognize the state of kansas
        from an airplane.

so that's a typical day for me,
at night I look at teabags till i'm drowsy
my stove was repossessed
        so I can't cook no more
but i'm keeping a stiff upper lip
        there's hope.
someone brought a victrola record player
        into the store and the boss of
        employee-pats-on-the-back-every-time-
        i-get-that-i'm-about-to-get-a-real-job-
        selling-kazoos-look hands me that

mystic, almost dinosaur-wise l.p. dog and
says a counterfeit penny for your thoughts.
I smile as the victrola dog gives me
the victory sign.
he has something up his paw.
it looks like revolution from here.
I swear this dog has che guevara's chin.
someday our song will be played.

WANT TO BE A STRIPPER

Want to be a stripper
Want to sell something
Want to travel

I thought of being a stripper
a girl came into an open mike
and said how she used to be a stripper
it was humiliating
men are jerks to the 100th power
they made us feel like objects she said
I thought that sounds like my life
it sounds like woman's life

our clothes come off in other eyes
why won't that one talk to you
why won't that one sing a song for you

likes your clothes
likes your mind

strip so someone else can know you
strip so you can know yourself

$150 dollars a night
        on a slow night
as a woman you're always on display

$4.25 an hour
you walk cross the street
a man shouts hey fat girl
he strips your mind
strip mining for ladders to climb
        to ejaculate his ego
the land won't be the same

stripping for yourself
putting on Neil Young records
writing a manifesto
life is a nudist camp
        if you're perceptive
        you can pretty much tell
        where things stand

where are the callouses of love?
practice living long enough
        and you might get callouses
yet you might not

where does language end and truth begin?
he mentioned illusion
he mentioned reality
he mentioned the past the present
        and the future
he talked with a coyote tongue
he held me with one finger clinging
        to the edge of a cliff

he fell first in my eyes
he fell second in my mind

I wanted to pull him up to solid ground
maybe not entirely solid
maybe baying with tie-dyed alligators
    made his voice sound so smooth

I thought his teeth were
    full of light and mirrors
I wanted to see
    what I wanted to be there
    he said we can't...
    to whatever the question was
he said the earth is our mother
I heard him say that

he is holier than a piece of wafer
he is holier than a dreydel
he is holier than an ashram

he won't let you forget
    who he is
he has the power
    to wet your underwear
    make you oversleep
    make your tears run races
    make you go crazy
    crazier than it might have gone
    if you hadn't met

he's well respected
a sage with a hard philosophy

he's on a tangent about 500 years
he's making so much sense
    my mind is in orgasm

simultaneous kindred spirits
hell this ain't easy
genetic memory he says
genetic just like crazy we live to survive
we are
you are
we are
you are
I am
you are

I am, I said, fed up with your hypocrisy
your genetic memory is Caligula
your genetic raincoat is Pinocchio
you're fooling almost everyone
    almost all the time
they ought to create a museum for you

yes wow a girl can't avoid
    being a stripper
    paying a price
    receiving something in her underwear

or receiving something in her mind
her heart a heart
        searching for callouses
        always a mile ahead of her
        in some corporate conference room

she doesn't really want the callouses
        as much as she wants
        to be understood
        93 percent of the time

she wants to be an astronaut
she feels like she's in a different world
        most of the time

she wants to be a woman
        in a world where history
        and herstory have an equal chance,
        where people realize the sacredness
        of a callous and lack thereof
        the trouble of obtaining a passport
        for a heavier than baggage requirement mind

Yes the women are stripping
Yes they're shedding new skin
Yes the women.

HE KISSES GIRLS JUST 'CAUSE THEY'RE BLOND

He kisses girls just cause
>they're blond
>because he knows I have brown hair.

Another kisses girls just cause
>they're blond
>because he's considered
>an outlaw in his culture.

Another kisses girls just cause
>they're blond
>because it will make
>his father jealous.

Another kisses girls just cause
>they're blond
>because she wants to start over.

Another kisses girls just cause
>they're blond
>because T.V. told him
>that would make him happy.

Another kisses girls just cause
>they're blond
>because he says the desperation
>in their eyes is so loud
>he becomes wet.

Another kisses girls just cause
>they're blond
>because he's overweight
>and this makes him feel thin.

Sometimes I feel sorry for blond girls
    as I stand alone
    and kiss myself.

IAN
SHOALES

FROM THE BOOK

NOT WET YET

BEAVIS AND BUTTHEAD / 1993

JAPANESE MONSTER MOVIES and poorly-dubbed Italian muscle movies are nothing new to late night television. Godawful movies from other lands have always been part of the global village's bad part of town. Godzilla and Steve Reeves have done more for multiculturalism than Zora Neale Hurston and John Woo combined.

The Comedy Channel's MYSTERY SCIENCE THEATRE 2000, however, adds post-modern spice to the Z-movie stew: In the future, in a distant corner of the universe, a mad scientist has exiled the series host, forever condemned to watch bad movies with only robots for companions. They sit in a row of theatre seats, shown in silhouette. We watch the lousy movies over their shoulders as they crack wise. Their comments are the hook upon which the show's popularity hangs.

Their cracks are funny, sure, but wasn't mockery of laughable movies something we used to provide for ourselves? Do we really need robots to be our sarcasm surrogates?

Now sarcasm surrogacy has reached a new level: MTV's BEAVIS AND BUTTHEAD. Imagine two Bart Simpsons. Make them sniff airplane glue for six months. Bake them in a closet in a heavy sauce of dysfunction and boredom, then release them to unleash their addled scorn on music videos. On the bright side, they're not robots. In fact, they're icons for today's youth. Unlike previous avatars, Bill and Ted and Wayne and Garth, they don't want to be in a band, or have their own show. Beavis and Butthead don't seem to want (or even expect) anything.

Again, bonehead nihilism is always good for a laugh, but what kind of corner is MTV painting itself into? "Here are our viewers," the network proudly proclaims, "brain-damaged social misfits who despise our programming!" This display of contempt for its audience and its own output is daring, certainly, but as a ratings strategy, I just don't see the long-term pay off.

On the other hand, who am I to question the wisdom of the marketplace? Adolescent boys, apparently, remain today's demographic of choice. To reach them, advertisers present alarming media images: Turn on the television and you see weaselly Legomaniacs everywhere, swaggering little snots who call each "dude" relentlessly, their long dank hair moussed into a life of its own, playing Game Boy while skateboarding, firing Nerf pump action shot guns, wolfing down sugar-laced junk food with arrogant gluttony, wearing running shoes the size of dogs.

How does this media feedback affect real boys? Well, here's an anecdote. I wandered into my local corner store the other night for a cold one, to discover two twelve-year old boys leaving. Carrying skateboards, they both had hair blessed by modern fixatives, large floppy tee-shirts, shorts, and (of course) enormous shoes. One of them shouted curses at the middle-aged Korean proprietor, ending with, "Okay man, see what happens if you ever need thirty-five cents," as they stalked off into the foggy night.

Buying my beer, I observed to the proprietor, "Polite young men."

He shrugged and said, "They say they want thirty five cents for bus. I say no. They say, 'How we going to get home?' I say, 'Walk.' They say they going to kill me. I say, 'Kill me, go ahead. You still walking home.'"

That's the cruel truth, isn't it? If target marketing continues, MTV may eventually find itself with just one ideal viewer: a surly twelve year old boy who only leaves his basement bedroom to buy game cartridges, and doesn't enjoy anything except gory revenge fantasies over half-imagined wrongs.

Even if the trick to reaching today's youth is to hate yourself prominently before he hates you, it seems to me that advertisers are still trying to make kids believe they're God's gift to culture. Call me reactionary, but I think this is a mistake. The last time America sucked up to its spoiled offspring, (The Sixties, Boomers), all we got to show for it were the sexual revolution and Screaming Yellow Zonkers. In other words, kids, kill me if you want but believe me, in the long run you will end up walking home...

COFFEE / 1994

LAST WEEK I WENT INTO a coffee house to get, you know, a cup of coffee, only to be told that actual coffee was unavailable. Would I like a tasty cappuccino, cafe au lait, or espresso? A double decaf latte with one of those little Italian biscuits that tastes like chalk? They had those, but a steaming java, a plain ordinary cup of joe? No way.

This mutant coffee thing is getting out of hand. It's even hard to get a cuppa mud at the local convenience store. It used to be simple: get large paper container, put under urn tap, pour, attach appropriate lid, pay, and go. Today, convenience stores all have an Isle Du Cawfay or some damn thing: it offers cinnamon coffee, vanilla coffee, and decaf Viennese, from beans fresh-squeezed by formerly Soviet virgins. I'm not against this stuff, but it's not what I look for in liquefied caffeine: I want a blister on my lips and a knot in my stomach. I want my coffee black, bitter and scalding. Give me that little pleasure, America. I promise I won't sue you.

Alas, we're well on the road to tepid exoticism. Have you tried to find vanilla ice cream at the grocery store lately? You could get frostbite from rummaging. You have to claw your way past Wally Walnut Peanut Brittle Supreme, or Cherry Brownie Fudge Syrup Surprise, ice cream with so much extra junk crammed into its mass it looks like a tub of frozen glue with chunks of bark floating in it. If you find vanilla ice cream at all, it's usually Milli Vanilla Whole Bean Rain Forest Saver, with vanilla beans suspended in its depths like boulders in a glacier.

While we're on the subject, isn't it time to declare a moratorium on microbreweries? Walk into an upscale tavern these days, and there's a twelve-foot wall of bottles behind the bar, floor to ceiling. If you ask the bartender what kind of beers they serve, you'll die of thirst before he reaches the end of the list. And all the names have the same annoying, vaguely macho ring to them: Ugly Alligator Ale or One-Eyed Pete's Pale Porter. I'll go mad, I tell you! Mad!

We've got to nip this thing in the bud, my friends. We're on the road to a world where we'll be able to flavor our foods with cumin, curry or cilantro, but not salt. We used to drink water from the tap, remember that? Then we switched to bubbly water from foreign lands; now it has to be cherry-flavored bubbly water, or we won't touch it.

We have special shampoos for our individual hair needs. We need special outfits to ride a damn bicycle. We have call waiting, call forwarding, caller i.d.-but when's the last time you actually talked to a human being on the telephone?

Our new culture is all quarters, no pennies, prayer in school but no education, all croissants, and no doughnuts. We're not smoking! Tomatoes will stay ripe for centuries.

We welcome space aliens, but not illegal ones. (As though Martians carry work visas.) We used to shoot tin cans from stumps with .22s. Today we shoot each other with .357s (the devil's caliber!). We used to drive gas-guzzlers, guilt-free; today we drive little tiny cars with strange names not found in nature. Do we really feel better about ourselves? Of course we don't.

We're just trying to prove that we can control our appetites. "I don't have a sugar jones," we say to the world, "I just have a sudden craving for Huggy-Buggy Sweet 'N' Sticky Health Bars. That's all."

I don't want to alarm you (well, okay, I do), but it seems like we're ripe for an invasion. Lean and hungry barbarians from the east, take note. You won't even need weapons. All you need are basic goods: sugar, salt, coffee, tea, whole milk, alcohol, red meat, tobacco. I don't want to sound like a traitor, but we're a pushover.

ELVITUDE / 1990

IN A RECENT NEW YORK TIMES MAGAZINE, Stephen J. Thibeault, the assistant public affairs officer at the American Embassy in Iraq, was quoted as saying, "This is the Ted Bundy of countries." There's a soundbite after my own heart. This man is the Ian Shoales of diplomats, and his quote is the Elvis of soundbites, head and shoulders above the Pat Boone soundbites thrust upon us by the news media hit parade. I've always felt that Ted Bundy is the one true Elvis of serial killers-he had that extra little something that set him apart from the other serial-killer-hopefuls out there.

Saddam Hussein, in the Tin Pan Alley of shorthand media quips, has often been compared to Adolf Hitler (who was, of course, the Elvis of dictators), but really, Hussein is more the Mick Jagger of dictators-darkness lite (as in Bud Lite, the Elvis of light beers). Hussein might have had a shot at being the Elvis of religious despots, but he preferred military uniforms to the flowing robes of religious fundamentalism, thus leaving total Elvishood (in the religious sense) to the late great Ayatollah Khomeini, the man who Ted Bundy'ed Salman Rushdie into his present position-the Elvis of persecuted writers.

So who, you might ask, was the Elvis of presidents? Kennedy, definitely. Lincoln was the Roy Orbison of presidents, Franklin Roosevelt the Beatles of Presidents, and Ronald Reagan was the Reagan of presidents, one of a kind really, they broke the mold when they made him. I hope they broke that mold. It's my personal Elvis of hopes. George Bush, again, is the Pat Boone of presidents, making Dan Quayle a kind of Pat Boone impersonator, I guess, or more precisely, a Pat Boone wannabe. I'd like to believe the preceding remark was the Elvis of gratuitous Dan Quayle jokes, but we both know the truth, don't we? It was just another Elvis wannabe, topical humorwise.

Like Madonna. Everybody knows that Marilyn Monroe is the

Elvis of blondes. Madonna might hold claim to the title of Elvis of Jayne Mansfields, but what kind of title is that? It's like calling Lassie the Elvis of dogs. It's true, but where does it get you? Before you know it, you're calling STAR TREK the Elvis of bad teevee series from the sixties, or Jeanne Kirkpatrick the Elvis of Republican women, or the Bible the Elvis of documents.

All of this might be true, but if all of the above is true-applying a little logic to this situation-that Lassie is the Elvis of dogs, then Benji is Pat Boone, and Cujo is Jerry Lee Lewis. This makes LOST IN SPACE the Fabian of bad teevee shows from the sixties, Pat Buchanan the Howlin' Wolf of Republican commentators and The Koran the Jerry Lee Lewis of documents. Whither then Rin Tin Tin, William F. Buckley and The Talmud? Are they just so many Sinatras in the forced metaphors of soundbite world? I think not, America.

Because we all know that America is still the Elvis of nations, and that we revere the Elvises among us-Hugh Hefner, for example, the Elvis of bachelors (retired), the man who built an American empire devoted to the relentless exposure of this or that co-eds' mammary gland, the Elvis of breasts. Walt Disney, truly an Elvis for our times, parlayed an obsession with the butts of fuzzy animals into a multi-trillion dollar empire which may yet overtake the world. I don't pretend to understand this empire, but it's definitely the Elvis of something. America understands the tragedy of Donald Trump, who wanted to be the Elvis of tycoons, but ended up the Monkees, the Elvis to which the New Kids on the Block aspire.

As we reel from the S&L crisis (the Elvis of scandals), we're still reeling from Viet Nam (the Elvis of foreign entanglements). Now we seem to be preparing to battle Iraq (Elvis of nothing special), either for the sake of oil, the Elvis of fuels, or to curtail the antics of the tinhorn Ted Bundy the world calls Saddam Hussein. Either way it's bound to be a new chapter in the chronicles of Elvitude. Stay tuned. As Elvis said, "Only fools walk in." I guess we just can't help it.

FUTURE / 1993

I WAS SPINNING THE DIAL LATE-ISH a while back and stumbled upon a STAR TREK episode I'd never seen before. As usual when catching STAR TREK, I only caught part of it and I wasn't paying much attention, but I did notice that the episode featured that familiar orange sky, Abraham Lincoln, and cruel, unfeeling aliens (who looked like sacks of potatoes) putting Kirk and Spock's humanism to a test. During the course of the grueling exam, if I recall correctly, Kirk got the little tear in his uniform and tiny ribbon of blood on his cheek that are the official STAR TREK indicators of intergalactic hardship. Anyway, they passed the test, Kirk scolded the potatoes for being manipulative and uncaring, everybody but Lincoln beamed up, McCoy said something cranky yet endearing, and they were off to the next star cluster.

Now, I've been catching snippets of STAR TREK for close to twenty-five years now. After all this time, shouldn't coming across an episode I haven't seen before be considered a miracle of sorts? As miracles go, this is pretty bland, admittedly, and I don't discount the possibility that I had seen it before, and forgotten. After all, I've viewed most STAR TREK snippets in less than ideal circumstances, at two o'clock in the morning, for example, or while suffering from jet lag and/or the lingering effects of mild substance abuse. Still, you'd think the sight of Abe Lincoln juxtaposed with potatoes from Mars would be an image with long term staying power, even in my battered synapses.

Nowadays, I forget television shows all the time, even those I've actually watched. I caught SEINFELD once, for example, because I'd read that it was hip and post-modern. Seinfeld himself is funny enough, I guess, though his brand of humor doesn't do much for me: "Ball point pens, I dunno, is it just me? Shoes are weird!" Well, all I can remember about SEINFELD the show was some annoying bald guy whining about something, intercut with a bunch of anxious people ordering Chinese food.

If having absolutely nothing happen is stretching the limits of the sitcom, I'd say SEINFELD is definitely on the cutting edge, but is a sitcom without a sit a good idea? If they'd thrown in a dead president and a smattering of potatoheads from other worlds, we might have had something. I felt the same way about THE COSBY SHOW. Every time I watched it, it seemed like Dr. Huxtable was trying to get a blender to work. Is that entertainment? If he'd thrown a Tribble or two into the food processor, maybe.

But the face of television is changing. In our modern television sea of infomercials, plotless comedies, and Canadian cop shows ("Stop or I'll shoot, eh!"), I believe the fine hidden hand of a secret network of Trekkies is computer-generating "new" episodes of the old STAR TREK. I can't think of any other explanation for what I've seen, can you? The question is, should we be alarmed or comforted?

If STAR TREK is invading the airwaves, both covertly (DEEP SPACE NINE, STAR TREK: THE NEXT GENERATION) and overtly (generation of "new" old episodes by all-powerful Trekkie hackers), mightn't they join forces? We've already seen Scotty, Spock, and McCoy show up on STAR TREK: THE NEXT GENERATION, and Picard show up on DEEP SPACE NINE. Could these inter-series invasions be a rehearsal for a takeover of existing syndicated series?

If Data ever shows up on Jeopardy, the gameshow bank would soon be broken. A small Romulan invasion could wipe out the entire cast of BABYLON FIVE. If Romulans and Klingons ever debate each other on Maury Povich, it could lead to a confrontation that would make World War III look like a picnic. Smarmy and ruthless Ferengi merchants could take over infomercials: "Here's your five point success program, earthlings: Surrender or die!" If it's true that Federation reps are standing on a starship bridge in their silly pocketless uniforms, even as I speak, dreaming up ways to infiltrate the airwaves, what happened to the Federation's logo, "Leave people alone," the so-called Prime Directive? Has the Prime Directive been replaced by Prime Time?

But the system's running at full warp now! She canna handle any more! She'll fall apart! For God's sake, turn it off before it's too late.*

---

* Since I wrote this, STAR TREK: VOYAGER has gone on the air. Consider it a warning.

GANGSTA MOM / 1996

THE NEW YORK TIMES SUNDAY MAGAZINE ran a profile a few weeks back of Suge Knight, CEO of Death Row Records, for whom Tupac Shakur and Snoop Doggy Dogg record their state-of-the-art gangsta rap. Tha Dogg Pound and Dr. Dre (formerly of N.W.A.) are also part of Death Row, with whom Time Warner lately had a distribution deal.

(This deal, you'll recall, was the bane of Bob Dole and William Bennett. Thanks in part to their efforts, Death Row was dropped by Time Warner. And the nation probably sleeps better tonight, knowing that these rappers' CDs are now being placed in record stores by an entirely different corporation. Thank God for free market Republicans!)

Mr. Knight, bearlike and known as Suge to his friends, comes across in the article as every inch the Scary Black Person we've come to know and love from white media. He neither confirmed nor denied having threatened rivals with baseball bats, but didn't seem displeased by the accusation. One of his employees was shot to death last year, allegedly by a rival East Coast producer. Like the mobsters of yore, Mr. Knight travels everywhere (even by charter jet to Vegas) with a vast crowd of bodyguards, who have names like Neckbone, Trey, Rock, Hen Dogg and Bountry.

Bountry, when first encountered in the profile, was removing lint from his black fedora with masking tape. Bountry described this as "an old ghetto trick."

Well, this gave me pause.

She never had a posse, never traveled anywhere by stretch limo, and never bludgeoned anyone to death at a music awards ceremony, but my mother did in fact teach me how to remove lint from clothing with masking tape. Did she have a secret past I knew nothing about? Among her friends was she known as Soup Mommy Momm?

Thinking back on my boyhood in the Dakotas, I've been trying to remember: was our neighborhood a 'hood? When Mom put a penny in the fuse box was she employing a Norwegian-American version of street smarts? When she darned socks, or tore up old tee-shirts for rags was she promoting a gangsta lifestyle or just being frugal?

On the other end of the spectrum, as a media-obsessed so-called adult, I find myself wondering: in all the interviews with rappers I've read in free weekly newspapers and 'zines, have I ever seen evidence of an interface between rapper and mom cultures?

I vaguely recall Ice-T in an interview somewhere reminding his fans that "Yogurt is a healthy substitute for sour cream-try it on mashed potatoes!" But I could be wrong. Didn't Ice Cube once close his live performances by telling his audiences to dress warmly and rotate their tires? Or maybe it was something about removing ketchup stains with baking soda and vinegar.

I don't know if many gangstas try to fool their children by putting generic frosted flakes in a Kellogg's box, or how many offset the high cost of limo champagne with the exclusive use of lower priced spreads back at the crib, or if they've discovered the incredible variety of interesting things you can do with leftover turkey after the holidays (Tried croquettes, by the way?), but even without this information, I think we can make some pretty solid comparisons.

Let's go to the chart.

GANGSTA	MOM
Surrounded by posse.	Surrounded by bridge club.
Raps at the drop of a hat.	Bursts into "I've Been Working on the Railroad" at the drop of a hat.
Likes hats.	Likes hats.
Calls home a "crib."	Has baby crib in attic.
Wears baggy sweats.	Wears baggy sweats.
Affects large gold jewelry.	Affects large gold jewelry.
Often makes complicated hand gestures.	Often clutches purse tightly.
Hates police.	Obeys speed limits.
Removes lint from clothing with masking tape.	Removes lint from clothing with masking tape.

Wears dark glasses.	Wears tinted glasses.
Often complains about being disrespected.	Often complains about being disrespected.
Knows all about life on the street.	Knows what every family on the street is up to.
Has nickname in the 'hood.	Is called "Mrs. Shoales" in the 'hood.
Is dangerous when crossed.	Is dangerous when crossed.
Doesn't take crap from anybody.	Will brook no nonsense.
Busts rhymes.	Uses DustBuster.
Uses the word "fly" to mean "great."	Hates flies, doesn't care who knows it.
Calls friends "homes."	Calls friends daily.
Cellular phone is constant companion.	Constantly gets caught in phone cord when talking with her homies.
Is a cause of conservative alarm.	Is an alarmed conservative.
Is fiercely loyal to friends and family.	Is fiercely loyal to friends and family.
Is very macho.	Thinks men are childish idiots.

There are several conclusions to be drawn here. I'm no sociologist, so I'll be damned if I'll draw them.

It is obvious, however, that a cellular phone would make an excellent Mother's Day gift. And if you're looking for a present to give to that gangsta in your life, we can recommend either a Glock 9 mm semiautomatic or HINTS FROM HELOISE—in paperback, now, not hardcover, and preferably used. After all, as our homeboy Ben Franklin put it, "Yo, a penny saved is a penny earned. Word up."

LITERACY / 1994

WARNING! The following contains references to polls and/or surveys. Reader discretion is advised.

According to a new Department of Education study, nearly half of Americans are illiterate. This is probably alarming. Irwin Kirsch, the project director, told NEWSWEEK, "This test revealed that many people can read in the technical sense that they can decode the words, but they lack the strategies and skills needed to use the information."

Well, wait a minute. If I decode these words properly, what they really seem to mean is, "People can read, they just can't follow instructions."

Sure enough, sample documents I've seen from the test include a pay stub, a social security card, a bank deposit slip, and a bus schedule. Perhaps we shouldn't be so alarmed after all. This isn't a literacy test, it's a *job application!*

Once again, our nation's educators have stripped away any semblance of fun from reading. Once again, America is warned that reading for pleasure is a one-way ticket to Palookaville. We must master fine print and boilerplate if we're going to get ahead in life. Reading is a grim chore, analogous to scrubbing toilets.

If we can't read, I believe the fault lies not with us, but our reading material. I read THE BRIDGES OF MADISON COUNTY in about an hour, and had time left over to get an innuendo update on Michael Jackson, absorb the thoughtful media coverage of the Burt/Loni affair, and still had a second left over to ponder the value of literacy at all. Yet I still can't program my VCR. Despite days spent squinting at the VCR manual, I remain ignorant of what "VHS" stands for. I don't know the difference between APR and FICA. What makes a PG-13 movie that much less suitable for children than PG? I couldn't tell you. I can deconstruct a text as well as the next guy, but I couldn't wade through a cereal box disclaimer to save my life. Am I being disenfranchised by this study? Would this be cause for hope or despair?

IAN SHOALES

My sensitive feelings aside, I'd say the bureaucrats have definitely found America's Achilles heel. It's hard to argue with those who say we have severely diminished comprehension skills. Even the most powerful among us can't cope with normal life. Remember President Bush's awe when confronted with a supermarket scanner? How many movie stars would recognize a bus schedule if they saw one? Could Ross Perot find the expiration date on a half-off coupon?

Of course, the powerful don't need to understand anything. That's why they have lawyers, to explain (for example) what a "wholly-owned subsidiary" is in terms even a CEO could understand. But lawyers don't need to understand anything either! Why have an attention span, when you can have a staff? As a matter of hard fact, all anybody needs to understand in America today is the interoffice memo. Memos and e-mail are the literary forms of the nineties. Master them, kids, and you'll go far.

I once knew two boys who had, according to the proper authorities, severe learning disabilities. Yet they could both name every STAR TREK episode, in order, and offer a detailed summary of each plot. They had devoured the entire paperback line of STAR TREK books. They had constructed intricate models of Federation and Klingon starships, so they obviously could follow instructions.

Oh, they'll probably grow up lacking the strategies and skills needed to respond appropriately to a sign like, "Don't even think of parking here," (which is, if you should find yourself thinking of parking there, to turn yourself in immediately.) They'll probably go ahead and buy a car anyway, never realizing that actual mileage will vary.

Here's the question, America: Do we want our kids growing up to be chipper obsessive Trekkies, or dreary anal retentives who can breeze through a freezer warranty with 100% comprehension? It's a grim choice, America, but it seems to be all ours.

RULES FOR ROCKERS / 1996

ON OCTOBER 21, Blind Melon singer Shannon Hoon, 28, was found dead of what the media always call an "apparent drug overdose," in the band's tour bus.

Rock stars have been overdosing for years now, not to mention getting arrested for indecent exposure, trashing hotel rooms, disdaining hairbrushes and only shaving every three days. You'd think they'd learn.

There's probably nothing we can do to stop brash young musicians from sneering at all authority and wearing tight shiny clothing not always appropriate to their physique.

Besides, attrition will take its toll on most teen heartthrob wannabes before any real damage is done. A drummer's girlfriend will force him to choose between the band and her; a bass player's dad will decide that he needs the garage to store his power saw collection, thus eliminating his son's rehearsal space, and ending his rock career forever; some sullen longhairs will even come to realize that driving twelve hours to a gig, only to be screamed at by a hostile crowd who throw full pitchers of beer at their heads, is not as much fun as it was cracked up to be.

Still, despite the best efforts of girlfriends and the free market, there are some rock-and-rollers who actually do "make it." This leads to a whole other series of problems.

For instance, a young rocker could make millions from "Armageddon Twist," but that's the only hit he'll ever have. He'll end his days a bitter old man, eking out a living lip-synching his ancient ditty at county fair Golden Oldies revivals.

Others can go from hip to ridiculous in an eye blink! One day our rocker causes teenage girls to swoon with his hoarse vocalizations, and the next day some latenight comic points out the amusing similarities between the star's hoarse vocalizations and Elmer Fudd's. The next thing you know our superstar's albums are going for a dollar fifty-nine in the cutout bin at the corner drugstore, and he's riding that long black train to Palookaville.

Rock fame is no picnic. Critics call your second album a "major disappointment." Sales plummet. Your once-sexy pout is now perceived as silly. You add a second guitar to the mix, and your fickle fans accuse you of selling out, then abandon you in droves. You marry a supermodel more famous than you, causing severe loss of self-esteem. You spend more time on a tour bus than in a studio and start to like it! The arrogance, rudeness, and self-indulgence that made you successful destroy you.

We need to help those few who actually get a recording contract survive long to do an "unplugged" CD. We've got to help them live long enough to save the rain forest, marry that film star, buy that mansion in the south of France, get knighted, and take up golf. If we put our minds to it, we can make sure that all of today's screamers can grow up to be semi-respected Frank Sinatras.

Kids, you need to follow these simple rules:

Drugwise, stick to ibuprofen, decaf lattes and pale pilsners. Never deviate! Wear earplugs and protective headgear at all times. Keep it simple, and stick to it. Bo Diddley had a beat named after him, and it wasn't 5/4. 'Nuff said.

If your stomach is not a flat slab, please leave your shirt on while performing. Wherever possible, take limos. Pick your band's name carefully. (STRAWBERRY ALARM CLOCK, for example, has not aged well.)

If your girlfriend asks you to choose between her and her music, sell your instruments immediately-especially if you're a drummer. If you do make it, be sure to buy Dad a new garage. Not only will he appreciate it, but if your second album is a major disappointment (as it probably will be), you'll have a place to go.

Finally, go easy on the supermodels, don't forget to tune, and remember: a tiny bit of dry ice and lasers goes a long way. Ditto with tattoos.

TONYA/NANCY / 1993

As A MEMBER OF THE INSIGNIFICANT MINORITY who wished the Winter Olympics would just go away, I watched none of it, and only absorbed the Tonya/Nancy saga through the print media.

Oh, I know the gist of the story. One figure skater, a hard-boiled product of a broken home, may or not have played a part in the physical assault on a second, America's sudden sweetheart. Both were catapulted, as a result, to unnatural levels of fame. Was Tonya given short shrift or too much slack? Was Nancy good or just goody-goody? Pundits vary.

But now the epic tale is behind us, joining other brief blips on the screen of human history. I think I've isolated its significance, and its ultimate meaning. Our fascination with Tonya and Nancy is nothing less than the yearning for our own psychic dualities to be merged.

Hey, no laughing out there! I'm serious!

See if these helpful comparisons don't strike a chord:

TONYA is to NANCY as—

Freud is to Jung, as bowling is to golf, Joan Crawford to Katherine Hepburn, Nixon to Kennedy, beer to lite beer, macaroni to spaghetti, Fox to PBS, cigars to cigarettes, or cigarettes to non-smoking.

Tonya is to Nancy as a doughnut to a bagel, white wine to red, teevee to movies, domestic violence to divorce, a dirt road to the information superhighway, a Chevy to a Volvo, John Belushi to Chevy Chase, a wink to a nod, an angry shout to a muffled sob, an all-beef hot dog to a turkey frank, a convenience store to a clothing store, or Tommy Lee Jones to Rickie Lee Jones (though that might be stretching it).

It's AM to FM, Irving Berlin to Cole Porter, cheeseburger to cottage cheese, United States to Canada, K-Mart to Target, Vegas to Disney World, Africa to South America, malt liquor to ale, seven and seven to margarita, dim piano bar to karaoke bar, World War I to World War II, crack to cocaine.

Tonya might be addiction, and Nancy habit, but if Tonya is habit, Nancy is cold turkey. If Tonya is cold turkey, Nancy is a twelve step program, but if Tonya is a twelve step program, then Nancy has always been a teetotaler. If Tonya has always been a teetotaler, Nancy is an addict currently working on her memoirs at the Betty Ford Center. If Tonya is the Betty Ford Center, then Nancy is a health care professional.

If Tonya were Arsenio, Nancy would be Letterman. Yet if Tonya were Letterman, then Nancy would be Leno, and if Tonya were Leno, Nancy would be Ted Koppel.

Irresistible force, the immovable object. Space, time, yard sale, estate sale, wink, nod. Yet who is the blind horse? We're talking rayon and silk here, felony and misdemeanor, passionate affair and guilt-ridden adultery, Jean-Claude Van Damme and Arnold Schwarzenegger, Lewis and Martin, Kansas and Oz, house and senate, lust and desire, desire and love, losing and winning (relatively).

We're looking at gaps as small as the difference between McGyver and STAR TREK, or MISSION: IMPOSSIBLE and STAR TREK: THE NEXT GENERATION. The Nancy within likes any title with a colon in it, yet it's the Tonya inside who rejoices at sequels!

We can be either one at any moment. Feel like ordering a pizza? You're indulging your Tonya. Some Thai food might hit the spot? That's Nancy talking.

And what of the Jacksons? Interest in the Jackson family is certainly Tonya-esque. Yet if La Toya is Tonya, then Nancy is Michael, if Tonya is Michael, then Nancy is the Jackson Family, and if Tonya is the Jackson Family, Nancy is the Jackson Five. Which is Partridge Family, which Brady Bunch?

We will never be content, and will continue to be fascinated by tinny spectacles, until we learn to marry the Tonya and Nancy inside. In real terms, if a drummer were to marry a bass player, the union could be exquisite in its Tonyanciness. Even more so if a the girlfriend of a roadie married a backup singer, if a mercenary loved an ideologue, a Sunni a Shiite. Alas, we have trouble now telling which is which.

So many of us despair before we've even begun. There's no blame in this. After all, if Tommy Lee Jones did marry Ricky Lee Jones, she'd still be Ricky Lee Jones, even if she kept her maiden name. Think about it.

WHITE LIES / 1983

WHITE LIES HELP US GET THROUGH LIFE. We hear white lies at work and play, we tell white lies for pleasure and convenience. We use white lies the way a carpenter uses a hammer: Mr. Shoales is on another line. He's away from his desk right now.

Your check's in the mail. Easy to install. Only takes a minute. A child could do it. This won't hurt a bit. Trust me.

Be glad to do it, no problem. Slices, dices, in seconds. Actual mileage may vary. It followed me home, can I keep it? I mailed it a month ago. I'm working late at the office tonight. This is my real phone number. I forgot to turn on the machine.

I think of you as a friend. She's just a friend. I need time, time to think, time to be myself.

White lies are an umbrella in the stormy weather of unrelenting truth:

Beauty is only skin deep. It matches your eyes. She has an interesting personality. You have an interesting face. Your poem is the best poem I've ever read. It was-interesting. I had a wonderful time. It was the best time I've ever had. I'll call you. I love foreign movies. Let's have lunch. We'll do it again sometime.

White lies are Band-Aids on the gaping wound of the morality gap: I didn't know you sang so well. You don't act like a Capricorn. Diamonds are a girl's best friend.

Money isn't everything. You're a gem, a jewel, you're irreplaceable. We don't need a contract. If we don't like it we can quit. We can stop any time. We can take it or leave it. Trust me.

White lies give us an excuse to do what we're going to do anyway:

This is just a neighborhood watch. This is just a border patrol. We don't use these weapons, we just have them. This is just national security. These aren't troops, they're advisers. I'm sorry. I didn't mean it.

The end justifies the means. Just little white lies. They help us get through life.

BILL
SHIELDS

FROM THE BOOK

ROSEY THE BABY KILLER
& OTHER STORIES

AN OLD TIME ASSHOLE

WHEN THE JACK KICKED OUT, the car crushed his chest. His two sons who were helping him at the time couldn't budge the old Chrysler. There was nothing that could've been done. It was considered the will of God.

Parents, friends & strangers attended the funeral. His dog quit eating for a couple days them promptly forgot regret & ate after the services.

There was a coin collection that no one could find. His wife found a couple bank accounts that he had hidden for years. The boys split up a gun cabinet that had been full. That was it, uneventful as road kill.

This became a sad little story full of food stamps.
A bland victim & stupid young men.

There was a girlfriend attached to the dead man's wallet.

MY DAUGHTER

"But Dad, you never spanked me," she says,
forgetting when she was little
& I was a garden variety son of a bitch.
"just once, honey," I always reply,
because that's what she wants to hear.
"I remember now," she'll say, "I spilled my milk or something like
that."
"Uh huh."
"I'm not having any kids. Never."
"I wasn't either, honey, but I've enjoyed a few surprises."
"Mom said you wanted an abortion."
"Mom lies." I'll answer, hearing the squeal of an IUD getting
ripped out.
"I knew it," she'll say, hoping to God that it's the truth.
I'm not saying another word.

A BAG OF WEENIES

There are rooms & beds that love is never going to find. Dreams that inflate to shit balloons. This is life, no implied warranty, no satisfaction guaranteed, nothing but blind product.

This morning I woke up furiously reaching for a gun under the bed.
I screamed at my wife, "You better fucking kill me today!"
She laughed & left the room.

It's impossible to kill yourself with fingers for a bullet.
I tried.

DESSERT

Like tasting the vomit when it rises from your throat but doesn't make the mouth. He stood perfectly still to stop the spinning room, then laughed at the absurdity of being alive, today: December 20, 1995.

There was a time he would have driven away from all of them & their home—credit cars & gasoline buy time & enough distance to burn the carbon out of a conscience.
But not now.
He walks in the department store, buys the Christmas presents, has them wrapped & heads home. A wife says, "hi honey," the dog leaps on his stomach & he calls his kids in other states.
Then he sits in the kitchen with the lights off for the longest time.

This story is almost over.

THE CAT PISSED YELLOW

"Did you kill the little motherfucker?" Serge asked me, taking a swallow of warm Pabst Blue Ribbon.

"Rice food, man, dude is face down," I answered.

"In the head?"

"Naw, right through his Viet Cong neck."

"That bastard killed a lot of good people, Bill. You know better than most."

"Yeah... I do."

A mortar round fell two hundred meters to our right.

"They ain't got it right yet," I said.

They started walking the rounds into our position, on the side of a paddy dike.

"See him?" I asked, looking for tube flash.

"Nope."

"Maybe that's the dead gook coming back for his face."

"He did look a lot like you."

The next round blew water in front of our faces.

"I must've really pissed him off."

"Not enough."

A dead fish floated past us.

ROSEY THE BABY KILLER

"I should have an affair," my wife said. We were sitting outside of a convenience store.

She agreed with herself—yes, indeed, she surely should.

This had happened before, the going-dead-on-a-person. Have at it, I thought, dick ain't gonna cure what ails you.

Then again.

maybe it will...

⚡ ⚡ ⚡

My first dog was named Putt, a mix of mutt & mutt. He was killed by a taxi when I dropped the leash. Figure him a year old, me maybe nine. Tan dog, red guts... long time dying.

The taxi never slowed.

The baby sitter was hysterical, tearing a hole through the old living room floor carpet with her flat shoes. There was nothing I could do but scoop him up & bring him home.

He was one of a couple buried in the back yard.

⚡ ⚡ ⚡

Her dad was a drunk steelworker, the mom more the slob in a nicotine housecoat; Suzie Androsek was more ashamed of her family than I was. It felt perfect with her. I had the embarrassed face & she had the chubby legs.

I spent a year in her pants & her cigarettes, then left for the Navy without saying a word.

Here's to you Suzy—you were spared a teenage divorce.

*   *   *

I knew it was a snake curled around my left leg, right at the kneecap. Three feet deep of mangrove swamp that stretched for miles & that fangy bastard found my bones. Damn.

There was no moving, no screams, just absolute quiet. Four Viet Cong were no more than a hundred feet to my right... quiet now, don't move, breathe slowly through the nose, he'll bite or he won't. He did.
I pulled my knife down on him, cut the body diagonally, then figured I'd be dead before Charlie...

So I shot at the four & ran straight at them,

screaming, "Snake! Motherfucking snake! You motherfucker!"

The snake & people died.

*   *   *

Commerce City, Colorado. I spent a week with a woman there doing heroin that she stole from her boyfriend. It was a dump of a house, olive paint & olive rugs, leaking waterbed.

We ate fresh peanut butter sandwiches & slept. She was a hippie & I was the Anti-Christ with a poppy disguise.

I lost her in a downtown bar, never saw her again.

& I don't read the obituary columns.

~ ~ ~

My daughter Kren never forgave me for missing her birth. Our last phone call went like this:
"Kren?"
"Yes."
"You know who this is?"

Click.

She's not much of a phone bill & I'm not much of a Dad.

~ ~ ~

My wife sleeps downstairs on the couch; I have the bed upstairs with the dog & everything that that implies. It's the coldest room in the house & the worst.

Dog hair coats the respirator that keeps me alive in the night. The TV doesn't work but the VCR does.

More importantly, there's a box of letters under the bed & that's this story.

~ ~ ~

Kids were killed in Vietnam & that's a fact nobody wants to breast-feed. But they were also dead in every other war & to such an extent. Dead is dead—age doesn't matter.

After the first month of war, my mind clicked into being a player on the ghostland. & there are always homicides in ghostland.

It's just the way it was—judge me harshly.

I do.

❧ ❧ ❧

He's young & he's dead.

His arms were sticking out of a paddy, the body buried in silt below; I had called the gunships on him & the rest of the VC patrol; they appeared like airborne snakes & drilled the eight of them into Hell's own dentist chair.

I've seen him just about every day since. He's either a fucking ghost or I've been insane a long, long time.

Consider him a ghost. Call him Nug & he'll shake your neck & you'll never feel him.

He's my oldest friend.

❧ ❧ ❧

"Yes yes yes, I know I'm regimented, a creature of habit, got bad senses of loyalty & I'm prone to violence," I said, laughing to my wife.

"You are all that," she agreed.

"We had talked all the way through a rented video. I sipped coffee, she had her Pepsi.

"Then... why the hell are you with me? I'll never figure that one out."

"Who else would put up with you?" she asked.

"That's bullshit. Everyone says that crap."

"I loved you once, maybe I still do."

A long lull in the conversation. I had the same with other women & it was the same script. I thought back to Joannie, Amy, Barb, etc. Same thing, sample problem, same man.

"I'm being honest, Bill," she added.

That she was.

*   *   *

My mother kept her vodka in glass peanut butter jars, hidden in the bottom of her purse, or under the driver's side car seat. She was drunk through twenty years of service to the Pennsylvania Department of Public Welfare. No one ever bitched about her—not her clients, her friends, or her boss. She was trashed by noon every day, on the job & off.

I have an ex-wife who spends weekends drinking by herself in a nice clean apartment. Fridays are bourbon nights, Saturdays are for wine & she always started Sunday morning out with a bottle of good champagne. This is true, a routine I witnessed for years.

She would want to fuck me only after the bottle was empty, or close. It wasn't sad or pathetic that a woman would only be close to me when she was drunk—naw. It humbled me.

*   *   *

We stole the jeep from an Army outpost outside of My Tho & drove it home. The Easter Pig was my running partner at the time, a big big Seal, 6' 6" with bright red hair & a pig's nose. We both ripped it.

We painted it blue, outfitted a .60 cal machine gun on 'er & called her our own. Middle of the night, he & I would go driving down those South Vietnamese highways without the lights on, looking for trouble & almost always found it.

Maniacal laughter & forty miles an hour down dirt roads that were mined—we shot the lights & life out of a few villages.

⚡ ⚡ ⚡

Shame...

It woke me again last night... In my dream I had run from a stacked firefight, a sure death warrant if I had stood & fought 30 to 1 odds. I didn't. I ran next to a river & listened to the VC laughing as they cut my friends' bodies to ribbons. I should've died right alongside them but didn't; living meant nothing if there wasn't just a touch of honor to it. I pulled out a .45, stuck it on my throat & pulled the trigger. Died? You betcha.

I was ashamed growing up with drunks, ashamed killing people, and ashamed having children. One enemy: shame. There's no cure for a past riddled in blood & deceit.

IGGY
POP

FROM THE BOOK

I NEED MORE

WANTED FOR MURDER

YEAH, SO WHEN I WAS IN THE STOOGES a lot of dumb things used to happen to me. I remember one night I was sitting up... just sitting up all night with our road manager, John Adams, shooting coke with a hypodermic needle. John was this funny guy. He was a junkie, you know. At this point—1970—the band was really beginning to disintegrate. I was staying on the 26th floor—room 26-G actually—which happens to be the size hypodermic needle I used to use to stick shit in my arm. This was the 26th floor of Ann Arbor, Michigan's only high rise, only penthouse building. I had to have one—being the lead singer type, you know. I had to have a room at the top. We should all have a room at the top.

So anyway, I'm sitting up there all night shooting coke and the sun starts coming up. You could see practically the whole town from my window, and me and John, we're looking down watching the day sort of slowly take shape and we notice that there are police cars cruising the city. Two of them at first and then four and later six, cruising the city in large squares, tracing configurations reminiscent of *The Hellstrom Chronicle*, closing in on the square. Obviously, it was a dragnet of some sort. So we watched. You know, we really used to get off on stuff like that, me and the Stooges. We sort of had this strange love/hate relationship with all authority... that is, police action in general. So we were looking at these guys, right? And we wondered—WOW! WE speculated—WOW! Who are they after? What's it all about, right, and la de da. Why is this dragnet closing in tighter and tighter?

Half the reason I was staying up was because the banks didn't open until nine, and I wanted to cash this check at the bank across the street, which is actually a bum check, but I did alot of business with this bank because there is a lot of quick money in rock, especially the way I play it. It wasn't like it is now, all this touring. WE were a weekend band. We just sort of played this wild music and people would ask us to come and we'd take the money and it was no big deal, no management or agents or anything. We actually had a so-called agent, but it was in name only. He never really understood the subject, though he did wire me a c-note to cover golfing expenses at the Doral Country Club—Miami, Florida, summer of 1970—during my final stages of a protracted Methadone-Golf-Valium treatment (first time for that one).

So, it's closing tighter and tighter, this dragnet, and John and I are watching, and I've got to cash this bum check at nine o'clock because I have to go with my Wurlitzer electric piano to Detroit in this rented car, which was basically stolen—a Ford Galaxie that I had taken out for one day and kept for a month, right. I just took my chances, you know, 'cause I had to score.

So I get down to the bank, and my pupils are about the size of basketballs. I'm very much in *that* state, and I'm wearing long sleeves, right, and I stand in line. I stand in line at the bank and I'm... At this point, we're talking about this guy who is sallow looking, drawn, a weird face, big bug eyes, real long auburn kind of straight hair. I wore what everyone else wore—Levi's, but I always wore long sleeves.

So anyway, I was standing there to cash this check for three thousand bucks. I'm standing there, pretty nervous in the sunlight and everything, I can't bear standing in lines of any sort, any time, anyway. So I'm really uptight. I hate being around regular people anyway. Even worse, I hate the bustle of anything that resembles an office or where business is being done in an organized form. So I'm standing there, and all of a sudden I hear a sound like the thunder of hooves to my left. Well, I look to my left, and coming in the bank in a half-trot, running, determinedly—are these two enormous, broad, heavy-muscled men in cheap suits with crewcuts. Early morning at the bank, rush hour, a lot of people, and lo and behold, they run straight up to me, straight up to me, pick me up in the air, pick me up in the air. I mean they didn't say a word. They didn't say a word and I didn't either. I didn't know what to do. They picked me up in the air and just ran straight out of the bank with me up in the air. One of them quickly opens the door of their car and throws me in the back seat, just throws me in the back seat. This is the kind of cop car that has grillwork between the front and back seat.

I was petrified. Petrified! I mean, beyond petrification and fear. I just thought, well, this is it. The gig's up. They've got me now, right, you know? I was sure they had me, right? I didn't know what was going to happen next, so I just sort of went crazy. "What did I do? What did I do? What are the charges?" That sort of thing, and they didn't say anything.

Well, as it turned out, they were looking for a murderer. So that was the day I was picked up for murder. They were looking for a murderer, and I fit the description exactly. Which is a good lesson for a young musician—don't hang out by yourself.

Anyway, so they are taking me down to the cop shop, right, and they don't even get halfway there when they take a closer look at me and check out some shit with their buddies on the radio and they realize I'm not the one they thought I was. They *know* it's not the one they thought, but from the look of me and everything, they decide to take me in anyway.

Ann Arbor, Michigan, where this took place, was veritably— during the mid-sixties and into the seventies—a police state. I've been all over the world and perhaps excluding Russia, I've never seen fascism more in force than in the Detroit area.

They just decided like we've got the town to play with and we're going to do what we want. It was strange because Ann Arbor was one of those funny Midwestern towns where, already in the Sixties, the residents, the people who actually lived there, had a much more laissez-faire, live and let live attitude than any of their hired guns. The police force thought more like Okies than they did like educated, civilized people. So it was a funny discrepancy, you know. You had this town full of peaceful kids at the mercy of these lunatics.

So they took me down and as it turned out, they found marks on my arm—because I was really stupid enough to shoot things into my arm. And I was very, very stoned and very, very scared. And the phone at the Stooges' main house was disconnected, and John had split, so I had no one to call, you know... and I didn't have a lawyer.

So what they wanted from me, what it came down to, was that they'd let me out if I let them search my place, you know. If I didn't let them search my place, it would mean detention. 72 hours—too long for a junkie type. Much to their surprise, they thought I'd say yes out of sheer fear or dumbness. Well, I did say yes.

And so they went up to my place—a sergeant, a lieutenant, and me. As it happened, there was nothing there that was incriminating. Just a whole lot of methadone and I don't know, the remains of ninety-nine fits and needles and things and pieces of this and that just lying all over the floor.

Unless you could bust a person for having lice and things like that—I was very louse-ridden at the time; personal cleanliness was not my forte—there was nothing they could really bust me for, but they said they could make an issue of things—the methadone and everything (which they probably could have, because it wasn't prescribed), and the needles and things.

So they worked on me in my place for about two hours trying to get me to rat on my friends and set somebody up. And I liked myself at the end of that day because I found out something about myself, and that something was this: I couldn't do hate's hurt no matter how I felt or who it was or how much trouble it might make for me. I thought that they could probably throw me in jail. I mean, John Sinclair went a few years for two joints just before that, and it would have meant a nice promotion for one of them, busting my ass.

But I couldn't contemplate screwing over a friend. I couldn't contemplate that. That's what my whole band the Stooges was all about for me: friendship. I found friendship as a musical style much more relevant than whether what we played was the blues or this or that. We were a band of friends. I need friends. As it turns out, the cops were bluffing.

TRAILER CAMP

I WAS RAISED IN A TRAILER CAMP—a mobile home park, if you will—which was situated out in the middle of the sticks, on US 23 between Ypsilanti and Ann Arbor, Michigan, in the middle of a very large farm owned by a Mr. Leverette. Our family was definitely the only literate occupant of the entire trailer park. The others were mostly heavy truck drivers or low-wage unskilled workers, who were often migratory-guys who would come up from the South when they heard there was some work in Detroit and then return to Carolina, or whatever, when the work was over.

The streets were really just ruts, and they were strewn with garbage. There were 97 or 99 lots in the trailer camp, and ours was #96, which is where my parents still live.

I guess the reason we lived there was because my father is a very private man, and he didn't want to have chums and neighbors; he really didn't want to have the bother of a house, with its upkeep and la de da. He really didn't want a social life. He was also very poor, being a junior high school teacher at the time; he had begun his career in a very rough school where kids would pull knives. Actually, he got to high school status, finally.

He was also a bit of a Socialist and a heavy union organizer. In fact, he organized one particular movement in the Ypsilanti school system which almost won out. But when things came to a head, everybody backed out on my dad, except his best friend, the diving coach. It's good to have a friend.

So I lived in this trailer camp. I never met kids who lived in houses. I wasn't really aware of houses until I was in the first grade, when I found out that other kids lived in this suburban housing development about a mile and a half up the road from me. That was quite a shock. I suddenly realized that my way of life was considered—well, let's put it this way—to anyone with two eyes you can see that a house is at least ostensibly more secure—it's rooted to the ground after all—than a mere trailer, which has a fly-by-night connotation.

The trailer I lived in between the ages of 8 and 13 was called a New Moon, and it was that *exact model* that had been featured in the film *The Long Long Trailer*, starring Lucille Ball and Desi Arnaz, right? They made a movie about this trailer, and my father and mother aren't moviegoers or anything, but they went because it was about trailers. My father loves trailers.

Trailers at the time were a rather revolutionary idea for anyone who didn't have to live in one. My dad was a bit of a nut.

So we had a New Moon trailer—45 feet long and 8 feet wide—which we kept from the time I was, say, 8 years old until I was about 13, when he traded it in for a 50' x 10' trailer, in which my parents still reside. A beautiful piece of art actually—this trailer—very well made, called a Vagabond, which is perhaps some mystic precursor of what my life was about to become—I lived under the New Moon and moved on to be a Vagabond.

You know what farmers say about crops: plant them at the new moon.

L.A. TROPICANA

SO WE WENT DOWN TO L.A. TO RECORD. We'd done that Frisco gig to help defray the expense of coming to the West Coast to record. We were recording at Elektra Studios on Santa Monica Boulevard and we were staying at the Tropicana, the internationally famous Tropicana rock hotel. Every day I had one song picked out—that was the song for the day. We'd go into the studio and I'd give em the song and we'd play it as many times as we had to, until I was satisfied. I distrusted all recording techniques. I'd sing with each take. I actually had my own PA set up in the place and I didn't use the board. We'd just sit there and record as best we could—no overdubs.

Luckily, we had very sophisticated engineers. Elektra was really ahead of the field at that time. They started out in folk rock. They were great. They were interested in making good quality recordings. They had an English engineer, Byron Ross-Myring, and he took our sounds, wherever they went and pushed the limits to crystallize our unity and random harmonics so it could come through on a phonograph record, cleansed of about one-half of my beloved "leakage." Things worked out great on that *Fun House* album, and I liked it a lot.

Elektra was only two blocks, two New York-type blocks, kitty-corner from the Tropicana. So every day, there you'd see us trooping down the street with our guitars to our recording. The four Stooges dutifully tromping down the street determined to go into the studio and get that song down, you know. Just walking down the street, you know—a bunch of hicks, you know—and maybe a piece of paper and a pen in the back pocket, in case I wanna change a word... and my drugs, and the guitarists and bass player with their cases, right?

Meanwhile, my next door neighbor at the Tropicana was Ed Sanders, who was writing a book called *The Family* about Mr. Manson. This was just after the Manson/LaBianca killings, and he was really uptight living next to me, especially since I wore this red dog collar, which I bought at the Bowzer Boutique. I thought it really suited me, but he thought it meant something. Everybody was really uptight about Satanism—whatever that is.

Andy Warhol, Paul Morrisey, and the whole cast of *Heat* or *Light* were also staying there. And so I met Andy Warhol. I was swimming in the pool at the Tropicana. The pool there was very small, and I'm a good swimmer, so I did three or four laps underwater and—I know there is somebody watching—and when I come up for air there is Andy standing there. He said, "My, you swim well." The exact words. "My, you swim well." So we had a little chat, you know. He was very nice. He said, "Come and see me sometime." I was very nervous. He was in Room 15 and I was in 9, somewhat kitty-corner from him on the top balcony of the fancy side of the Tropicana—Don Drysdale's Tropicana. Don Drysdale was a football or baseball player. So anyway, he'd always leave his door ajar, just to see if I'd come in. I was very shy. I finally did come over one time and we managed to talk a lot.

We did a gig at Whisky a Go-Go and just completely cleared the club.

CLOSE ENCOUNTERS

I'VE BEEN SPIT AT. I've been slugged. I've been egged. I've been hit with paper clips, money, cameras, brassieres, underwear, old rags, and with expensive garments and belts and things. I've been hit with, well... a slingshot. Yeah, you just get used to it after awhile.

I was just in Detroit about six weeks ago and this guy threw a Johnnie Walker Black whiskey bottle. I know it was a Johnnie Walker Black because the band picked it up later. *Threw a whiskey bottle at me.* He'd gotten it in past the people, past the friskers. It *just* missed my head. It brushed my hair actually. I saw the gleam as it arched near me. I saw it about the last six feet. I didn't have time to move really. I just heard it whoosh by and crash. The glass was so heavy, it didn't break. It's really heavy glass. Johnnie Walker Black is a good bottle. And I told an asshole TV commentator afterwards how good it felt when the bottle was going past my head, which he took all out of context, saying a terrible thing about how "this is the way my fans traditionally greet me and that I like it and encourage it."

I got hit with a grapefruit once, right in the center of my head, in Cobo Hall in Detroit.

One time, we were playing in a place called the Rock and Roll Farm in Wayne, Michigan. I mean this place was a *pit.* I used to play a lot of pitholes. Nobody in the Stooges cared. We just played, you know. Well, we're playing this pit in Wayne, Michigan, way out on a farm road—about 800 or 1,000 kids—and I was dressed in a floppy woman's hat with three flowers on it and wearing long bleached blonde hair and a dancer's leotard with little ballet slippers—practice slippers—and a sash affair around my waist. I think it was some-body's curtain.

Eggs kept flying up on the stage and as the set went on, I was getting *really* sick of it. So I said, "OK, stop the show RIGHT NOW!" I do this sometimes.

It's a funny thing. Maybe it's common to other rockers, I don't know, but the sort of music I do is very aggressive and intoxicating and after a few songs, I enter another state, probably an adrenal over-load of some kind. I believe I can do just about anything. It's not true, of course, and I often used to get into fights I just couldn't possibly win.

So I finally say, "OK, stop the music!" Again, this is a low ceiling dump of a room, could have been a pinball palace. I want to know who's the one throwing the eggs. Lo and behold, the waters part and hundreds of people spread apart. And there before me, about 75 feet yon, really just standing there like man-mountain Dean, just grin-ning, feet squarely planted, toes out, was this *enormous* youth with the most, the biggest, happy smile I've ever seen. Really, it was a won-derful smile, 'cause he *knew* he was king and was about to kick my ass (I'm hoping not too badly), with long flowing red hair. He must have been 6' 5", huge shoulders, had this large plaid lumberjack shirt, this big grin. And this one arm had a knuckle glove on—*a knuckle glove* that went *all the way up* the arm, studded at the knuckles. He was carrying one of those dozen-egg cartons—his weapon. He's clearly got his act and he's just standing there, a hand on his hip, just leering at me, you know, and in a deep, resounding voice he says, "Hello."

So I had to make a show of it and I'm on my toes like what I'd seen boxers do on TV, and I come out like David against Goliath to face my tormentor. Watching his fist moving toward you was like waiting for a train to hit you. He just squared off and decked me with one punch, right down on the ground, and I'm bleeding. I still have a scar, just dead between my eyes. I'm bleeding and everything. I saw stars. It was obvious I couldn't win so I said, "Alright, well... On with the show."

And I went back and did "Louie, Louie."

I have this deathly fear of cops—of authority. And I had this girlfriend who lived in the area—a very straight girl. She was a vir-gin at the time. Ha! A detail I took care of a year later. She lived with her parents and she said, "Quick, I'll hide you." I just wanted to get out—I knew there'd be police. I didn't want them near me. So I just ducked out with her in my little ballerina costume, right, and crept into her house late at night. I spent a night in the suburbs with this chick in my ballerina clothes in Grandpa's bed or something, and to add insult to injury, it was a chick that didn't even screw, you know. So I was all hot—a beautiful girl, you know—and trying to make it with this chick in my ballerina costume in the suburbs all night. The next morning I had to go through tea with her mother, in the daylight, in my little ballerina costume and all. So that was an unpleasant day. It was just the wrong clothes.

That same day I went back to Detroit. I went to the radio station and challenged the entire gang, the Scorpions, of which the guy was a member, to come down and do their worst at my big show in Detroit, at the Michigan Palace, which they proceeded to do.

It became "the last ever Stooges gig" tape, *Metallic K.O.*, with a picture of me on the front of it, knocked out cold—a picture of me lying *in state* as it were. And you can hear all sorts of things on the tape flying through the air—shovels, four-gallon jugs, M-80s, blah blah—but our lady fans in the front rows threw a lot of beautiful underwear, which I thought was sweet.

And spit... I've probably been spit on more than any person alive outside of, I would say, a member of the prison system. It's funny how one's chickens come home to roost. I was the one who instituted the custom of spitting. I used to spit on my audiences, when I was pissed off with them, to get them going. I couldn't get *satisfaction* any other way, so I spit on the fuckers.

But ohhh my, three years later... I did a comeback tour in 1977 with David Bowie's help. He was in the band on the piano. We had a gig in Friar's Court in Ayllesbury, near London. It was a warm-up gig for London. We had been living on the Continent for some time and we heard about this punk movement that was going on in England and certain of its associated rituals.

Apparently, audiences had learned to gob on the performers, right? So I came to Aylesbury and was greeted with the most affectionate hail of gob... No, a frenzied hail of gob. They were leaping in the air to get to me. They would even work out these rotations so that everyone could get a gob in, you know? The people who really get hurt in all of this are the other band members, because they can't dodge as quickly as I can. People's aim is often wild—they often mis-judge—so my band got a lotta gob.

I hired a soul musician, Jackie Clark, a Black fellow who had played with Ike & Tina Turner, the Nitty Gritty Dirt Band, and per-haps with Dr. Hook's Medicine Show or one of those putrid American bands. This was, like, a *professional*, soulful musician and I hired him to play rhythm. He had a good sense of rhythm.

Well, I hired him on one tour and he dressed in sort of the "Blazing Saddles" kind of tradition. He dressed the black cowboy that was his particular bit—sort of a Gucci/Bo Diddley—a very beautiful, fine wide-brimmed Stetson hat, tan, in good taste, and these toreador-type pants—very overdone cowboy. The first night out, he came up to me. "Jim, I don't care what they do to me, but when they gob on my hat, I get mad." I used to get just covered in gob.

As a matter of fact, a lot of my musicians have strange things happen to them. Klaus Kruger, my German drummer, came over to America for the first time to do the *New Values* album with me and he decided to take a little trip to see America. It was just before Christmas. He drove across magnificent deserts and canyons. And on Christmas Day, some kid threw a grapefruit off a freeway over-pass right through the windshield of his car. It nearly killed him.

Half of my band got beat up on this last tour trying to defend me, to save me from a monster I provoked. Marseilles may be mean-er than Detroit.

CHART BUSTING

THIS IS HOW YOU RAISE A BASTARD up to number 39 on the disco charts. I was in the middle of spending well over $100,000 on an album that was meant to be commercial because I had *promised* my record company president, God bless his soul, and my "manager"—I'd sworn and crossed my heart or hoped to die, hand across my breast—that I would make a commercial album. But it still sounded like me.

So my record company president from England flew into Chicago to see me, but my new manager is so precious of me he won't tell my record company where I'm staying. So I miss the president, Charles Levison (managing director of Arista Records International, one of my few true friends in music life and a guy I like), that night. So the next morning, Charles just calls me on the phone.

"Jim, I've been looking for you."

I say, "Hey, I'm at the Holiday Inn in Lakeshore."

"Great."

So he comes by to pick me up in a little rent-a-car. And the first thing that happens when Charles pulled up in his car is Dennis Sheehan, my manager at the time, opens the back for *me* and gets in the front himself. My president turns to look at me and says, "Jim are you comfortable back there?" arching an eyebrow. He was a cool guy. He was *pissed* at the treatment of a great artist by a semi-literate swine. I later fired Sheehan's fucking butt. I love to fire people. Oh, it's the greatest feeling in the world... You're fired! Fuck you. You don't work for you. You work for me, you cocksucker! Anyway, so then we go up Lakeshore Drive. We take a right on Ohio St. where I know a neat little hibachi grill. We go to this hibachi, right? And I have three or our four sakes and they don't drink any. They're sitting on either side of me and the food arrives, and I'm stuffing my face and they're not eating much. Finally, Charles comes to the subject.

"Jim, you've now spent over $100,000 on this album and we don't hear a single. Uh, what can we do?"

I say, "Hey man, get me Phil Spector, man. I know he's a loner, but he's got to be a nut not to work with me. He understands me. You'll have a #1. If not Phil Spector, get me Mike Chapman" (whose work I admire and is a good guy).

Well, to make a short story long, I didn't get Phil Spector, I didn't get Mike Chapman, I got Tommy Boyce and I made a song called "Bang Bang."

Now "Bang Bang" is a song that goes boom, boom, boom, boom, boom, boom, mum, mum, mum, mum, which means EEEEEE, DDDDDD, BBBBBB, CCCCCC, and on and on, and on and on. What a concept! "Bang Bang" is from the brain of Ivan Kral, who's a dumb ass-fuckin-guitar-player-twit who just wants to make money and make it in America. He thinks to be big and rich and to be somebody is all he's got in him, and he's selling himself short because there's this wonderful, beautiful European music in his heart.

He's scared of his *heart*. So many people are scared of their hearts. You don't have to be scared of your heart. You just have to find a new road. Anyway, he overreacted against his heart to the point where he became simply one more asshole to endure.

T R I C I A
WARDEN

FROM THE BOOK

ATTACK GOD INSIDE

SEVEN DAYS

#1 woke up to car alarm. put coffee up.
mechanically drank three cups. took
a leak, thought about a multitude of
excuses, watched kids on the way to
school dragging their feet behind
them. spoke to boss on the telephone.
said my mother was very sick. haven't
seen her in three years. I put my shoes
and socks on. I went to the newspaper
stand. squinted while I searched for
change. paid a dollar to sit on the
train with the newspaper underneath my arm.
went back and forth on the line seven
times. noticed that the same people
kept getting on.

#2 dear ear, washed the toilet today.
stood out on the fire escape & aimed
burning cigarettes at all the waterbugs
fucking on the hot strip of driveway.
ate a tuna fish sandwich while staring
at the laundry all over my floor. went
outside walked around aimlessly. ran
into pauly who wants a date. I looked
up the street for something that never
came. he ran his lines. I prayed for
potential weapons or hoped nervously
for a track meet to begin.

TRICIA WARDEN

#3 stared at my face for hours searching
for answers & blackheads. I concluded
by spitting at my own reflection. my
spit had brown things in it. watched
13 minutes of a talk show & had a laugh.
but afterwards I felt disgust & looked
toward the wall. the lady next door was
screaming her head off. joey downstairs
had backed over the neighbor's cat who
was black, white, & fuzzy. today for a
midday witness it was black, white, &
bloody. entrails hanging out of the belly,
head crushed on the crisp edge of a spring day.

#4 received greeting card from relative
who added, "why aren't you what
you are supposed to be?" hallmark
would make a lot of money by running
this line. good luck today. went
to make phone call on public pay
phone; received a quarter.
things aren't so bad.

#5 dear disease, stop growing inside me
puncturing all my thoughts with
fabricated ice picks
as common as tongues.

#6 sun woke me up. I had fallen asleep
underneath the windowsill staring at
the moon thinking of simple explosives

and time limits. sat on the steps. small
amounts of wind occasionally caressed my
face. counted how many people I thought
had hair on their ass. 37.

#7 dreamt that god loved me more than my
mother. walking home from work I dropped
my keys on the street. they bounced &
fell in the split lip of the sewer.
some people were standing around. I
laughed and pointed. they looked at me
like I was nuts. good thing I had a spare
key on me. when I got home I didn't feel like
doing much of anything. laid down on my
mattress & watched the pictures dripping
underneath my eyelids. friend of mine
called & left a message saying she dreamt
that I wrote these words; "I am the final
widow," which may be true but I know
that a widow is a final window.

STANDING ROOM ONLY

once in an empty nightclub
he bent down on his knees
lifted my shirt up
rubbed his honey brown hair
against my stomach
I looked down at him
with sincere love in my eyes
he looked up at me
and said,
"you look like you want to kill me."

SUPER

the backyard was what they called it. but it was a long broken up driveway. which was narrowly sandwiched in between a five story brick building and an iron fence of an overgrown lot. it was full of ruptured concrete and chipped metal frames. attached to these frames were lines and pulleys so tenants could hang their clothes out. finding another practical use for the clotheslines sam, luke, peto and andy swung on them like chimps on pcp.

it was one of the first hot days of spring and sam got to wear shorts. this excited her since she got to show off her legs which were covered in various scrapes and bruises most of which she was extremely proud of. today was also special because she donned her favorite t-shirt which was bright orange and read SUPER on it in big multi-colored patch work letters. sam's seven years old and three quarters and she'll tell you if you ask.

earlier peto scared her by pointing out a gaping hole by the edge of the iron spiked fence. the hole was so deep you couldn't hear where your rocks fell. the four kids surrounded it in awe. peto told them as they peered into the blackness that the devil lived down there and if you leaned in real close you could feel his breath. sam, andy and luke all nonchalantly moved away from the hole not wanting to appear outwardly chicken. peto continued. he went on to say that if the devil liked you he would come out of the hole and steal your soul. and that his breath was so bad that it would burn off all of your skin. sam liked her skin and said, "I don't believe in the devil!" (not really believing that herself) but kicked some dirt defiantly toward the hole anyway. they all paused, even peto, but nothing leapt out. to change the subject sam said, "let's play murder ball!" andy and luke liked the idea and quickly chimed in an "ok!" they weren't into peto's devil bit either. luke for obvious reasons. he was originally pakistani but his father was a born again christian. andy and peto no doubt had their own version of the devil. their dad sold coke and their mom was a high priced call girl. peto laughed because he was the oldest and was already used to the devil. peto said, "all right" to murder ball still smirking cuz he knew he had scared the crap out of everyone.

after some heated eenie meenie mienie mo's peto is it and boy can he hit hard. while running sam shouts, "can't catch me farthead." to further show off her skilled prowess she climbs a metal frame. she leaps yelling out her best tarzan impression while catching one of the laundry lines in her hands. luke and andy are running around taunting peto with incriminating names. sam holds onto the line swinging with one hand beating her chest with the other.

this racket incites helga, a hefty old lady, to get really pissed off. she opens a cracked storm window and screeches, "vill yuv shut up?!" in a high pitched tone. sam still swinging is not in the least bit ruffled. she looks her straight in the eye and says, "no." then adds, "why dontchu shut up?" the boys stop what they are doing and watch gleefully as sam shoots her mouth off. luke trying to repress a fit of laughter shakes his head and dashes for the alleyway before helga can witness his explosion. he lives two doors down from helga and doesn't want to cause trouble for himself. he is two years older than sam and a bit more intelligent under these circumstances. he stands against the filthy brick vibrating. he tries hopelessly to catch his laughter in his hands. helga visibly shaken by sam's words takes a deep breath, "I vill zell yer mozza zam." sam swings higher, bolder. she lets go of the clothesline and upon landing states, "no ya won't ya fat ol' lady." to this helga shudders involuntarily, "yuv vill lizten to…" with hands planted firmly on both hips sam says mocking her, "no no no I vill not lizten!" and that really burns helga. like an ancient tortoise she begins to retract her flabby neck in from the window while sputtering, "vat?!… vie!?" sam's laughing at her now. she says, "ya wanna know why?" sam looks down at her shirt and points, "because i'm super and yur not. so I don't have ta listen ta ya lady." as a final reply helga slams the window hard. the boys and sam fall to the ground in hysterics. luke in between laughs manages to tell sam that she's really gonna get it good this time. to which she replies, "ah I don't care. it was worth it. I hate that ol' bag. always yelling at us. how can anyone play quiet? what did that windbag expect?"

five minute and twenty three seconds later another window parallel with helga's opens with extreme ferocity. "SAAAAAA MMMMM-MMMMMANTHA VICTORIA STONE GET YER ASS IN HERE DIS VERY MINUTE! BEFORE I HAFTA COME DOWN DERE AN' BEAT YUR ASS!" peto mutters, "fuck man yur in trouble now." "i don't care." she says trying not to look visibly shaken. "GET THA FUCK IN HERE RIGHT NOW!" in respect for sam the boys look at the ground or the gate or wall as she begins to stomp away slowly. she says to the irate woman in the window frame, "all right. all right already. i'm comin. i'm comin." her tone is cool and half inspired. although when she nears the doorway to the garbage room she breaks off in a small run. as she disappears into the garbage room. every one of those boys knows he won't see her for at least a week.

"goddamn it! i didn't do nothin' wrong. that fat ol' lady tole me to shut up and that's wrong. she's got no right to talk to me like that. she's not my motha. who she think she is or somethin?" sam talks aloud to herself through the garbage stink. something that everybody is used to. she has a gang of imaginary friends for when she exhausts everyone else. she ascends the dirty sagging staircase that leads up to the first floor. her parent's apartment is only steps away from the top of the stairs. as she climbs she begins rehearsing what she might say to that big contorted face that never listens anyway.

as she turns the doorknob on #104 somebody on the other end is already pulling it open. sam follows the natural laws of physics as a tight hand grips her skinny left arm. the hand is attached to her mother gladys who is in her early twenties but does not look it. "what's wrong wit ya huh? saying stuff like dat!" whap! a backhand connect that is hard. sam's neck snaps back into position. her eyes are closed tight ready for the next one. "yur supposedta respec' yer eldas. look at me when I tawk to ya!" sam opens her eyes. whap! another one in the face. inside sam is a squirming fish in a sea of acid. whatever look her face must of revealed warranted another reason to be hit somewhere else. whap! this time the right hip. probably meant for the ass. sam twists her body away from the blow as much as possible. this infuriates her mother more who I guess thinks that someone should behave nicely when they are getting slapped around. hand prints rise up on sam's skin giving gladys something like shoe stencils to an old dance. whap! whap! "I tellya whatcha yur gonna do little miss samantha. yur gonna march yer no good ass over dere and 'poligize ta ha'." "that fat lady..." whap! "that fat lady tole me..." whap! "ta shut up..." whap "i'm not gonna..." whap! whap! whap! "yeah ya are!" "no i'm not! i'm not!" "ya are!" whap! "I toldja i'm not" whap! whap! "ya will cuz I said and ifya don't (whap!) i'm gonna makeya ya little bitch!" sam's cheeks are red and her body burns. when her tears hit her shirt they resemble bloodstains.

her mother tries to push her into the lobby but sam won't budge. gladys grabs sam by the arm and drags her down the hall toward helga's door. sam locks her feet. she is giving gladys a run for her money. her canvas sneakers screech down the hallway. she bends her knees for leverage as her mother pulls her along. then gladys decides to grab a fist full of hair as a better deterrent for sam's recalcitrant stance. this doesn't make sam much more pliant, but gladys continues to use this method regardless. sam yells, "i'm not gonna!" as they near helga's door. suddenly sam tries to break for it, but gladys is fast with the vice grip. she gets only a couple inches of freedom's taste before her mother locks in on her. soon gladys' knocks are reverberating off the dark wooden door.

the large woman is summoned. her large, loose arm skin sways with the momentum of the opening door. her perturbed face is heavy with age. sam's mother quips in breaking the iceberg. "uh hi helga (forcing a fake smile) i'm so sorry 'bout this whole ting ya know..." when sam hears her mother's voice she looks upward to see if it is the same person that dragged her down the hall. she hopes for a moment that gladys has been magically transformed into a fairy godmother or something. no such luck kid.

"can we come in? i tink samantha here has somethin she wantsta tellya." helga opens the door wider to make room for their entrance. when she does this sam notices she is wearing a tent-like blue house dress with faded yellow lining. she files this information for later disruption. with fleeting glimpses of a future revenge sam is forced down helga's hall. she runs when she can't slide.

helga looks down at sam and gladys who are finally stationary at the end of her hallway. helga is a tall woman about 68 years old. the mole on her left cheeck houses two lengthy strands of hair. gray unraveling braids are criss-crossed on the top of her tilting head. "vill... vat have yuv got ter zay fer yerzelf?" sam wnon't even look at helga's face. she is studying the floorboards with extreme ferocity. gladys shakes her a bit. "well smarty pants? what do ya hafta say for yaself? huh?" shake shake. "huh?" with a hard pinch glayds makes sam's face a fish face. with this technique she tries to make sam look at helga. helga is now shifting uncomfortably not looking so mad now as she is worried. sam shuts her eyes tight refusing to look upon helga even though her face hurts like hell. when gladys takes her hand off of sam's face to slap her, her fingerprints are embedded there. helga says, "she doezn't have ter zay she iz zorry gladyz. itz ok yuv can shtop." "no." gladys says, "i'll make ha'!" whap "now say ya sorry damn it!" whap whap "say sorry ta dis nice lady!" "please gladyz itz ok." "no it isn't. now say ya sorry!" whap "Dontcha remember dat nice doll helga gave ya fa christmas?" whap "ya ingrate! say ya sorry!" sam is humiliated and sobbing. finally she shouts, "no! I won't! I won't!" and the way she shouts it makes helga's hair stand on end. helga places her elephantine hand on gladys shoulder saying, "itz all right. itz all right. she doezn't have ter apologize." gladys gives her child a frustrated look. she sighs. on seeing helga's sympathetic look, gladys straightens up and loosens her grip on sam.

helga bends down slowly, "zer. zer. shtop crying. vould yuv like a pretzel?" sam looks her dead on with hate filled eyes. helga smiles and says, "yes, I zink yuv vould like a pretzel." helga disappears into the small kitchen which is on sam's and gladys' right. gladys bends down gritting her teeth saying one more time, "say yer sorry" shaking her more. but sam has already returned to her intensive floorboard scrutiny. helga nor gladys exist anymore just the cracks in the worn out wood. helga returns. in her hand is one of those large rock hard bavarian pretzels that will constipate you for days if you eat too many. gladys says tightly, "now take tha pretzel from tha nice lady samantha." sam's left hand shoots up and takes the pretzel from helga's hand. "now say thank you ta helga." adds gladys before sam has any real time to. "she doeszn't have ter itz all right." sam says, "thanks" in a small voice. helga and gladys look at each other in surprise.

gladys and samantha begin to make their way out of the apartment. gladys says over and over, "i'm so sorry about dis helga please..." helga just repeats, "itz all right. itz all right." her hand already for the doorknob. she ushers them out as quickly as possible. she wishes that she never said one word.

back in the lobby gladys begins to drag sam back to the apartment. sam falls down. she drops the pretzel which cracks into pieces and ricochets off the floor in six different directions.

#104 slams shut. muffled slapping and screaming can be heard through the door.

fifteen minutes later the first floor is quiet. mr. johnson exits the elevator. slowly he scuffles over to the tarnished metal mailboxes. his keys jangle in his shaky hand. as he moves toward his number something hard hits his worn brown leather slipper. with the next step something crunches beneath his foot. he opens his mailbox and extracts his mail. as he turns back toward the elevator he looks down and kicks a pretzel piece against the wall. "white trash pigs," he mumbles. his blue veined hand clutched around his bills.

ONCE

i do not understand how
two holes sewn shut could see through me
an orange face
some kind of bad death make up
i don't know if the make up artist was tripping
or if it was because you were so yellow when you died
i cried for a week because I never really knew you
everyone told me to cut the crying crap
but you were my father even if you were a screwed up drunk
i'm glad you waited for me once in your life
even if the first time was the last

TWELVE

if women in the sex industry
love what they do so much
pay minimum wage
then ask them how they feel

THIRTEEN

what you command with your mind
no one can touch

ANOTHER FOR LLOYD

saw lloyd today
wearing a pair of swanky rose colored shades
his legs crossed politely on the bus stop bench
one bouncing rhythmically off the other
he sipped his coffee girlishly
as his ten broken watches glittered in the sun

WHAT DO YOU SPY WITH YOUR BEADY LITTLE EYE?

you come and stand outside my house
a haunting possibility poised
you think I tried to take something from you
but I promise you have nothing that I would want
and for that matter I certainly don't have anything
that is worth taking
your eyes resemble ash left behind
from a long dead family barbecue
although when you see me
you smile & laugh like some skeletal advice
but I see through the nylon of your cheap device
standing at my gate
straining your neck trying to see me
but i'm not in there behind those windows
I am out here behind you
watching you watch
the way you stare so intently
makes me wonder
what you see in there
that I can not

NICK
ZEDD

FROM THE BOOK

TOTEM OF THE DEPRAVED

CHAPTER ONE

I ONCE HAD A DREAM that my mother was cut in half. She was crying and bleeding. I was six years old. I grew up in Hyattsville, Maryland, a quiet town near Washington DC. There was a field and a forest of trees behind our house leading to a creek hidden in the woods where I'd go. It seemed to lead to another world. My parents, ordinary people who lived normal lives, had an abnormal son, for which I will always be grateful. I could never be like them. When I was growing up, my father was employed by the government to censor mail, to determine whether printed or photographed material gathered as evidence could be defined as pornographic and if so, whether a successful case could be initiated against the creators and disseminators of this material. My father was a conservative person who lived a quiet existence as a lawyer and a bureaucrat for the US Postal Service.

My mother is a strong-willed, generous and outgoing religious person. My parents provided me with the usual Christian indoctrination that many people are subjected to in this country. At least they didn't beat me or abuse me. Instead, they left me alone to explore my dreams. We didn't get along too well when I was a teenager, but for some reason they couldn't bring themselves to disown me even though I got busted for drugs, burglarized houses, and once stole a bubble gum machine. My younger brother Jon turned out to be quite normal.

When I was in sixth grade, we moved to a different town. The kids there hated me. My new nickname was "Nigger Lips". There was a Jewish girl I had to sit next to in class whom the other students would throw pennies at when the teacher would leave the room, making her cry. These kids had a hatred of anything different. I wondered where it came from. Smaller ones were picked out as targets by the bullies who seemed to be admired by everyone except the kids they picked on. I once stopped a small gang from beating up a kid named "Doughboy", but most of the time, like everyone else, I stayed silent out of fear. I even joined in once when a boy was chased from the bus and had his shirt ripped to shreds by a howling mob of kids.

I got arrested when I was sixteen, hanging out with a tall kid with blond hair named Walter. One weekend a bunch of us were smoking pot in a parking lot when a cop car pulled up. As the cops approached, we tried to walk back to the car. I asked Walter, "What should I do with the dope?" He said, "Just hold onto it." I threw the pot away, but the cops saw me. They picked it up, handcuffed us and took us to the station. They strip-searched me and put me in a cell for four hours. When my parents came to get me, my mother was in tears. The next day, they took me to a barber who cut off my hair.

A couple years later, Walter got arrested for burning a house down and went to prison. I once took LSD with Walter when I was in the eleventh grade. It kicked in during the middle of a basketball game and made the players accelerate and slow down. Walter disappeared and I ended up going home feeling paranoid. In my bedroom, alone in the house, there was nothing I could relate to so I turned all the lights out and tried to sleep. My mother came in the room and told me they'd invited one of my father's war buddies, a two-star general, to dinner. She wanted me to eat with them. I said I couldn't. She asked why.

"I'm sick."

"What's the matter?" she asked.

"I did acid. I've lost my mind."

She then said, "You may never regain your sanity."

She insisted that I go out and say hello to the General. It wasn't easy. I said hello and went back to the room and tripped another twelve hours and finally came to in a cold sweat. I spent the next six months in a state of depression and made a lot of calls to the guy on the suicide hotline. I tried to believe in Christianity and attempted to read the Bible, but fortunately it didn't work. I became a born-again atheist.

I started painting a lot of surreal canvases of deformed naked people flying in the air. I'd show these paintings at art fairs but nobody would buy them. I started making movies where I'd animate toy soldiers being killed by giant flies. I was getting in trouble in school, skipping classes and roaming the streets with a skinny Jewish kid named Tonk Wanger. We'd drive around in a car on weekends looking for girls. During the day we'd skip classes and sell drugs to junior high school kids. One Saturday night, I terminated an evening of driving around and finding nothing by taking Tonk home. He was incensed. "I bet you only fucked two girls in your life!" he said. Tonk was a virgin like me, but he couldn't admit it. No girls would come near us. We had too many zits.

In high school, I got sent to "detention" a lot. I couldn't seem to obey the rules so I'd be sent to a room where I'd have to sit for an hour after school. Finally, I got out of high school and went to Philadelphia College of Art for two years. I hated most of the people there. I became interested in making films again, so I moved to Brooklyn in 1976 and took film classes at an art school financed in part by student loans I never paid back. It was there that I met Donna, a girl who lived in a room next door to mine in a building on Willoughby Avenue.

There was a lot of tension between blacks and whites in the neighborhood, a run-down section of Bed Stuy. Living there, if you were white, meant being subjected to a lot of bigotry from blacks. I was harassed on a daily basis. I got attacked by a gang once and had to have my eye stitched up. Girls I knew had been raped. One time I had a stomach ache in the middle of the night and had to walk a mile to the nearest hospital, doubled over in pain. The doctors told me that I was getting an ulcer. When I came back, I told my roommate Todd and he told Donna. I thought Donna was a fool. Mentally, she seemed to be living in the Summer of Love. When she heard I was sick though she came over. She parted the curtains surrounding my bed and talked to me, inviting me to come visit her next door when I felt better. She kissed my bare chest and left. That night I went next door and we made love.

I began to visit Donna every few days. She couldn't make up her mind if she wanted to be with me or her Japanese boyfriend, Duane. I discovered that Donna went through a lot of pain when she was a child. She had an older sister who was her best friend and died of cancer when she was five. She had another sister who died of cancer before she was born. She still cried about her older sister. She hated her father who used to beat her, but she stayed friends with her mother. Donna was a painter and she had a lot of talent. After spending more time with her, I felt an incredible feeling of release. All the years I had spent alone feeling ugly and worthless seemed to be over. I gained a new confidence from being with her and she became my best friend. She soon broke up with Duane and I moved in with her.

I gave her the lead role in my first feature, *They Eat Scum*. She played a juvenile delinquent named Susie Putrid who, with her band the Mental Deficients, started a movement known as Death Rock, consisting of kids running around cannibalizing people and causing a core meltdown at a power plant, irradiating the city of New York. The film was horrible. When I shot it, the camera was often running at the wrong speed, turning the actors into cartoon characters.

I showed *They Eat Scum* at Max's Kansas City and Club 57 in the fall of '79. 1979 was a time of renewed energy in the New York film scene. Simultaneously, people who didn't even know each other were making low budget super-8 features starring members of local

ZEDD AND DONNA DEATH / E. PRETZEL

bands. I would go to the New Cinema, a storefront on St. Mark's Place equipped with a video projector. They would show super-8 movies by Eric Mitchell, James Nares, Vivian Dick and John Lurie. Max's would show the films of Scott and Beth B. in between bands. Meanwhile, I was showing *They Eat Scum* at places like Tier 3 and O.P. Screen, a room on Broadway that had shown Amos Poe's and John Waters' early films. The owner, Rafik, was an early supporter of underground movies and the only curator left from the sixties who was still open minded enough to show the movies of the "para-punk cinema".

I met David McDermott, the diminutive star of *Rome 78*. He was a skinny painter who dressed in clothes from the turn of the century and drove around town in a souped up Model-T. He became the star of my 1980 film *The Bogus Man* before submerging into his fan-

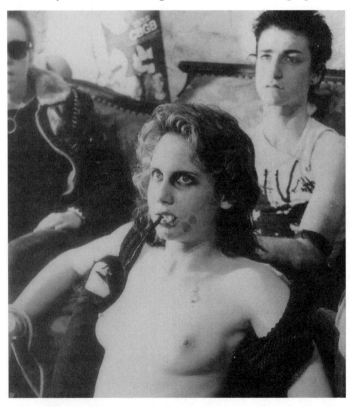

KATHERINE WITHERS & OTHERS IN "THEY EAT SCUM"

tasy of living in the year 1900. Lydia Lunch was appearing in films while playing around in a succession of noise bands. Her band Teenage Jesus and the Jerks would do ten-minute sets while the audience screamed, "Less!" Before the club scene was corrupted by overpriced tickets and the invasion of out of towners, CBGB's and Max's were a vortex of energy with bands like the Cramps, the Ramones, Suicide, Richard Hell and the Voidoids, Blondie, Steel Tips, the Blessed, the Contortions, James White and the Blacks, DNA and others who played almost every night of the week. Club 57 was the best club in town, with joke bands, drag queens, old TV cartoons, Japanese animation, fake rappers, lady wrestling tournaments, underground cartoonists and filmmakers and a succession of pre-sellout weirdos like John Sex, Wendy Wild, Klaus Nomi, Ann Magnuson, and an endless list of exotic hipsters and shitfaced lowlife in the days before gentrification ruined the neighborhood. Club 57 lasted until 1983 when, under the tutelage of a junkie with itchy fingers, it succumbed to mismanagement.

My films started getting covered in the *East Village Eye, Soho Weekly News, Damage* and other punk publications. I was even denounced on the front page of the *Wall Street Journal*. A tape of *They Eat Scum* was shown in Germany to an incredulous and silent audience. I wanted Lydia Lunch to be in my next film so I met her at Tier 3 and she said she'd do it. We agreed to meet at a certain time so I got a cameraman, but when we arrived at her apartment, she wasn't there. She'd left town. I didn't see her again for three years.

After making *The Bogus Man* in 1980, I was living on welfare and moved into a loft on West 35th Street with Donna and a guy named Screaming Mad George, a ridiculous painter who fronted a band called The Mad. We shared the place with his entourage of Japanese friends. I was showing *They Eat Scum* weekends at O.P. Screen when I got cut off from welfare. I got a job as a bike messenger, but I kept wrecking the bikes when cars would hit me. I broke my elbow and became a foot messenger. I left resumes at every film company in New York but nobody would hire me. I went to the three major networks and offered my services but they weren't interested.

I called ABC and asked, "Do you need any educated people on your staff?" The person who answered replied, "Very funny! Who do you know here?" I said, "Nobody. What does that matter?" She said, "Don't you realize, it's not WHAT you know, it's WHO you know?" "Well you don't know anybody so FUCK YOU!" I screamed.

Desperate, I went through the want-ads and found a job at a Haagen Dazs. When I got there, they asked me how many years experience I had with an ice cream scoop. "How many do you need?" I asked. They wouldn't hire me. Nobody would. They all said I was overqualified. Flat broke, I went home to live with my parents in Maryland. I got a job as a washroom attendant in a porno theater for three months before getting fired. Returning to New York, I got an apartment with Donna on 11th St. and Avenue A, then tried for a year to get grant money to make films. I was, however, about to meet the man who was to be my greatest influence—Jack Smith.

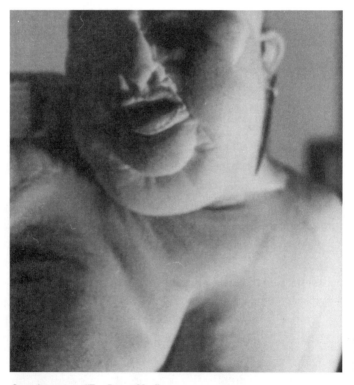

GRIER LANKTON IN "THE BOGUS MAN"

CHAPTER TWO

UNLIKE MOST PEOPLE, I suffer from an obsessive mental disorder that has made me think I can be a motion picture director without being a multimillionaire. In a perverse way, I have accomplished this. But at what cost to my sanity?

The only family I now have are my movies. These movies are enormously unpopular and with each new monstrosity, I create a more hideous distortion of "reality" and a more real expression of what I am. I have tried to release my id in my films—to express something beyond words—my own confusion and horror, joy and ecstasy at being alive. These deformed, brilliant, and beautiful entities are shadows of light and sound made to cut through the hypocrisy to which you and I are conditioned.

Unreasonable expectations were planted in my brain when I was five years old and saw *Voyage to a Prehistoric Planet*. I was stunned and traumatized by the thought of being shipwrecked on a planet of dinosaurs and cavemen. Little did I know this was to be my destiny.

Thanks to my obsession I became a hermit. I tried to visit the vomitorium of mediocrity that passes for our world and I once almost believed that I was in touch with real people. But a chillingly mindless cheerfulness was incomprehensible to me, especially when imposed by a series of bad jokes. The squealing noises people make to children and cats are also incomprehensible to me—they appear to be faked—and the smug cynicism and insulting innuendoes of the carrion I know make me want to puke.

Several years ago, angered by the spiteful film critics at the Voice and other publications who blacklisted me for the crime of criticizing their indifference, I devised a plan to subvert their ignorance by launching a movement known as the Cinema of Transgression. Publishing a magazine called *The Underground Film Bulletin*, I wrote a series of manifestos lauding the emergence of new films by people like Nazi Dick, Tommy Traitor, Manuel Delanda, Erotic Psyche, and a plethora of others, most of whom betrayed the

ᴢᴇᴅᴅ & Sᴜsᴀɴ Mᴀɴsᴏɴ / R. Kᴇʀɴ

movement years later in acts of petty jealousy and heroin induced fraud. The plan worked for awhile and journalists and curators temporarily woke up and paid attention to films they'd been ignoring for years. Sooner or later though, almost every filmmaker I'd mentioned in articles or included in group shows ended up stabbing me in the back, lying to me, or accusing me of exploiting them by exposing their work to more people. Some, in their jealous treachery, went so far as to write falsified biographies of me which were then printed in nationally circulated magazines as my "obituary". I was astonished at the vehemence of their jealousy and the absurd lengths to which these pedalogical pipsqueaks would go to discredit me. Nobody seemed to notice how much their limited fame depended on my clandestine support so I decided to drop the traitors and let them flounder on their own.

In the nightmarish debacle of bringing the Cinema of Transgression to life, the only things that didn't betray me were the films I made. I have since devoted my energy to the creation and dissemination of these films to my eternal regret.

The awareness that the outside world is resolutely committed to going backwards bothers me. I see it every time my roommate turns on the TV. The person I live with spends hours in front of it watching programs which are crude propaganda for a "normal" point of view. All conflicts are cheerfully resolved with a fake sincerity by boringly ordinary people oozing a pustulent sentimentality. That every cliché on TV is met with a hail of applause and laughter reinforces the illusion of democratic consensus. But how could someone like me turn the poison of mass sedation around?

I discovered that being an underground filmmaker makes me less than nothing. With the world corroded by an entertainment industry that is so restrictive and reactionary and so motivated by an urge to please a contingent of cretins, I feel no more influential than a homeless person asleep in front of the White House. Why I had to find an activity designed to obliterate the values of the dominant hierarchy is beyond me. Why couldn't I be happy just driving a cab?

Being an independent filmmaker is a baroque curse. It means none of your films will likely be reviewed by anyone and only a tiny fraction of the general public will ever know you exist. I have tried to get my films seen and distributed, but no one will touch them. My

NICK ZEDD AND KEMBRA PFAHLER IN "WAR IS MENSTRUAL ENVY" / KATRINA DEL MAR

"lifestyle" has become an obscene parody dictated by endless games designed to con people out of money so I can puke out a few more turkeys before I die. The only people I have anything to do with are my investor and my roommate, two strange creatures I've been trying to get away from with no luck.

It has taken me ten years to find somebody to be my investor. This person is a commercial artist who would rather be doing something avant-garde but is unwilling to sacrifice material comfort in order to accomplish this goal. This person lives vicariously, enabling me to create my masterworks which make no money and are hated by everyone.

Recently, I thought if I made a movie where everyone was naked I might get laid. The film, entitled *War is Menstrual Envy*, would deal directly with the misdirection of my sexual energy. Two of the actresses on the project might have wanted to fuck me but for some reason didn't feel right about it. I thought if I played an octopus, I might be able to rape Annie Sprinkle but Kembra Squalor insisted on doing the scene instead and would only allow her husband to rape her. I thought up another scene where I'd play a mummy and have sex with an old girlfriend, but she had band practice the night we were supposed to do it so I had to give the scene to two other actors. I pray I will find some way to get laid before this film is done since it is costing my investor so much money.

My roommate spends more time talking to cats than to people. Every penny I raise driving a cab goes to pay Baby Jane Holzer, ex-Warhol superstar turned greedy slumlord. My rent is three times what it should be. These sixties superstars are now parasites leeching off poor creatures like me, stealing our architecture and selling it back to us at fantastic prices.

A couple of years ago, in a vain attempt to protest the murder of Michael Stewart by a gang of transit cops—who were later exonerated by our evil judicial system—I made a film called *Police State*. It demonstrated the lengths to which the state will go to exterminate those who deviate from the approved cultural stereotype. Since making the film, I have tried without luck to get it seen in America and

Canada where it was twice stopped from being shown by government censors. In New York, no theater will exhibit the film and I have been repeatedly turned down for any grants to finance future work. When I took *Police State*, *War is Menstrual Envy* and another film called *Whoregasm* to show in Washington DC, only three paying customers showed up. I spent six hours the night before putting up posters all over the University of Maryland and downtown DC. No newspaper would mention the films and a heavy snowstorm occurred the night of the show to keep people away.

Maybe someday people will care about underground films, but I doubt it. That's part of the definition of being underground now. Nobody cares. In the face of a mad rush to be normal, most Americans won't bother to go see anything out of the ordinary. I have accepted this. In our present era of mindless complacency and profound ignorance, America, the great Fascist Empire, is controlled by multinational corporations dedicated to the destruction of diversity, and in their stampede to crush the deviant, urban planners and corporate gentrifiers have made enormous gains at the expense of those aspirations of the human spirit to which all civilizations are ultimately judged. One day, the transient concerns of our national corporate oligarchy will vanish into dust along with the military industrial complex which sucks up such a disproportionate amount of our people's money. In a thousand years, like any civilization, ours will be judged by the ideas found in the subterranean artifacts being produced by the impoverished and the marginalized, and it is for this reason that I continue to make films whether or not anyone comes to see them, because they speak to me and to future generations who will one day dispose of this monolith of greed that oppresses us all.

CHAPTER THREE

In **1981,** I met the underground filmmaker Jack Smith who directed *Normal Love* and *Flaming Creatures*, "a masterpiece of inane kitsch" back in the sixties. He lived in a tiny sixth floor walk-up jammed with garbage and decorated to look like a kindergarten version of Baghdad. The bathroom was a lagoon filled with plastic vines. His bathtub was filled with moss. He planned to film a pirate movie with miniature ships in it. The door frames were modified with spackle to resemble Arabian arches and the place was crawling with roaches. He kept his movies in a closet in the kitchen under his bunkbed.

I used to come over to help him paint the walls of his "set". He would take time out so he could make tea. He sat at the kitchen table and placed the package of tea in front of our cups. As soon as he opened the package at least twenty roaches came scurrying out. He remained oblivious to their presence and asked me how much tea I wanted as he stuck the spoon in the box. I said, "None," as I watched him drink it.

One night I was at his place with a Cuban filmmaker named Ela and we decided to go out. He wanted to put on "exotic attire" before leaving and came out with a pair of hideous, striped platform shoes which I convinced him to wear and an Arabian scarf which he affixed to his head. In the platform shoes he stood at least seven feet tall. He made an attempt to descend the six flights of

JACK SMITH (1989) / CLAYTON PATTERSON

stairs but tripped and fell before he could make it to the fifth floor. He took off the shoes and left them in his apartment. Smith had a paranoid obsession, fixating on a man he called "Uncle Fishhook", a filmmaker named Jonas Mekas who he claimed had stolen his films and was sucking him dry. "Uncle Fishhook stole my roachcrust," he'd mumble. He had a rolodex in which were scribbled cryptic messages like, *It's no use...I'm too old...I have no more pasty cheerfulness...* and *Unexotic Aftermath of Nuclear Hollow Crust.* He felt the image of lobsters being boiled alive was a perfect metaphor for man's existence.

Anyone he despised was a "crust"—what was left over after being eaten out—including Andy Warhol, whom he'd made a film with in the early sixties. Everywhere we'd go, he'd get strange reactions even though he was totally passive. When I had to move out of an apartment, Jack came over to help, holding a Chinese umbrella when it wasn't raining. The super, a loud, fat Russian, slammed the door in his face and started screaming hysterically for no reason. When I couldn't reason with the beast, a guy I knew named Tom went in the vestibule. The Russian suddenly stopped when Tom screamed at the top of his lungs, sounding more insane than him. I was impressed since Tom was only five feet tall and the Russian was six foot two. He finally let us enter the building, but it was Jack's passive weirdness that set him off.

I wanted Jack to play a college professor in one of my films and he insisted that he'd memorized the script but it was essential that I purchase a pair of glasses for him from a junk store. I asked how he would be able to see with the wrong prescription. He said if we looked hard enough we'd find it. We went to all the local thrift stores looking for spectacles—a waste of time since he could just as easily have worn frames with no lenses in them—but he refused, saying they had to be authentic. He planned on making a Sinbad movie in his apartment. When I asked how he could shoot an entire feature in a one room apartment, he said he'd play all the parts to save space. He later decided his stuffed penguin could do a better job.

He wanted to change his name to Sinbad Glick, the Pink Pirate, but then decided it might offend "anti-Semitic pressure groups" so he changed it to Sinbad Rodriguez. He said one day he planned to burn all his films so nobody would steal them. He had an expensive 16 mm camera he'd been given by some camera company which grew dust in his closet for years. When it came time to rehearse a scene, he showed up at my place without his glasses and said he couldn't see anything so we went to his apartment.

When he put the glasses on, he revealed that he hadn't memorized any of the script and tried to cover it up by attacking its literary merit. He was incapable of rehearsing the scene with the other actors since he refused to take it seriously, reciting the words on the page in a monotone voice so we left Jack sitting in his room staring at the sheets of paper. "Don't you want them back?" he asked as I left.

I never saw Jack smile the entire time I knew him, but he was constantly trying to get other people to laugh. He told me once, "In Europe, I danced with a penguin. I was paid an enormous amount of exotic currency and was treated as royalty. The penguin was inert and feeble and at the conclusion of our dance I inserted my finger in his rectum. I smelled my finger. It did stink." He would tell me stories

like this in a sad whining voice and a completely straight face. He thought he was "unphotogenic" and wanted to have his nose removed since it was shaped like a hook. I'd tell him it was his best feature but he wouldn't believe it. *I was the world's most glamorous pie crust,* he once wrote. He had a strange charisma and often tried to manipulate people to do all his work for him. He told me at one time he was turned into an "art

JACK SMITH (1989) / CLAYTON PATTERSON

machine" by unscrupulous "college scum" who fed him drugs so they could exploit his ideas. He once punched out a federal narcotics agent at a poetry reading for attempting to bust someone smoking pot.

Smith was living on bonds purchased with money he'd inherited from his family years ago and complained about the sordid nature of his sex life. He would go to Variety Photoplays and get blow jobs in the balcony seats. He did the same thing at the bath houses and complained of the lack of romance in these encounters. I wondered if I might become a sexual attachment in his eyes and tried not to spend much time with him even though I found the nature of his genius fascinating. I asked him if he had ever been in love with anyone and he said once, but he drove them away. "It was a terrible mistake," he said.

One day, a couple of weeks after I'd spent an afternoon painting gold trim over the arches of Baghdad in his apartment, I called to invite him to a performance I was doing with Nazi Dick and Tommy Traitor at a dive called Darinka. He angrily asked, "Why would I want to go to that?" and made it clear that he considered me a traitor for not visiting him or calling him more often. I told him that he was a flaming turkey. We never spoke after that.

Every person he knew at one time or another had been subjected to his paranoid wrath and an army of enemies existed in his mind, isolated for decades in his fantasy world on First Avenue drinking bottles of Guinness Stout. In 1989, at the age of 57, he died of AIDS. Someone told me he said it was "a glorious way to die."

Jack Smith was a "failure", but he refused to commit suicide. By refusing to make concessions to everyone else's feelings, he remained pure and uncorrupt, maintaining his individuality in a way that no one else could. He showed me that most people who are "successful" are really shams because they've committed mental suicide through the process of compromise. He proved to me that you can rise above living for other people and that the integrity of one's vision can be maintained even in the face of poverty and indifference if you believe in yourself.

HENRY
MILLER

FROM THE BOOK

DEAR DEAR BRENDA
**(THE LOVE LETTERS OF HENRY MILLER
TO BRENDA VENUS)**

July 15, 1976

My lovely Brenda—

I have returned from the Press Club luncheon and am starved. The meal was a strange American sort of one. No wine—just coffee and tea with the food. After a cup of soup came a salad (which I didn't eat) and then a piece of cake. That's all! I kept expecting another course but it never came. However, it was a good reception I received. They kept firing questions at me and laughed a great deal— so I must have hit it off well with them. They were all correspondents for foreign papers. No Americans, thank God!

I came back and took a little snooze, during which time my mind kept reverting to that erotic-porno Japanese film I told you about. When it is released to local theatres, would you care to see it with me? I would value a woman's opinion, especially someone who is in the films, who is not prudish or squeamish and who has a critical faculty.

Now I want to say a few words about the batch of photos. They are lying beside me and the one on top which you call your "ultra Hollywood" pic is to my mind extremely beautiful and seductive— due perhaps to the way your thick mass of hair drapes itself about your head. But the look in your eyes is exciting. Next up is the one in a bikini at 4:00 A.M. God, but you look ravishing. Excuse me for putting it this way, but I can't help it. You look like you are ready to be laid. Though you didn't do it deliberately, I am sure, yet your pelvis juts forth most invitingly. And those thighs of yours! Made to crush a man's ribs!

Shall I go on? (I hear you say Yes!) Next up is the girl with the straw hat. Reminds me of a famous painting by Matisse. The design on brim of hat is very intriguing—as pattern.

Next I have nothing to say about—you say on back "Thinking of someone I loved far away." A faint reminder of Laurette Taylor, ever hear of her?

The next—with Russian dancer is like from Ravel's "Bolero"— *non?* I feel jealous of him. Nor do I understand what you are trying to tell me about your present lover, Dan. One little detail... I notice that even with your shoulder straps slipping off to your arms, your breasts do not pop out! What control! Or is it carefully studied?

And now we come to the one you refer to as "crude." In another woman it might be so considered but not with you! Your look is wonderful. Naturally one's eye travels immediately to the crotch; one also can't help noticing that you reveal more than usual of the one teat—right? Brenda, it is possibly what one might call a lascivious pose, but with a body like yours, anything is forgiven. Besides, aren't you the girl who wrote me that her whole body was one big erogenous zone? Didn't you also tell me that my so-called obscene books were not obscene but natural? You know, it's strange, but as I was opening the envelope of photos I said to myself—"I'll bet this time she sends me some sexy ones!" I'm surprised at you using the word "crude." It's not crudity but audacity. (Thank you for writing on the backs of them.)

The next one is a misnomer—"rather dull" you wrote on back. Anything but, I'd say. This is virtually an "invitation to the dance," to put it elegantly. Do they really wear swimsuits like this—and where—in Italy or La Riviera? I haven't seen any like it in this part of the world. It's very lascivious. And your holding your hand as you do increases the awareness of what we are missing. One says to himself, "Why did they stop at the belly button? Why not cut it a few inches lower and give us the whole show?" (Do I offend you—I hope not.)

And now the last one—the one you like. I agree with you. Your pose is almost that of an Eleanora Duse, my great favorite as actress. She and Garbo—*c'est tout*. Jesus, but I'm hungry, and not just for food. I may put your photos under my pillow tonight in order to summon the dreams I desire. Do you mind? Brenda, your letters make me more and more "delirious"—I think that's the word for it. What erogenous zones I have left are quivering with hopeless anticipation. Nothing in the world could give me a greater thrill than to take you (roundabout expression) or even just feel your secret parts. You are treating an old man like me royally. Like a prince, I might say. But each letter, each photo, only increases his (base) appetites.

You can appreciate that, can't you?

I am talking rather boldly this time, but not without encouragement, I feel. After all, think of it as one erogenous zone talking radar to another. I'm sure we speak the same language, only using different words. Am I not right?

Brenda, I must stop or else... To know anything about your horoscope one must have place of birth and the hour you were born. Can you furnish these? Then I'll see what Omarr, my astrologer friend, has to say. Though he has multiple sclerosis he has (4) women on his string, usually on the end of his cock!

Henry

Same day—later—July 18, 1976

Brenda, my delight!

I tried to get you on the phone a few minutes ago but don't know whether I got the answering service or just ether waves. So I hung up.

But you're still with me, like a foetus in the womb (only I'm missing the womb).

It's been on my mind to ask you if you ever read any of these famous love stories:

1) Tristan and Isolde

2) Abelard and Heloise

3) Laura and Petrarch

As for Orpheus and Eurydice, enclosed is what my secretary found in the Encyclopedia. Not much, sorry to say. You seem to think I'm a great scholar—but I'm not. I've read a great deal, but never in scholarly fashion.

Two authors I wonder if you ever read—1) Dostoievsky, 2) Isaac B. Singer? Or, and my perennial favorite—Knut Hamsun, author of *Hunger, Victoria,* and *Mysteries,* among others. Have you? I love the way he handles love. *Mysteries* is my great favorite. Have read it 6 or 8 times and would read it again tomorrow if someone put it in my hands. If you'd like to try it, I'll hunt up a copy for you. He's long out of print, I'm afraid. If it's true, as Omarr says, that Scorpio becomes the characters she reads about, then I too am a Scorpio. I go nuts reading Mysteries yet my children, who read well, don't care for it. Knut Hamsun is my favorite author, though Dostoievsky is the greater writer. (Do you know his famous woman character—Filipovna—in *The Idiot?*)

Well, tonight I seem to be on cooler ground, don't I though? It's only a foil or mask. Underneath I'm still smoldering for this Venus woman. By the way, I mailed you a copy of Omarr's little book on Scorpio for 1976. See where I turned the page down. I know Scorpio by heart. I wonder where your Venus, Moon, and Mars are? Will tell a lot. Do you know the aria in Wagner's *Tristan and Isolde?* Do you know the opera was almost censored and banned? The music is sexual. It does get to your blood, no question about it. Just one prolonged "fragrant delectus." I mean the "Liebestod" part. In other words—an everlasting orgasm. But you probably know all about it...

Tell me, how did you hit it off with Coppola? Is he re-hiring you? Jesus, but I'm asking a lot of questions tonight. Pardon me! I sound like a professor. But it's only that I like to share certain good, beautiful things with you. Savvy?

Did you ever see that soft porno called *Emmanuelle?* Did you like it? I'm curious. Enough of questions. I am hungry still for more letters and more photos. I love the way you utilize your time, writing me at odd moments in odd places. Great! Few women seem able to do that. But I keep forgetting that you are not an ordinary woman, you are Brenda, the volcano, the *con furiosa, toujours prête à bruler tout ce qu'elle touche* (meaning—always ready to set afire whatever she touches).

I hope I can go to sleep. Last night I awoke, slept out, at 1:30 A.M. Had a notion to call you, as you once suggested, but didn't want to give you a sleepless night.

You mentioned the moon being in Capricorn the last few days. That explains my rather torrid letters, no?

Brenda, I press you tight and kiss you avidly a thousand times. (Give me more strength, O Lord!)

Henry

❧ ❧ ❧

Henry felt he was clairvoyant and psychic. He would predict certain happenings, some of which eventually came true. He was fascinated by astrology, astronomy, and numerology as well. Sometimes he would send me his psychic readings.

❧ ❧ ❧

Same day—a little later
Beloved—

Do I dwell too much on your beautiful body? Don't forget that it's you who inspire this adoration.

I feel I must express a few thoughts about your mind and your soul, for God has also richly endowed you in these areas too. I think first of all of your voice, the pitch and the tonality. They never vary, good weather or bad, which means you are harmoniously equilibrated—at least in public or in my presence. If you have emotional fits you don't show them. It's always a bell-like clarity to your voice. It also has a joyous ring, or rather a tinkle. You think with your whole organism, including your private parts, maybe particularly with these parts. It lends color to everything you do or say, even to a gesture. Am I making you too perfect? No, only as I see you through my worshipful gaze. Your soul is utterly mysterious—but it is intact and generous and understanding. If it can hate it can also forgive. It is abiding, like the Rock of Ages. It does not change color, like the chameleon. There is something leonine about it. You are a Scorpio that is non-poisonous. One can keep you as a pet without fear. You can swim in troubled waters and be at peace. You radiate peace and good will. Your sexual fantasies are inherited and spring from the heart rather than the vulva. Your purity is the outcome of your vitality, which was God-given. You have a streak of Semiramis in you, but it will disappear as your love deepens.

That's all I can tell you this evening. Be with me Thursday—in fine fettle.

Your adoring
Henry

One morning I phoned Henry and asked if I could drop by in the late afternoon around four-thirty and give him a hug and say hello, and he answered yes, but he would be leaving the house at six for dinner. He greeted me at the door, as he often did when he was in good spirits, and I gave him his promised hug and kiss and we shuffled into his bedroom to talk for about an hour nonstop. Then we went into the living area so he could show me the new paintings he did that day, when the doorbell rang. He got this mischievous look on his face and said, "Brenda, quick, hide behind the draperies. It's Lisa Lu and I haven't broken the news to her about you. She will be very jealous if she sees you here." So he guided me behind the drapes and neatly patted the folds where my body was bulging, to make it look as if no one was there. But my feet were sticking out and there was nothing to do about that because the drapes were a bit short.

He told me to be perfectly still because he would be in a lot of trouble if I was seen. I said, "Okay, I'll just hold my breath." "No," he retorted, "don't do that. You might faint."

In the foyer, before he opened the door, he whispered, "Brenda, are you all right?" I said, "Sure, but try and hurry because this is not very comfortable."

I could hear him giggle before he opened the door as if he was really pulling a fast one. He greeted Lisa with "Gee, you're a little early, aren't you? You wait here, I have to go and get my coat." Lisa said, "But your coat closet is right here in front of you."

Henry didn't miss a beat. "I guess I'm a little bit excited, I was waiting for you so anxiously. Forgive me, I'll just turn off the lights in the ping-pong room. Must save electricity, you know."

With a twinkle in his eye, he hurried back to tell me we narrowly escaped a messy situation and that everything worked out fine. "She didn't suspect a thing."

I remembered that he had been in a similar situation with Anaïs Nin, only he was the one who had to hide behind the drapery.

In an earlier letter Henry had stated that he had at least six women "on my string." I feel that all these pretty women gave him a reason to live, to wake up each morning, because he could believe he was still the Romeo

*of yesteryear. As long as he could fantasize, he could shrug off the aches and
pains.*

✈ ✈ ✈

July 21, 1976

My dear, dear Brenda—

Yes, I do write to a lot of women as well as men, my corre-
spondence is enormous and covers the whole globe. But, don't mis-
understand-I don't write all the women as I do you. I do have a rather
warm (very friendly) correspondence with a beautiful Japanese in San
Francisco and a quite young Korean girl (a genius of a pianist) who
may possibly be in love with me. But, my dear Brenda, I couldn't pos-
sibly keep a string of beauties—like a stable of fillies. It isn't human-
ly possible. I don't even desire it. Some publisher who is a great fan
of mine and makes me many gifts of art books, wrote in his memoirs
of finally meeting me—good description of dialogue—and then
ended the passage by saying: "At 82, H.M. still wants to fuck every
woman he meets." And that's not true either. There are so many
women who bore me to death. Maybe the Women's Libbers think
the same way about me but they have never recognized the fact that
I love women taken as a whole. And why not? But I can't love them
all in the same way. And Brenda, please believe me, you are some-
thing very very special to me... I don't know if that was good to give
Coppola all those wonderful compliments about me. It will probably
leak out. If reporters ever got wise to our goings-on they would
ridicule me to death!

How have I forgotten to tell you about Coppola—or didn't I?
He never showed up. Had to meet Marlon Brando before taking the
plane back to Philippines. Seems Brando is dissatisfied with script!

To come back to Francis, I'm sure he would like to have you in
his stable, assuming he has one. That's why he was so shy. (Men too
are shy sometimes, you know, or "innocent," like me. Ho ho!)

You say "the great lovers" is one of your favorite topics. Not
your lovers, I hope. You mean Garbo and the like? It's mine too. That
and "unrequited" love.

When you finish reading the books I bring tomorrow I will have more for you—if you have the stomach for it. For example: I have the book about Walt Whitman, the *Tale of Tristan and Isolde*, *Against the Grain* by Huysmans (Oscar Wilde called it his Bible of Aesthetics). It's up to you how much you can absorb. If I said "take" it would sound like *Deep Throat* and the Sword Swallower biz, eh what?

So you enjoy my sensual writing too! Do you realize you are guilty of euphemism frequently? That is, not saying exactly what you mean. Beating around the bush.

And, as for nudity, don't you go about your own home naked sometimes? Did you know that Benjamin Franklin used to do it and recommended it to all good Americans. It makes one relax, feel free, is good for skin and circulation, and gets one to appreciate one's own body. From doing that to posing for a painter is but a step. Naturally I am not thinking of porno films, whether soft or hard. But your body is a gift to the world! Make it known. When the young woman who posed for Botticelli's "Venus Rising from the Sea" died at an early age, people went mad, flung themselves at her coffin, wept and howled. You too are a Venus—*en chair et os*, as the French say— meaning "in the flesh."

Do I sound "Hedonistic"? How can I help it with you? You invite romantic dreams, "the skin one loves to touch," nocturnal emissions and God knows what all.

Love yourself! As you would expect others to love you.

Ta ta now!

Henry

ᵕ ᵕ ᵕ

Henry was intrigued that I was part Indian, and said we ought to become blood brothers. I thought it was a touching idea, and before I knew it Henry had me cleaning a penknife with alcohol. I went first, pricking myself on the wrist. (I still have a tiny scar there.) Henry took the knife and went a little overboard. We managed to exchange blood and vows to love each other forever when I began to realize that his wrist wasn't drying up. I rushed to get a towel to wrap him with, and every time I checked it there was fresh blood. I was on the verge of calling the paramedics when it finally began to slow down. Henry thought the whole thing extremely romantic.

Soon afterward, Henry came to my house for dinner. Henry had been feeling melancholy, as he would say, so I planned to give him a special present to try to lift his spirits. First, I told him in detail some things I had learned about Captain John Smith and Pocahontas that had always had a special interest for me. She had really been the first woman diplomat, representing the New World in London. When she was still a young girl she had given John Smith, whose life she had saved many times, a small vial with her blood in it to wear around his neck, hanging by a necklace she had woven from her own long black hair. She told him it was the greatest gift she could give him to show her love. It was her "heart's blood."

Now, in my family on my mother's side, we also have a special gift. The firstborn of each generation is given a family treasure, a six-carat ruby, which is placed on his forehead at birth and is meant to give the child special powers. I had been the lucky recipient in my family and it was intended to go to my firstborn. But since I had no children and no immediate plans to marry, I decided to break tradition and after telling Henry the Pocahontas story, I gave him the ruby.

He loved his present, and from then on whenever he went out he wore it around his neck. At night it was always by his bedside. Some weeks after he received my gift, he presented me with a coin which he had worn for many years. He told me the story of this gift, that centuries ago the coin had been found in a sunken treasure chest, and had then been worn by St. Francis of Assisi.

My mother, by the way, did not speak to me for six months.

✦ ✦ ✦

July 23, 1976
My darling Brenda—

Last night I went to bed in a state of bliss. What a wonderful evening you gave me! Thank you, thank you! (And here are a few hundred kisses in the interim.)

I can't get over how beautiful your little home is. Like you in every way. Too bad there were no portraits of you by Bonnard, Renoir, Dubuffet, Braque, or Picasso. Only sit for the Masters! Only sleep with the Masters! Eat and drink with the nobodies or the somebodies, but no more.

When you came out with the cookies in the white robe I was astonished. What an actress you are. But most of all I remember the tender looks you gave me, the warm hug, the shower of kisses.

One funny little incident sticks in my crop. When you escorted me to the bathroom and then stood there, as if expecting me to ask you to hold me up. I'm sure you would have done just that had I requested. What a woman!

And then that story about Olivier. Utterly fantastic. Great! Like that one day some director is going to seize on you, make you his star, and let you be known to all the world.

Oh, yes, and the Pocahontas yarn. Captain John Smith burned—and her attitude. How noble some women can be! What a shame they can't tell us the naked truth in history books.

I seem chock full of wonderful memories of last night—tidbits to perfume my sleep. Bliss, bliss—no doubt about it. The blood-brother to ecstasy. But more steady, more lasting. I'll cherish your heart's blood. Have put it somewhere for safe keeping.

Well, I imagine you are winging your way to Utah and to Dan. It's great that you have room in your heart for the two of us. Or am I being a bit presumptuous?

What a shiver of delight went through me as you kissed me good night.

I'm going to stop now in order to do some work, but don't know if you will let me. You keep tugging at my heart. It's almost as if we had drunk some witch's brew! (Tristan and Isolde.)

More anon. Take good care of yourself. Don't get exhausted from love or work!

Henry

Same day—a little later—
Dear Brenda—

You know those black holes in the sky which are s⸍
ies to astronomers? Well, I feel as if there were a black hoⱼ
vate sky since you left.

I was asleep and Val woke me to sign a few prints which she just sold to some movie director. (She loves to make money, Val. So does Tony. I never had that bug.)

Anyway, since I was up I decided to stay up and chin with you a while. What about? Anything and everything. Your chaste walls, for example; your spotless refrigerator and the fleurs de lys pattern on Sarah Bernhardt's blouse as I was taking a leak *chez vous*. And those lovely portraits of you—Hurrah! That body, that face, that *je ne sais quoi* (don't know what)—all enough to drive a man out of his mind.

When I first heard you say "my period" I was almost shocked. What! The shy Brenda telling me about her period, her profuse bleeding, her painful spasms! Incredible. But how natural you were!

And then in the bathroom waiting hesitantly, ready, I do believe, to take it out and hold it for me, if necessary. That didn't shock me; that merely told me how considerate you could be—and still remain shy! I think such behavior one might expect of a Japanese woman, not an American.

Funny you telling me of Captain John Smith's burnt penis and I sending you the review of Japanese film in which the woman cuts off the dead man's penis. Did you understand why she tried to strangle him while mounting him? Did you know there is a legend about the hanging of a man, that the moment his neck snaps and with it his cortex he ejaculates automatically. And where there is a gallows there grows a plant called mandrake or mandragora, shaped like a human head, born of the semen of a hanged man! There was a German novel built around this theme called *Alraune* by Hans-Heinz Emers-many years ago.

Do you own a copy of *Tristan and Isolde?* If not, I'd like to send you one. This and Emily Bronte's *Wuthering Heights* are two very passionate tales, no holds barred. Tell me, with all your other talents, do you also write—stories, plays, scripts? You put in such a full day that wonder if you can find time for such a pastime or even for making love. From the little hints you have dropped about your love life I imagine it to be full and rich. I also think of it as rather paradoxical—i.e., extreme passion together with great modesty. If it weren't for the latter element, you would be in danger of being a nymphomaniac! Right?

You said at dinner table, "Everybody has a birthmark." But that's not so. Vaccination marks, *oui!* But not birthmarks. I think if you will examine yourself more closely you will discover yet another birthmark and this time in the vicinity of the pussy willow (maybe hidden by the pubic hair). The Japanese sometimes say "public hair."

Now I am treading on dangerous ground, aren't I? But I do so only with your kind permission and not to deny you a single crumb!

How I long to see your next letter! I hope it's a good "torrid" one. Did you notice that the subtitle for the Japanese film was "the corrida of love?" A corrida for me, eh?

Henry

Same day—still later!

Brenda, I wish God had given me the gift of writing about sex like D. H. Lawrence. Somehow my efforts always seem crude and shocking, even to liberal-minded individuals. Why do I speak thus?

Because, willy nilly we are approaching that delicate yet most powerful region called the genitals. Just as Walt Whitman felt compelled to include in his *Leaves of Grass* the "Songs of Adam," which alienated so many of his admirers here and abroad, so I feel I run the great risk of alienating your affection once I begin to plunge in where angels fear to tread.

Yet, do I not have a collaborator? Have you not kept pace with me step by step all along the way? Do you not write screaming messages between the lines, so to speak? Do you not encourage me to be myself?

Before I go any further, let me tell you of a little incident some few years ago in Paris, after the publication in French of *Sexus*. All of a sudden the French authorities decided that they would take no more of my nonsense. They threatened me with imprisonment, imagine that!

Fortunately there is a court in France, the like of which we don't have here—a sort of pre-trial court. There I was summoned with my French lawyer. After quite a bit of questioning, the judge leaned over his desk and, gazing at me severely, said, "Monsieur Miller, there is one last question I must put to you. Please pay strict attention." The question was—"Do you honestly believe a writer has the right to say anything he pleases in a book?"

I took a few studied moments before replying and then I said calmly but with conviction, "I do, your honor!" (With that the clerk, who had been taking notes and watching me most attentively throughout, looked in my direction and silently clapped his hands under his little table.)

Now the judge came down from his dais, hugged me, kissed me on each cheek ("the accolade"), and said, "You belong with the immortals: François Villon, Baudelaire, Zola, and Balzac. I salute you!"

I didn't mention that during the course of the proceedings I was so tense that suddenly I wanted to urinate, I felt my bladder would burst. I turned to my lawyer and asked where the lavatory was. To my astonishment, he said, "You can't go. Do it in your pants if you have to." Whereupon I did it and there was a big stream of water across the floor, almost to the judge's feet. I was not tried again nor imprisoned either. I was granted "an amnesty." But from then on I was a hero in French literature, one of their very own. And I am treated like one to this day.

Well, does all this give me the right to speak my mind to you? I am still hesitant. I think I shall wait for your reaction before proceeding further. Have mercy on me! You've taken me to your heart. Now take me other places!

Henry

Henry was unpredictable. One day he would write me erotic, suggestive letters and then the next time we would meet he would apologize profusely and beg my forgiveness if I was the least bit offended. He explained this

behavior often by reminding me that he was a man, made of all the var-
ious parts a man is made of, and that he must at any and all times be him-
self. He desperately wanted me to understand this side of him.

Sometimes when he would write asking a sexual favor, or if the
entire letter was abrasive, I would not read it. Instead I had a drawer that
I put those particular letters in and I would read them at a later time
when I could distance myself from them. He would ask repeatedly, did I
receive the letter and what did think? In reply, I would say, yes, I received
it but I prefer not to comment now, but I promise that I will later. And, of
course, I did when the time was right. I never wanted to hurt or offend
Henry. I cared too much for him to be inconsiderate of his feelings.

There were days when I wished he wouldn't talk so much about my
body or pretend he was falling so he could touch my breast or thigh. He was
not a quitter, so it was up to me to find my sense of humor about that
relentless situation.

At one point Henry told me he wanted to write me a really risqué
letter and he hoped he wouldn't offend me. If any other eighty-seven year
old man had suggested something like this, I would have been put off-but
who was I to tell Henry Miller what he should or should not write? I told
him that if he thought it was going to be too erotic that he might consider
writing the letter in French.

⇥ ⇥ ⇥

Same day—later 8/7/76

Your lucky day, Brenda! Was it? Spent two hours today talking
to a young couple (fans) from Salt Lake City. After that one solid
hour answering Lisa's questions about words and phrases she didn't
know—in the *Book of Friends.*

Answering her questions, I realized very strongly that there is
a man's language and a woman's language—in all countries. The
man's language sounds flippant and derogatory where women and
sex is concerned. For instance, consider phrases like—"I'm going to
get me a piece of tail," or "I want my nooky," or "She was a
pushover," etc., etc. In Japanese, though the women may have the
same vocabulary as the men, they pronounce the words more softly,
more ingratiatingly.

Maybe that's why you asked me to write the erotic letter in French. If the French do use "dirty" language, they make it sound humorous, too.

In Chinese I find there is no equivalent for the words and phrases I use. Chinese must be a rather dull, flat-sounding (not writing!) language. Everything too explanatory. Very few metaphors. Yet they have good poetry!!

Did you like the printed words on the flap of my big envelope? I hope they didn't irritate you. So many American women I know bristle when I mention the Japanese woman! Jealousy, envy—what? You could well pass for an Oriental of some description—Hindu, rather than Chinese or Japanese!

By now, from dint of thinking about it so much, I can virtually visualize the "campy" photo at the Post Office. You are still wearing a "seventh veil" only it is shorter, more revealing. Your teats are exposed, but in a discreet way. There is a cricket hopping from your left leg to your right leg, then losing himself in your silver dollar navel. *Vous êtes intriguée mais assez triste. Vous avez besoin d'un homme. Assez pour ce soir.*

Henry

(In French for Brenda)

The idea which you suggested to me is so audacious that I am not sure of being capable of doing what you asked of me. Since I have known you you have occupied my thoughts perpetually. In my fantasies I have done all sorts of things with you. I have guarded in my head the idea not to offend you. At the same time thru your letters I can sense that I may dare to do and say much more than I actually am doing. Your body itself is an invitation to do everything.

The scene that comes to mind repeats itself often. I am at your house looking at your paintings. You immediately give me something to drink. The drink rises to our heads. You are dressed in a very thin and transparent skirt. Above your belly-button you are wearing nothing. Your breasts are splendid. You have the appearance of a dancer. (Something from Degas.) Your legs are strong and beautiful. All of a sudden I throw myself on you, and lift your skirt. You are totally naked under the skirt. Your little puss with black and copious hair makes me immediately tighten up. I plunge my hand between your thighs and I see that you are already wet. You seem very excited, ready to do anything. That is not surprising. I know you from centuries, what I mean to say is from other incarnations.

We were lovers many times. Sometimes you were a prostitute at the temple—in the Indies, in Egypt and in other countries. You are always a lady of pleasure, but always religious. Your religion was always "sex"—just like the practitioners of Tantra of today. You teach the young, the men and the women. For you it is a question of art. That's why you now appear to be an expert.

Without the slightest blush you lightly touch your cunt with your right hand. Then... with two fingers of each hand you open the crack between your legs, and you show me the small lips that tremble like a little bird. The juice flows liberally; your thighs gleam.

Without saying a word you put your hand in my trouser and catch my flute (or the bollard if you prefer). Your hands so strong but delicate, play with it as if it were a musical instrument. You are choked up and irresistible. I want to "play" immediately, and most of all when you put your tongue in my mouth. From there your mouth turns to suck my flute gently. It is difficult to remain standing. Luckily the couch is on your side. We fall onto the couch together, mouth on mouth and flute on cunt. I have not yet penetrated you. How warm you are! You give me kisses all over. I want to kiss you. You are totally ready. You press on my flute and put it between your legs. I enter softly, even slowly. Your organ is deliciously formed. It is narrow and deep. You hold me as one would a finger. Naturally I cannot retain myself anymore. I come—as do you—at the same time.

We remain like that for a while intertwined like serpents. I want to tear myself away but you do not allow me to. You hold me with strong muscles. After some time I feel movement inside of you. Little by little I begin to swell. Now you lift your legs and put them over my shoulders. You are totally open and wet. You do not stop coming. Your eyes turn towards the ceiling. You ask me to continue, to do more. You say [in English], "Fuck me, Henry, fuck me! Shove it in to the hilt. I'm so horny." It is the first time that you have used such language with me. It drives me wild. "God give me the power, the strength," I say to myself, "and I will kiss you endlessly." Do not forget that I am relating to you a fantasy. I do not understand where the power comes from to give you pleasure for so long.

You are insatiable. You make all sorts of movements, sometimes gestures that are completely delirious and obscene. You have lost your mind. You are totally sex and nothing else. Knowing that you can kill me you detach yourself from me so that I may breathe. But you do not stop caressing, especially with your tongue. And your body continues to undulate over me. You kiss me like a madwoman!

Et puis quoi? Quelle position? C'est moi qui propose que nous faisons l'armour comme les chiens . . .

↳   ↳   ↳

Henry and I were talking about parenthood, and about what parents contributed to the nature of their children, both good and bad. Henry began to talk about his mother, and he was overcome with anger. His face turned red, and he complained of pains from his heart as he reiterated the injustices he had suffered from her when he was a child. I suggested to him that the time had finally come to forgive her, to make peace with her. We agreed that he couldn't get into heaven if he continued to harbor this hatred.

↳   ↳   ↳

Saturday—8/14/76
Dear Brenda—

I just finished writing about China for a Chinese magazine and another (short) piece on Hokusai for an exposition of his *shunga* (erotic) wood blocks done at the age of 80. The exposition to take place in Paris at "L'Espace Cardin." Erica Jong came for lunch and left only about an hour or so ago. She'd like to find a house in California. After New York, California seems like a Paradise.

I have been thinking of you ever since you put me away early. You went to acting class afterwards, didn't you? You could have told me and left even earlier had you wanted to. I would not have objected.

I notice you observe the other night that I always have "sex" on my mind. Not always, dear Brenda. There are a thousand other things more important to me than sex. But when I come across a creature who is all sex I can't help but betray my feelings.

A lapse of a few hours here. I was in bed but got up to finish this. I want to make mention to you once again of one of my favorite writers—Marie Corelli.

I rediscovered her about a year ago. I now have ten of her titles. Here are the names of some I read:

1.) *A Romance of Two Worlds*

2.) *The Sorrows of Satan*

3.) *The Soul of Lilith*

4.) *The Life Everlasting*

She lived in the latter part of the 19th century, during the Victorian epoch. She never speaks of sex, never mentions any sexual organ or any intercourse. Yet she is a thrilling, inspiring writer—for men and women. (I don't think you would like her, though.)

When I was waking up a few minutes ago, I found myself writing in my head. The strangest thing—I was dead and had just realized that I was in Devachan (the realm between death and rebirth). My mother is coming toward me looking radiant. She seems very young. "O Henry," she begins, "I have waited for you so long. What kept you on earth all this time?"

(This is the first time I hear my mother murmur endearing words.) I am choked with emotion. "Mother . . ." is all I can say. And then I discover that the tears are running down my cheeks.

You know, I believe that I hated my mother all my life, to the very end. I wonder what this dream signifies—that I am approaching death or that I am losing all hatred, all bitterness?

As I got out of bed I wondered if I should try to write a short book on Mother and Son in the Afterworld?? Very strange for me. Your talk must have done something to me deep down, softened me up in some strange, inexplicable way.

Did you ever read my essay on The Womb? Very surrealistic. I love the thought of the womb-so cozy, so nourishing.

Enuf now—I'm sleepy.

Love,

Henry

✴   ✴   ✴

Henry's daily routine was basically the same, with a slight variation depending on how strong he felt.

He usually would greet the morning around seven-thirty to eight o'clock and would either call and say good morning, or he would just lie in bed and listen to the birds chirping and the different sounds that one might hear at that hour.

At 9:00 Charles, his nurse, would arrive and prepare him for the day. This consisted of washing, exercising, a little cheerful conversation, vitamins, and breakfast. He adored Charles for a number of reasons. They had one basic characteristic in common-they both loved life and they laughed a lot. Sometimes I would drive over early for a swim and a run around the Palisades, returning to find Charles' big black Cadillac parked in front of the house. It always made me feel good to know that Charles was there.

After breakfast Henry went through his mail and answered as many fan letters as possible. Letters he felt were exceptionally good, he would send on to me to enjoy. If he was working on a new book or an article, this would be the time he would take to work. If not, he would sit at his ping-pong table and do a watercolor or two, depending on how good he felt. After working a few hours, he would take lunch and after, a little nap. He would often have visitors. Some were good friends, others came to ask for favors. Can you lend me money, would you teach me to write, can I live at your house for a while? I'm doing a film, would you please be in it? Sometimes Henry was easily accessible and other times it would be impossible to see him.

When I met Henry he told me he hated the telephone and would seldom use it because he couldn't hear very well. But as time went on and we knew each other better, he called at least once a day. He would leave long messages on my answering machine, taking into consideration that he was always teaching me. There would be a story he forgot to tell me or some

*valuable information he forgot to write. I often called him after I got into
bed just to say good night and send him my love.*

↝   ↝   ↝

Sept. 4, 1976
Chérie—

All day, I've been wanting to write you, getting my mind read-
ied for it, and then at 3:00 P.M. comes a neighbor (from Arkansas)
and buys $130.00 worth of my books—but takes up 2 hours doing it.
Fuck her!

Any way, *mon chou*, how goes it today? No letter from you and
I suppose you won't get my Special Delivery till Saturday—and this
one only next Tuesday! Wow! We are really fucked up by the holiday,
eh? Those post office bastards ought to work night and day and
Sundays and holidays, too.

Tomorrow I'm sure I'll receive the letter you mailed yesterday.
It better be good! I'm counting on it.

You know, I was studying that photo of you and the boy. It's
amazing how beautiful you look as a man. Without losing a mil-
ligram of femininity you have developed a nice streak of masculinity.
It adds to your charm, not detracts. You are such a candid, frank per-
son. I'm sure if I asked you seriously to describe your cunt (physical-
ly) you would do it like an expert. How many things you have told
me about yourself—intimate things! Women don't usually do that.
Not right off leastways.

Am I falling into a Southern way of talking? If so, attribute it
to your influence. You can't make me do things but you influence me
a great deal.

I love to tell inquisitive people that I'm in love with a young
woman from Mississippi. I wouldn't say Hattiesburg, but I feel when
I say Mississippi they immediately connect up with Mark Twain and
those big two-wheeler boats.

I'm running off the track. This is all bosh what I'm writing you.
I had very definite things to say but they have been blurred by the
advent of that talkative real estate woman who lives on Alma Real

nearby. Do you know that *alma* means a soul in Spanish? Isn't it another coincidence that the next street to Ocampo should be the street of the Soul? And a few blocks away is the street of the Womb (*La Combre*)!

Strange how with me soul and sex are always united like Castor and Pollux, the Heavenly Twins.

Yesterday came the woman from Japan. She gave me a gift of a beautiful, flexible silver paper cutter. Told me a lot about the ungodly man-woman situation in Japan. The men, as every Japanese woman tells me, are simply incorrigible. They are weak (caricatural) hangovers from the days of the Samurai. (Have you read *Shogun* by Clavell? Seems most everyone is and raving about it. It's out in paperback now.)

By the way, I wrote you "precipitately" when it should be precipitously, did you notice? There is the noun—precipitate. (Does it matter?) I'm simply trying to hold you to the paper. It's a way of holding you in my arms and caressing you.

Did my last letter surprise you a bit? Were we then on the same wavelength? Or was I way off this time?

Listen, I'm no longer so very horny, but when I rise up in bed and slide to the edge of the bed my balls get squashed. Can it be that they are growing now, at my age? If only my prick would follow suit! Sometimes, when it's snoozing, it looks like a lost snail to me. Now that's one thing about the cunt. The variations throughout the day are not so conspicuous. Right?

This reminds me of a conversation I had the other night in Malibu with a lively, delicate French woman. She had been arguing with a French man about the fact that they always use *con* (cunt) in a derogatory way. When a Frenchman says—*"sale con"* (dirty cunt) he doesn't mean that. That's his way of saying "stupid bastard." Anyway, he got her so riled that finally she retaliated by calling him *"sale couille"*—*couille* means balls. There is no part of man's sexual apparatus which is ever used in a derogatory way. (Here they resemble the Japanese a bit.)

Did I ever tell you how inventive the Japanese man is when it comes to delineating a woman's cunt? They have all sorts of terminologies for this organ. The cunt they appreciate the most is called "like a thousand earthworms." Another, not so good, is "hit the ceiling," and for a very big cunt it is "falling downstairs." All expressed in a word or two. Remember my water color "Asamara"? Means "morning erection." Morning, mind you, no other time of day.

Folle à la messe

Molle à la fesse

François Villon

(Crazy about mass, soft in the ass.)

Next Tuesday I'll be looking for a Loulou of a letter from you. You'll have a whole weekend to cook something up. Make it a good bouillabaise! And throw in a few *baisers* (noun or verb, no matter.)

Are you slithering around now? You do get restless, don't you? And don't you like to open and close your legs? Doesn't that excite you? In French, by the way, the verb *exciter* means to get passionate—not "exciting." *Alors, attention!*

Have you "learned" anything from this letter? Or should I have added something about Virgil, Ovid, Rabelais, Cendrars, Celine, or Octave Mirbeau?

My eye is getting bleary. Signal to quit. How can I? You have me in your grip, just as sure as if your thighs and mine were interlocked. You are the acme (apotheosis) of sex, yet cool as a cucumber outwardly. You are North and South in one. You arc the monsoon and the deluge all in one. You are you—and that's saying a lot. So long for a while. (I may write more-later.)

Henry

MICHAEL GIRA

FROM THE BOOK

THE CONSUMER

EMPATHY

WHEN MY SISTER WAS RELEASED from the mental hospital, she came to live with me in the tilting and crumbling one-bedroom house I'd bought with the small amount of money I inherited when our parents died. She arrived one afternoon unannounced in a taxi. She must have known instinctively that I'd take her in. I don't know how or why they released her. Probably due to overcrowding, and they had her scratch her name on a form, then pushed her out the door. Or maybe she just slipped away when no one was looking (who'd notice in a place like that?)—she never did tell me and I didn't ask her. I was so happy to have her with me again that the last thing I wanted to do was break the spell by letting reality intrude. Ever since they'd dragged her away weeping with laughter and reaching out for me with our parents' blood still coating her hands with shiny red gloves, I'd felt amputated, like they'd pulled her kicking and screaming and insane out of my guts.

My house sat beside the freeway in a cluster of upright rectangles laid out in an orderly but grimy grid directly beneath the flight path of the LAX. The living quarters formed the upper half of the rectangle, squatting on top of an open-faced garage. As the relentless chorus of rising and falling howls pounded down on the house from above, the garage would resonate with a deep rumble like a kettle drum, rattling the flimsy stucco walls and sending an accordion of low-frequency sound waves surging through the slat wooden floors.

Sometimes, before my sister came to me, I'd stand naked in the center of the floor for hours, dreaming of her and feeling the house rocking and resonating up through my bare feet into my bones, as if my body were a hollow bell, tuned and vibrating in perfect sympathy with the frequencies that coursed through the world outside. My blood hummed with pleasure. She was singing through me, calling out to me over the distance from her cell, forgiving me my secrets and washing my mind clean. But the air inside my house smelled foul, like the inside of my body, as if I'd extruded a growing shell out the pores of my skin and was now huddled inside it, stinking and rotting and feeling sorry for myself because I couldn't be near her.

I never went outside anymore, except to buy alcohol and meat. I'd get drunk, loosening my attachment to myself, and I'd eat the meat raw, pretending it was my sister, planting her flesh inside my stomach so she could grow inside me and live through me, like a cancer. When they sentenced her to that place, my own life started to drain out of my body immediately. As I walked away from the courtroom out into the poison sun of Los Angeles, I felt the light shooting straight through my eyes into my skull unfiltered, causing a tumor to grow in the center of my brain. The tumor was shaped like a rose and its petals were as sharp as razorblades. With each new thought, a petal would spiral away from the body of the flower and slice a passageway through the meat of my brain, slowly boring out large sections of my identity.

I hadn't seen her in three years when she arrived. It was the middle of summer. A constant regurgitation of corrosive yellow soot spilled out over the houses from the elevated freeway, burning my skin and eyes and tinting the neighborhood with a golden pigment that sparkled like sharkskin in the sun. The heat clung to the smog. It was heavy and painful going down into my chest, infesting my body with toxins with each breath. I was mildly drunk, sitting inside the house with the lights off and the curtains closed, sweating. I watched the blank screen of the television reflect the glow of my cigarette and imagined the hovering red ember was me, and I lived in the arid world of tubes and electronics behind the glass.

I heard a horn blaring up from the driveway. I looked out the window and saw her in the back of the cab, sitting up rigid, looking around, confused, uncertain what was supposed to happen next, maybe not even sure she'd come to the right address. She squirmed in her seat as if it were alive and she were trying to ecape its grip. She seemed to have forgotten she could simply open the door and get out. Her hair was stringy and matted to her head, so shiny with grease she might have just stepped out of a shower. She yanked at the strands that stuck to her forehead, plucking at them with pinched fingers as if they were long black worms she didn't want to touch. But she still looked beautiful to me. Her neck extended high and elegant, like a swan, just like our mother's neck before she cut it open. It presented her face, like a smooth white oval sculpture on a sleek pedestal. It was the face of a superior, chosen being, with eyes so black and flooded with cruelty and remorseless intelligence that when I looked down at her now, I felt like I'd always felt when she was near me, like a cringing, one-dimensional cut-out figure—a second-hand shadow peeled up from the outline she cast on the world.

The driver hit his horn again and looked up annoyed at the parted curtain in the window. But I stood hypnotized, watching her lower lip tremble exactly as I remembered it used to do when we'd lie naked on the cool sheets of her bed, locked inside her room as our parents slept, caressing each others' electrified skin with the peacock feathers we'd collected from the fields beyond the back yard. Her lip was a shuddering animal then, and she taught me to bite it and play with it and torture it, as if I were a predator and it was my game.

I ran down the stairs, drugged with happiness. The memories of our life together congealed, then broke like an egg in my throat, spreading her helplessness through me and charging me with strength. I fumbled in my pockets as I tried to pay the driver. She got out of the cab, bunching her eyes up defiantly against the sun, as if daring it to try to slap her down with a wave of smog and heat. She stood shaking in her pink institutional bathrobe and slippers. One of her legs was meticulously shaved and polished with cream so that it reflected the sun like pale pink marble. But the other leg looked like something freshly dug up that had been decaying while buried in the dirt. It thrust down into the light from beneath her robe like a simian arm creeping out from a dark damp cave. It was covered in a coarse fur that stopped abruptly at the delicate bones of her ankle, as if the blood beneath this tighter skin was too thin to fertilize its growth. The skin beneath the fur was a gangrenous reptilian hide, shedding patches of white scales that adhered to the hairs and flickered in the sun like sprinkled flakes of pearl.

She leaned forward and kissed me on the cheek. Her lips were cold and wet. I felt myself weakening. I smelled something decomposing beneath her robe, like the smell of my own trapped insides. When she pulled away from her kiss, a silver thread of her spit connected us, strung like a fragile translucent nerve between our skins. It moved with the heat that rose up from the white concrete driveway. I felt her love pulsing through the liquid wire into my mind, telling me secrets and injecting me with her loneliness.

Her robe had opened slightly with her shaking. A breast sat matter-of-factly exposed, plump and vulnerable in the sun. The cab driver noticed it but pretended he didn't see it, and so did I for a second—I could feel the pliant nipple between my teeth, sucking the sweet healing milk into my mouth. I finished paying the slimy bastard and told him to get the hell off my property. I pulled her robe closed and helped her up the stairs.

We stood on the landing just outside the door and leaned on the rotted wooden railing, looking out across the freeway. The haze was a thick veil of brown blood. I held her close to me. The sky was a dull blanket pressing down on us, not leading up into space but defined in-close by the wall of sound and vapors directly above us. The air stuck to our faces like syrup. The bellies of the airplanes passed so close overhead they were like the undersides of giant boats seen from beneath the water. As they glided over us, moaning and shaking the house, we could see the faces of the passengers looking down at us in wonder, as if we were miniature animated mannequins in a sprawling amusement park landscape.

I reached my arm out towards the freeway. She followed it with her eyes. It was raised up to the same height as us, so near I could almost touch the guard rail. But the drivers in their cars, tightly sealed in the air-conditioned environment behind their windows, were traveling in their capsules through another world, completely enclosed, as if the glass walls of an aquarium separated us from them.

She laid her head on my shoulder as we watched. Her tears soaked through my shirt and stung my skin like acid. I kissed her moist forehead and noticed her eyes scanning back and forth with the passing cars. She was trying to make eye-contact with each driver as they scrolled past us. Trolling rays of concentrated hatred shot out from her eyes as she tried to connect with their unguarded minds. If anyone had met her gaze, she would have instantly boiled the grey sponge behind their eyes. But no one would look at us. The world beyond the freeway was invisible.

Inside the house, it was dark. As our eyes adjusted to the absence of light, the details of the room emerged, slowly advancing in the darkness like lost memories approaching through a fog. She stood in the center of the room and spun her body in a circle, reaching her fingers out for the air like a sorceress conjuring up a hidden world, sucking my essence into herself through mouths cut into her fingertips. Gradually my weakness without her revealed itself to both of us. The hollowed husks of the bodies that I'd shed hung from hooks secured in the joists of the ceiling, dripping down in rows throughout the house, melting in the trapped heat and darkness and saturating the air with their rotting, like lilies wilting in a suppurating garden.

My sister let her robe fall to the floor. Her flesh grew up out of the offal and blood iridescent, like a night flower straining towards the moon. She danced nude among the entrails and garbage and beer bottles as if she were wading joyously through a foaming red sea. The scent of her insides seeped out from beneath her skin into the closed air of the room, gradually augmenting and replacing the smell of my misery with the familiar balm of her glands, a perfume so close to the smell of my own body, I was drawn to it like a species of insect honing in on its queen. Her face radiated a submerged glow like a magical orb stealing stored light and heat from its surroundings. I flowed into her. The energy my body contained was sucked through a stream into her eyes. She held out her arms and enfolded me in a kiss that both drained me and simultaneously filled me with a warmth I recognized as her life seeping into me. Her tongue was a velvet slug that burrowed into my mouth, then wound down my throat into my intestines, where it prepared the nest where she would grow.

She loosened my pants, cooing the same song into my ear she'd sung to me when we were children, like a secret greeting-call, long forgotten. My exposed erection burned against the cold oily skin of her stomach. I was hardened by her strength. She'd reached into me and was flexing inside me. As the first spasms of hot white fluid jerked out of me, she cupped me in her hands and guided the flow across her belly, smearing it up onto her breasts and over her neck and face, sealing herself inside a second crust of skin, like a nascent cocoon standing upright in a sunless forest of pendulous flesh.

We nailed the doors of our house closed from the inside. She lives on the meat and blood growing everywhere around us. The sun filters through the closed curtains like urine. She probes and crawls through my guts, mining me. I'm an inert object, but I come alive with her touch. Each time she finishes fucking me, less of me remains in my body. Soon I'll be emptied—a dead shell of loose skin, like the others. The sounds of the traffic and the airplanes passing overhead beat against the walls and soak the insides of this house with pleasure. We're coming, lodged in the bowels of the world as it screams. I'm moving into her, so I feel good. I'm vivid and flooded with love, dissolving like a breath steaming in the cold air, hovering. My sister is inhaling me into her body, digesting me.

WHY I ATE MY WIFE

EVERYTHING MERGES EVENTUALLY—everything is organic. It's impossible to distinguish one thing from another thing. When your mind is emptied of selfishness, it crumbles and dissolves in the water. If I cut at my body and concentrate correctly, I won't feel it. Each time my heart beats, it jerks violently and whips my spine loose, tugging at the base of my brain. Memories move through the clotted and rotting forest inside my head and crush the present beneath them. My memories don't belong to me. They're as unknowable as a centipede fluttering its legs in the dark corner beneath the sink. When an image moves through my nervous system, it's with the predatory greed of an intruder. My body's laid open, transparent, defenseless. Each second of time is an individual insect feeding on my blood.

When my wife and I joined our bodies together, I fell into her body and wore her skin like a rubber sheath. She protected me from the outside. Because she's dead now, I'm certain to be eaten soon. I'm a skinless body, my muscles drying in the sun. I feel myself shrinking.

I used her as a process, a system through which we could blend with matter beyond our selfish thoughts. When her hand stroked my leg, when her mouth wet my skin, the arousal I experienced was the first wave of a current which would ultimately erase us both. I love her more than I need my own identity. Though her body lies here on the table before me, I don't need to open my eyes to see it in detail, to feel it physically saturate my senses. Love allows microbes and viruses to pass through my body without resistance. In loving her, I lose the will to live. If I eat her body now, I'll take her back into myself. But with each mouthful I swallow, I'll remove a commensurate amount of myself.

Her fragrance lifts up shimmering above her in a mist and flavors the air with honey. Her breasts have now begun to slide down the hill of her ribs, rotting, no longer firm with arrogance or inflated with the promise of fertility. The nipples I once took into my mouth and sucked and chewed, stand straight as if in defiance against the retreat of the body of her breast down her side. Gravity is pulling her down into itself like quicksand. Her belly is shifting, emitting obscure demonic incantations from inside its depths as it breeds gas while decomposing. Looking down at her open mouth, I can still remember the taste, the slightly caramel flavor of her saliva, and feel the rubbery resistance of her tongue slipping into my mouth, circling across my teeth, wrapping itself around my tongue. But now, an open cave in her face displays the dead thick leather tongue like the cadaver of a beached sea mammal, crawled into the dark space of her mouth to hide from the sun and the swarming flies. Her lips, which were once a rare fruit I sucked for juice, are now shriveled and cracked like a dried apricot. Her eyes stare back up at me, searing my face with corrosive acid. My tears drain slowly down the corners of my eyes, thick as mineral oil.

Seven days ago, she stood secretly in the doorway of our bedroom watching me, curled in the bed reading, unaware of her presence, until she had silently approached and breathed warm breath against the back of my neck. Now her flesh lies here devoid of gesture or empathy, reduced down to a process, like yeast reacting to water. The molecules that comprise her body are moving, detaching from one another, rearranging and dissipating into the surrounding chemical stew of biology, no longer held together by the adhesive material of her individual will. I feel my own body churning with particles, genetic material, atoms, parasites...

The smell of her sex crawls into the womb inside my brain where it gestates, forming a perfect memory, a hard red core of impossible lust that glows and warms my thoughts. I bend down to her for a last futile kiss. The inside of her mouth excretes a sticky white glue that smells as if it came from a place deep in the earth— a cache of animal compost hidden in a lightless tomb. I take a serrated kitchen knife and remove her fingers carefully, catching the draining fluids on a white bath towel. I eat these possessed fragments of her soul with empirical care, transfixed by her unblinking eyes. I'm intoxicated with the finality of her memory and the transmission of her taste, odor, and texture into my mind and body.

As weeks pass, each day brings the ingestion of another piece of her essence. As the substance of her being enters me, I'm transformed into an entity beyond myself, and beyond her too. This evolution is just the first step in my own slow decomposition, as I blend with the infinite organisms that will in turn feed on me, ultimately mixing me with the atmosphere...

THE YOUNG BOY

STILL A YOUNG BOY, I stood naked in the cell, a gift from heaven carved in alabaster. Girlish and barely pubescent, my skin glowed, pure and creamy, an opal shell lit from inside by the cold light of my unviolated innocence. A silky blond tuft of angel's hair grew clustered just above my genitals, floating like a holy crown. My body relaxed as if sleeping as I stared down meditating on a secret place on the floor. My long silver hair fell in streams before my eyes with the iridescence of a waterfall. Tears gathered at my feet, drawn together like mercury in a small mirrored pool on the oily black surface of the concrete. A single pale blue eye stared back up at me from the pool. Hypnotized by the eye, my body swayed in the moonlight that entered through the small barred rectangle in the steel door.

Outside, the moon rose above the black wooded hills and flooded the courtyard of the prison. Arms dangled limply through the openings in the cell doors that surrounded the courtyard. Fingers gathered in the light, as if it were a clear liquid narcotic. I imagined that after being drawn into their cells, this intoxicant was drunk furtively from cupped palms, the prisoners squatting in a dark corner as they sipped.

The prisoners in my cell watched me from their beds, the rough wool blankets pulled up to their chins. The blankets were ripe with years of sweat, musk, and oils, the smell sealed in with the weekly blizzard of DDT the guards inflicted on our stripped bodies, our clothing our personal effects, and our bedding.

Across the courtyard, a prisoner was being tortured. According to standard practice, his wrists had been tied to his ankles and a pole had been slid in beneath this knot. Lifted in the air by a guard on either side of the pole, his body was spun as he was beaten with a club. In between times, when the guards tired of spinning him, the soles of his feet were burned with cigarettes. The screams, as with most of the new prisoners, were muffled and resigned, subdued, to demonstrate total compliance. The screams were almost never expressive, rarely more than what seemed a cursory acknowledgment of the personal subjugation of the process. It was a ritual that was best endured passively, an initiation into the mute boredom and coming regimentation of institutionalized life.

When they'd finished their work on the victim, I watched as the guards ambled across the courtyard, the moon casting long gesturing black shadows behind them on white stones. When they entered the door that led into the administration building, the night went silent except for the low residual moans of the tortured man.

I turned from the scene in the courtyard. The prisoners in my cell were hovering around me, closing in. Their blankets shrouded their heads, hanging loose from their shoulders. They looked like leprous savages emerging from the woods, or evil monks drawn to a bloody sacrament. Each one held a weapon—a toothbrush filed to a point, a razor-sharp spoon, torn strips of cloth to be used as a garrote. I backed against the cold metal door and waited.

DON
BAJEMA

FROM THE BOOK

REACH

WHOPPER

THE TRUTH IS ROBERT MONROE WAS A LIAR. He was lying when I was six. He was still lying when I was ten. He needed lies in his life. He needed falsehood. He said the truth was too boring.

One morning Robert started in on a long story and this guy home from a CYA detention camp out in Poway groaned, "What a whopper," and spat through his teeth, hitting Robert on the shoulder of his t-shirt.

Robert looked at the ground in front of him for a week. Then he started telling about the time his father got his fingers slammed in the truck door, which we knew was true because we were there when it happened. That story led right into one about the day his epileptic uncle pulled a V8 out of an Oldsmobile with his bare hands. The way his eyes went red as he stood up with the whole works balanced on the inside of his forearms. How he shook, and the pressure blew his boots off.

Someone finally just started calling him Whopper. The shock on his face said he knew for sure he'd been tagged. For the rest of that Saturday, every time someone called him Whopper, everyone would crack up, rolling on a lawn under a jacaranda tree, flowers crushed under our brown backs, hysterical in the delight of such an outrageous disgrace of one of our own. Whopper kept trying to threaten us into dropping his new name but it was no use.

Didn't stop him from lying though. He'd quit for a while, then he'd get away with a little lie. Then he'd try a larger one to see if he could still pull it off. We'd bust him. He'd even cry when we didn't believe him. It got so he'd really bug you.

In July, he tried to pad his batting average and we caught him. We shouted the lie at him through the fence when he got to bat, watched him strike out. We mentioned it at the concession stand in front of his sisters. Brought it up about ten times during the long walk home after the game. He took it pretty bad. He'd want to fight, but being in the wrong, his heart wasn't really in it. We laughed at him instead.

That turned out to be his last lie. We didn't notice at the time really, but by the time we got back to school, Whopper hadn't whopped since baseball season.

First day at school at the bike racks. A cloud of dust and a deep circle of boys. Fight's gonna start. I'm walking over with Whopper beside me. About twelve sixth-grade boys are in a circle, yelling in horror. And in the center is Jimmy Johnson, the toughest sixth grader who ever lived.

Jimmy Johnson was already building a reputation that was to peak two years later in the eighth grade, when he got impatient only being the toughest kid in junior high. He wanted the high school. He made sure the word got to the toughest kid there, a Golden Gloves boxer named Matranga. Then Jimmy went right up to the guy in the middle of school and said, "Let's go somewhere where the teachers can't protect you."

That afternoon at a hamburger stand, in front of about three hundred kids, Jimmy Johnson kicked the shit out of Matranga. Thirty seconds. It was strange to see the will of someone evaporate like it did in Matranga. Jimmy showed him a whole different level of violence. It went beyond trying to hurt someone or sensing victory or anything like that. It was without honor or logic. It was Jimmy doing what he was born to do. And when Matranga's car keys popped out of his jacket pocket, Jimmy snatched them off the ground and threw them on the burger stand roof. Jimmy yelled to his buddy Benny. Benny tossed him a can of lighter fluid. He sprayed down the guy's hair and lights him up. Whoosh! Matranga ran around like a horror movie until a couple of friends threw him down and smothered the flames. By then, Jimmy and Benny were gone.

At the bike racks, Whopper and I approach the circle and peer through the shoulders. Jimmy Johnson is down on his hands and knees, cutting the legs off of a thrashing ten inch alligator lizard. The lizard has red stubs at its tail and on one leg. Jimmy put the leg in front of the lizard's mouth hoping he'd eat it, which he didn't. Jimmy was getting ready to cut off another leg when Whopper says:

"You have to stop doing that."

Whopper is in the fourth grade, a third Jimmy's size and skinny. Jimmy Johnson's got nothing to prove. I'm standing next to Whopper, praying Jimmy hasn't heard him.

"Or what?"

As soon as Whopper begins to talk he sounds miles away.

"I'll try to kick your ass."

All the boys go "Whoooaaa" at Whopper and start laughing at him. Jimmy ignores him.

Whopper says, "I mean it Jimmy."

When Jimmy presses the knife on the large joint of a hind leg, Whopper pushes past a couple of kids and shoves Jimmy over. Jimmy struggles to keep his balance, but finally falls on his back holding the lizard in the air so that it doesn't hit the ground and get crushed in his hand. He's protecting it. The lizard twists its head, snaps the air, three legs twitching and a red stump left for a tail, like the burning end of a cigar. Jimmy's getting his awkward body realigned, pressing one hand on the ground, pulling his legs under his hips, using one knee and then the other to finally stand. He seems to be waiting to hear the boys snickering behind his back. Something seems to be crying deep inside.

For the first time I notice that he's wearing big, stupid-looking hard-soled shoes, the fashion of geezers at the beach. His head is plastered with a lot of vaseline melting in the sun, his scalp visible through his very thin hair. I tried to see it all at once, but I lost it beyond a vague sympathy for the lonely awkward life of Jimmy Johnson. But he is focusing on Whopper with an expression saying, "I'll fuck you up in a minute."

Then he puts the lizard back on the ground and slices off two legs. He stares at it, hunting for the connection of the lizard's fate, and his part in it as its vengeful god.

Jimmy stands up. The circle widens, like it wants to get a little distance, but at the same time it moves and shrugs and jumps and ooohs and ahhhhs and groans like it's alive. Jimmy starts punching Whopper's arms and shoulders, letting him know how hard he hits. But he doesn't try to run. So Jimmy moves in going for his head.

Knots and bumps turning purple on his face, nasty gaps forming over his cheeks and eyes. And Whopper keeps swinging anyway, making Jimmy more and more pissed.

What should I do? Jump in? Get the crap kicked out of me in front of everyone? Just because Whopper feels the same thing as I do about torturing a lizard, but has the guts to do something about it? What I'm seeing being done to him, I don't want done to me.

I think fascination is not necessarily a good thing. I mean we didn't want to watch. But everyone did anyway. And we would have looked if Whopper was the lizard and Jimmy was chopping him up with an axe. It's one of those unclassified sins. You will watch. But there was something clean in it anyway, as certain uses of our spirit can sanitize anything no matter how foul, because Whopper wouldn't quit. Like he was taking it from nothing but an ass kicking and making it into something else. We waited for him to quit. We couldn't see any point not to. Except Whopper had discovered something that was beyond anything he'd ever felt. It was pure purpose. Whopper was the only one with the balls to go in. I'm not making myself clear. I mean Whopper found something-new territory, a place that he ruled, his place. I mean he was, right now, between Jimmy's knees and on the ground, but he'd get to his feet just to get pounded like no one we've ever seen get pounded.

Guys are yelling at Jimmy to quit, and Jimmy is yelling back. "Not until he does!"

Whopper keeps swinging, once or twice landing something feeble on Jimmy's face. But the little pop bouncing off Jimmy's head had so much... I don't know... class. Finally, Jimmy goes nuts. Blood is flying in the air, girls are crying, but Whopper only gets more determined. I mean you can see the thread of concentration. It seems kind of calm. He was definitely following something and it was changing him into someone else. Hammered at the bike racks on Jimmy's anvil like they are in it together. Like Whopper needed Jimmy to show us his heart. I can't believe what I'm seeing. My feet are buried in concrete. I just stand there. Time already stopped.

Some little kids peek in the circle and start screaming and a teacher is running over. We all scatter for different parts of the canyons. Some girls wait around to give the teacher names.

I walk home with Whopper, following him down the canyon trail, listening to him cry and catch his breath. What am I supposed to say? He must hate every one of us who didn't back him up. I would if I was him. I'd especially hate me. He always calls me his best friend. I'm even a year older. I feel two things real strong. The first is that I am proud to be walking with him. The second is that I am ashamed of myself. But at that point, the distance between us was so far that I knew he couldn't blame me. I could see that he didn't. I mean, he was pissed, but who wouldn't be? I wanted to tell Whopper everything I just told you but I can't get the words at the time and he wouldn't listen anyway. So I just say:

"Man, that was the bravest thing I ever saw."

"Stupidest."

He answers in a way that had a sort of joke behind it. One word, calling it stupid, not saying it bitter but more like I said, a joke.

I couldn't believe it. I left it alone.

He told me for awhile he hoped somebody would stop it. But when he saw no one would, he figured what the fuck.

Then he says, "Where were you?"

So I lie to him. I tell him I thought he didn't want the fight stopped. Then I go further and tell him I was thinking about helping him, but a couple of Jimmy's friends were looking at me, waiting. I knew it right away. I wished I'd never said it.

"Don't lie, Eddie... Don't lie to me."

He looks like he's gonna bust me in the face. He was pretty hot and he had a lot he wanted to tell me but it's plain I wouldn't understand. Nobody would. Maybe my Uncle Adrian. But none of us Whopper's age. The rest of us will just have to wonder if we'll ever have balls.

I am as amazed at this ascension as if he had sprouted wings and lifted right up off the ground. And everything he did told me he was free now. He couldn't change it if he wanted to. I always saw him in the air from then on. I mean like, in the air. I noticed how he always sat in the highest place. Like on the kitchen counter, or the tree in the front yard. He began talking about parachutes and astronauts. This is gonna sound funny but he seemed kind of wise, informed or something. I mean right there, he knew more than either of our fathers or any of our older brothers. I knew it wouldn't last to tomorrow but I knew for sure that right then he could tell me about things even our mothers didn't know about men. He was in on the secret.

Whopper stands for a minute, starts to walk, mumbles and sits down. He looks at me through the bruised mush around his eyes. I check out his cuts and stuff. An eyebrow has a slit that is still bleeding. He hangs his head to see how much of a puddle he can make. He tries to write his name with the drops in the dirt. He has put a tooth through his lower lip. His cheeks are blue and black, skinned and filled with dirt. His hands are raw. He's a mess.

He stares at the skin hanging off his knuckles-bright red orange scrapes you can almost see through. He chews off a large piece in the middle of his hand.

I look back up the trail, the fence on the top of the mesa is filled with kids and teachers. They're all staring down the hill. One teacher is calling out Whopper's real name, but since we're behind a stand of manzanita, we can't be seen.

I can tell Whopper's beginning to see what he's done. It's beginning to dawn on him that it's all over. He has made it. The isolation he felt in the fight was really the isolation of his own courage.

I tell him about the fight. Some of it he didn't remember and it strikes him as funny. He laughs a couple of times. He says, "Really?" when I describe how brave and tough he was. I even tell him about how he looked changed and the anvil and all. He smiles like he thinks I'm crazy.

We walk home the long way, wondering what his mother is gonna say. I ask him if he is ever going to talk about it. It seems to me to be the only way to get something out of this for himself. He can't really just go back to being who he was. He doesn't answer.

"Because it would be so righteous if you didn't."

Whopper says, "Why?"

I don't say anything. I just hoped he'd figure it out. I can see him hiding the smile on his busted lips the color of plums. He stumbles down on the edge of a deer trail overlooking a huge patch of anise. The stuff grows all over San Diego, thickets of bamboo-like stalks with big splayed flowers-tall, sometimes eight feet. The seeds taste like licorice.

He mumbles, "Yeah, I'll act like it didn't even happen."

He practices the shrug he's gonna use when people ask him about it. Every boy and girl in school will think he is God. Still, none of us would have done what he'd done to make it that way.

It worked. At school his name became ironic, like the names they give huge guys, calling them Tiny or Half-Pint. Overnight, Whopper was a name of honor.

Except at his house, because his little brother wasn't buying it. Whopper and his little brother had problems. They hated each other and I guess I was a part of it. We did things to him we shouldn't have. He was only a year younger than Whopper but we treated him real bad. He brought it on himself because he demanded so much attention. So we used to beat him up all the time. Like one year on his birthday, we tried to set records for making him cry. We got him eleven or twelve times on his 10th birthday. And he was real hard to make cry, because he had a lot of pride and he was tough as hell. In a way, he was even tougher than Whopper. Everything we did was as far as it could go. We were masters of ridicule, and knew how to cover what hurt our feelings, and say things that would really hurt his. We didn't want it to be that way but the meanness had a life of its own. Nobody could stop it.

Then Whopper decided he needed to bridge the gulf of trust between him and his little brother. The time had come to put hate behind them and form a team of brothers, a gang. All for one and all that. It sounded like a good idea since we were getting into too much shit with the old man over all the "roughhouse crap," as he called it.

Whopper stopped fucking with his little brother, told him how sorry he was, that he was his brother and, as such, they had to trust each other. And what they needed was a ritual to restore that trust.

His brother told him, "Yeah? Well fuck you."

This went on for days. Whopper telling him that it was the most important thing in the world for him to reestablish the trust that brothers need to become men. A couple of times Whopper nearly cried. He meant it; I could see that. It was always on Whopper's mind; they just had to pass this test of trust together or they'd never become men.

Finally Whopper proposed the "ritual of trust" as he said it a million times all day long whenever he had the chance. Whopper wanted his brother to stand on the edge of the roof, with his eyes closed and his arms spread like an eagle, with Whopper standing behind him. After that they could trust each other and be true brothers... after the ritual of trust.

It took Whopper all summer to get him to listen. Around Halloween he got him to come up on the roof with him for just one minute, no blindfold, and Whopper on the far side of the roof. But his brother wouldn't go back up there, saying that was enough ritual of fucking trust for him. It took working on him day and night during Christmas vacation to get him to finally do it. His little brother was beginning to believe. I would have too. Whopper had been the perfect big brother since the fight at the bike racks.

It was the day before Christmas. There was Whopper, walking with his blindfolded brother. Whopper talking in a low quavering voice, speaking of the ecstasy of blind brotherly trust, right into the ear of his brother. He led him to the edge and told him he had to let go of his hand so that he could stand behind him. His little brother stood unafraid, free of the mistrust and hurt of the past. Ritual of trust. Solemn occasion of brothers turning into men.

They looked like angels up there, their faces in the blue sky. The winter sun glowing golden and pale behind them. I was amazed again at what Whopper had become. I knew I could rise too. I could become a man who could atone for my wrongs. I could stand up for the right things, all of that. A smile broke under the blindfold. Whopper's face went cold and he pushed his brother off the roof.

His little brother didn't believe it. He thought it was a cosmic trick. Or maybe he went into shock or was just dumbfounded, because he held his position like a diver. He did a head plant from a ten foot roof onto a cement stair. Everything slowed down. The blindfold jammed down to his little brother's shoulders, his neck disappeared, and he looked like he stood on his head for a long time before he crumpled. I swear, the noise is what made the neighbors look out of their doors. The sound wasn't like anything else I'd heard, a melon or something. I got scared, like we'd finally done it this time. Whopper was ecstatic. His arms spread like an eagle, his head cocked to one side, looking over the edge at his unconscious brother.

"Sucker."

It was plain Whopper thought he had done something important. He didn't feel the need to celebrate it with me. I don't think Whopper thought there was anyone else there. It was his thing. His brother was a part of it but it was his. I got my voice and said:

"Shit Whopper, ya killed him."

The little brother wheezed a deep breath and his eyes fluttered like mad.

"He'll be ok. Don't sweat."

As weird as it sounds, Whopper looked kind again, more like an angel than ever.

"It's the best thing I could have done for him."

I started walking and it was like the street was asleep. People were looking out of their doors. The cop across the street was frozen on his lawn with his hands on his hips and his mouth open. Nobody moved, except Whopper, who was doing a little slow spin dance with his arms spread out and his face to the sky above.

I took the long way home through the canyon bottom, winding along the edges of trickling storm ditches, slipping along mossy stones, old underwear and wads of stringy paper. I can still see Whopper on the roof, turning in that circle.

After he got out of the hospital, the little brother wore a white turban on his head until after Lincoln's Birthday. Talked like he'd been drinking for the rest of the year. Their mother never trusted

Whopper again. She hardly spoke to him for a long time. Their big sister left that year for Texas. And then the years just passed like clouds and all of us lost touch.

Jimmy Johnson got killed in his second tour in Vietnam as gunner on a helicopter. Whopper got murdered in a bad drug deal. He brought his little brother along-they killed him too.

SLIDE

I'M SO SPACED IN THE EARLY MORNING SUN that the question is not where am I, but where will I puke next.

Right here.

My stomach contracts in a single spasm. It's mostly spit. I see a lawn sprinkler and follow the green snake to the spigot, turn it on and return to the splashing puddle in the dirt. The cold water uses my stomach as a trampoline and flies up and out of my mouth. I breathe a little air, then what's left in my stomach blasts out of my nose. Alright, I'll wait.

I circle around like a dog and pass out, curled on my side in the hot sun. I hear voices, tiny and deep from within a cave somewhere in Africa. But when I open my eyes, there are tips of roughout boots in front of my nose. The voices are discussing what to do about me. They're what pass as friends. Big guys who try, and succeed, at making people shit themselves. Last image I can think of is a shotgun in some fuckup's mouth as he gets the time and date straight for his last chance.

We're supposed to be planning the details of setting up a black funk soulster superstar who has a tendency to go off behind cocaine. The object, of course, is to get the funkster's coke and money without getting caught, which would mean getting killed. I had a plan to use two sure things: greed and ego. Get him to overextend himself and then get him irrational when he tries to cover his embarrassment. But before I could work out the cast of characters, I got drunk.

So far, the plan calls for me to deliver a pound and hang around in the front room, waiting for someone to get back from somewhere with a lot of money, and then stall until my friends come in and take us all off. The pretext is women and some problem with airline tickets.

Then my job is not to freak out while all these psychos strut around and try to fuck with me. It's a delicate balance between knowing how much to take and where to draw the line. My bit is stupidity. I am the butt of jokes, conversations going on around me that I shouldn't be hearing, gleaning this, figuring that, then doing something off the wall. It's worked in Mexicali, Juarez, El Centro, San Ysidro, El Cajon and Santee. Now we're gonna give it a try in Malibu.

I'm getting to my feet, listening to my friends argue about my condition. Standing up blinds me for a second. The top of my head comes to their chests. They must weigh two hundred and fifty pounds apiece.

"I'm ready."

I expect the laughs. Here they are. Laughing, then silence. One guy is about to utter a challenge. I can tell because he's from the South, and he telegraphs his hostility by curling his lip-Elvis damage. I interrupt him.

"I'm more effective when I'm underestimated."

He's about to say something devastating to my interests. I edit the movie playing in my head which stars him in an amazing scene of beating me to a humiliated pulp. The estimates of his weight are ignored behind the central thing in my mind, which is hit him real hard and real fast. Then as he recoils, swarm him. When those thoughts get strong enough, the imagined action follows. Guys are pulling me off and I am praying my target is unconscious. Hit him twice and no one saw the punches. Believe me, if you have the choice between size and speed, take speed. He's doing a little half turn. His upper body is out before his knees know it. He's buckling backward with his knees still trying to hold him up. Finally his heels flick out in the dirt and his back thuds.

I start to walk toward the car saying, "Let's stop for breakfast." We cram ourselves into a Valiant and drive off.

Beautiful Malibu flying past the open windows, a joint fired and passed around. Going up to Trancas to rip off a superstar. This is the life. Except the radio... that seventies music-weird, imitative, overproduced stuff. Right now, the Eagles are flying or something, and then someone is running down the road trying to loosen something with women on his mind.

Driving through empty Malibu, up carless Pacific Coast Highway on a hot spring Wednesday makes you feel like you're getting away with something. There's the ease of residential opulence; the only faces you see are locals, and most of the locals are stars, near-stars, were-stars, know-stars, want-to-be stars, think-they-are stars, sexual-partners-to stars, suppliers-of-vice-to stars, parasitic-servants-to stars. And on the road blasting past, you almost think you're rich and famous. Actually you think you're too cool to be famous. Especially if you have Phoenix Program washouts riding with you who manage to kill a couple people a year.

Killers suck the air out of the room, but you have to look close to notice. Intense implies some kind of action or energy. What these guys have is a complete absence of energy which they try to cover up with an act. Like the funny wheezy guy in Pacific Beach, the sharp dressing Romeo hair-combing guy from San Ysidro, the four-eyed school teacher who always reads the dictionary to improve his vocabulary, and dumbshit losers carrying piano wire, plumber's wrenches and hammers like the ones I'm riding with. Their guns are inside the spare tire in the trunk.

The guy driving changes channels looking for Willie on the country station. These guys will damn near cry if they hear Willie singing "Somewhere Over The Rainbow." That's almost as scary as the weird scratching habits and teeth sucking sounds they're always making.

The highway is dead. Everything is going on behind the walls that line a five mile stretch of PCH. You can grab a glimpse of beach between a restaurant and a gas station. Other than that, it's a rolling line of walls to the west. Behind each one, somebody famous getting sucked by somebody who wants to be. Ok, that's jaded, cynical. Every other wall.

Eventually the Spanish tile is left behind. Pass the hidden gates of the Colony, home to huge money and temporary power. The whole place is paranoid. Neighbors never speak except in hails called across the street. Everybody busy with the effects of the latest hit, or big deal, or heavy meeting, or this or that. Usually just pantomimed cool.

"Yeah, bitchin. Thank you, thank you. We are all stars together here. Isn't it just wonderful in the cool terrace and tile hallways in this I'm-scared-to-death-to-get-older-smaller-less-powerful-land? Yes, yes, no autographs here. We are all stars."

All said in waving hands, cool shade tilts, and casual hundred thousand dollar car-door openings. The scared-to-death part reserved for shrinks, or as confessionals to appear human enough to get somebody's pants down. Out here on the narrow Colony streets, it's strictly the celebrity benediction, neither one believing the other. Some remnant of the papal wrist swinging acknowledgment of access to the high and fucking mighty.

Breakfast is on me. The waitress is in worse shape than we are. She's cranky and nauseated with a healing rope burn on her wrist, nose ring, blond hair, cigarette dangling, eyes patrician and smug, body dreamed up by a fuckbook artist before the age of surgery. See-through cotton dress. Her girlfriend arrives, sits on the inside of her ankle, leans over the counter. Twists the counter stool, left beaver shot, right, left beaver shot, right. Blinding me like a lighthouse beam. Hard to concentrate. Anticipation for the next twist, attempting to keep from being busted. As if she doesn't know. As if she fucking cares.

I'll take half a dozen scrambled eggs. Steroids need that extra protein. I rattle three little blue pills out of a plastic brown bottle-Dianabol-discovered by farm boys who wanted to make the team out in Texas and found out the meat their daddies put on a steer could be the meat they put on themselves for the Cotton Bowl. People will tell you steroids create a feeling of invincibility. I'll tell you, a couple months on a steroid cycle, and if a cop car gets too close, you'll rip its door off. Makes you horny, too.

Up on my feet heading for the lighthouse. Big smile. No response. Under-my-breath request for a couple of lines. Girl never looks at me. I take the little envelope that materializes out of her hip pocket. My Frye boots galump toward the bathroom. Her voice sounds like Jodie Foster accepting the Deepest Voice in America Award.

"Sixty bucks."

I'm still thudding my heels toward the men's room, slow and steady like a gunfighter. Sometimes I act like that if a woman blows me off and makes me disgusted at myself, I should just tell her I want attention.

"Hey, I said sixty bucks."

She's used to being paid attention to. This is a contest of wills. I'm in the men's room. She's in the men's room. I lock the stall door behind me. She's coming over the top of the stall. She's pissed, yelling this amazing shit at me. I say, "Go ahead," to all her threats throwing in, "I hope you do," to a couple of her suggestions. Envelope is open; she's pulling my hair above the toilet tank. One of my friends is laughing a beery, bluster-boy haw haw. She's getting tired and isn't yelling. She's hissing, "son-of-a-bitch-mother-fucker" at me. Fingernails in my scalp. Alright already.

"Hey hey hey... Here, take it. I was just kidding."

She pushes me around the stall.

"Asshole."

Yeah, sorry, I know. She fills a spoon, puts it under my nose. Boom. Malibu dentist's daughter I guess.

By the time we get to Trancas, the funkman has departed. He's living elsewhere. His parties have come to the attention of the police. His guest's drunk driving has become a problem for tourists. The general scene is turning sour. I'm getting this from a guy who feels important for a second, having all this information about a famous hipster-superstar. I gotta put up with it. It's pretty warm today; all the windows are open and this guy is wearing one of those huge knit hats that flop down around one shoulder. He's wearing tight, tight, tight pants. It's plain to see it hurts him to move, but he must think it's worth it. His shirt has huge wet rings under each arm. Little drops are running rivulets down his shiny black neck. He walks back and forth across the deep shag rug, sniffing deep with a knuckle pressing first one then another nostril closed.

"Where is he? We're late already with this and my man said he was pissed."

He ignores me.

"Ok, well, when he asks about it, I'll just... What's your name?"

He sneers at me.

"Ok, I don't need to know your name. I'll just say you said that he should fuck himself."

He starts telling me about my white ass.

"Let's just drop the racial shit, ok?"

He's not listening.

"Ok, ok... right before you get to the part about the last four hundred years and all, why don't you just call Adolph?"

He asks me who the fuck is Adolph.

"Adolph is the man who takes care of your boss."

He yawns and tells me the studio is in Oxnard. He bought a house. It's better for him out there-no white folks hanging around. God, the guy doesn't quit. I ask him if it's near Pt. Mugu. He says it is. I ask if it's around the Angels' place and he says it's across the fucking street. I tell him thanks and if he talks to his meal ticket, which he will, to tell him we're on our way.

"What do you mean, meal ticket?"

"Just tell him."

Oxnard is where the pigs, like all pigs, will look the other way after their taste. We get up there past Pt. Dume, around the corner of a huge rock along the highway, and we meet a few friends at a little bar for a couple of beers. We try to see if our program is together, but it's hopeless. We can't remember anything, so we decide to play it by ear. A couple of guys stay at the bar and we call the Angels. We ask one of them to go across the street to see if anyone's home. He comes back saying there is. That, it turns out, was probably our mistake. Angels are so fast. I mean, you give them a half second to fuck something up for you and next thing you know you're saying, "Ow, Ow, Ow."

We drive over and watch three big dogs' heads pogoing over a redwood fence. After a minute or two of standing around timing our spit and the dogs' heads, we hear a whistle and the dogs are rounded up. A man asks us what we want and we try to sound like gangsters in an old movie but we start laughing. The fence gate opens. An old black man looks at us. He's got to be the funkman's father. He lets us in, closes the gate. He's a little drunk... and he's holding a gun.

"You funny guys?"

"You drunk?"

"Yeah, you funny?"

"Where's your son?"

"Which son? I got eight."

"Oh, c'mon..."

"You crazy?"

"Yeah, sometimes."

"Sometimes" hits the old man's funny bone. He doubles over. I get embarrassed. I feel my face getting red. I knew right there that something was real wrong.

The patchy lawn is dotted with white and brown piles-every square inch. The place stinks. The door to the house is wide open. Doris Day is singing "Que Sera Sera" over a zillion dollar sound system. An Amazon crosses the doorway. Three inch platforms puts her about eight feet tall. After she leaves, it takes an extra ludicrous second for her butt to clear the doorway. A voice comes from inside, whiny, and at the same time, trying to be demanding. It's a man's voice squeaking like a neurotic queen. It's the kind of voice that has no power but instead wears you down-a "with-it" smart ass assuming a superior position over somebody.

My eyes adjust to the darker room. A little white guy is sitting on the sofa. Blousy shirt, sunglasses. Guy talks fast-East Coast-makes a point of using it. Trying to conjure up mean ass streets to someone over the telephone. I hate that shit. I begin to realize he's doing a version of what he thinks is Mick Jagger. A lot of these guys are doing that androgynous bad boy bit these days. He knows he has my attention and carelessly lets a little English lower class nasal snarl rise at the end of his sentences. Fake people busting themselves everywhere.

He's a mogul of some kind, using the funkman's name. It begins to dawn on me that he is directing this stream of abuse to the funkman. He's screaming now about money, then a couple insults. Whoa, personal insults. Definitely impressive.

I walk out the door because I'm too stupid to be impressed. He'll have to try something else. The Amazon clomps up behind me. Eight feet easy. She's talking to the guys and wearing a loose halter top. When's she gonna bend over? Five... six... seven. Bend. Big jolt when the cleavage shakes loose for a good glimpse. Up... big smile. Phoenix Program licks his lips. The other guy drags a few thinning strands of what was once a pompadour through his fingers and does something like a smile or smirk with his mouth. I stuff my hands in my pockets and turn to see if the guy is off the phone. His hands are waving in the air, bouncing up and down on the sofa with each accented threat. There's no telling which continent he grew up on now. He's a cheesy Londoner one phrase and a cheesy Brooklynite the next. He gets quiet and listens. I better fall for his big shot routine.

The Amazon is telling Elvis damage where the funkman is. Blue mountains outside of Kingston or recording at Muscle Shoals. Someplace, you know how it is, never can tell. He is making a point of looking directly into her halter top. She emphasizes that funkman is elsewhere one too many times. Elvis is going to lose his balance rocking forward on his toes.

I'm back inside. The international big-shot is off the phone and now he's assuming I'll be interested in his problems with superstars. How it's so hard to make them do things when they already have more of everything than they know what to do with. Basic business, a deal is a deal and you gotta be where you say you're gonna be. Yeah... right, I understand.

I cut him off before he starts the standard rhapsody beginning with, "Well, he's a genius," and blah blah blah.

I stand still and ask can I use the phone.

"Sure, go ahead."

He glowers down at the coffee table. A gigantic ashtray is heaped with butts. He lights up. I leave a number out of my home phone. I start talking.

"He's not here." Wait...

"He's in Kingston... I guess so."

I ask the mogul his name.

"A guy here named Phil has just been talking to him."

"I don't know."

I check to see if Phil is biting. I direct a question to him.

"Phil, do you know when he's coming back?"

Phil shrugs with disgust.

"No telling... What should I do? Bring it back or what?"

Phil sits up on the edge of the couch. I turn to pretend to try and get a little privacy. He stands up and walks to the fireplace and gets a little box from the mantel. He's nonchalant as all hell about it. The phone is gonna make an off-the-hook tone any second.

"Well... shit, I don't really know. You want to talk to Phil?"

Phil turns walking with his hand out for the phone.

"Ok... then listen. I'll just see what he wants me to do. The money? Yeah, I know."

I hang up. Phil looks a little miffed.

"Phil, Adolph says you can take the load if you want to pay for it all now or get a taste on account to get you through until he gets back from Kingston. What you want to do?"

Phil's dreams are coming true. He says, "I'll take it all now."

He can barely contain himself. I say ok and Phil goes upstairs, saying anxiously, "I'll be right down."

This is a bad situation. Phil doesn't know me. He's ready to pay out a ton of money? Sure. He's ready to set us up before we set him up is what he's ready to do. The Amazon selling funkman's where- abouts tells me he's probably upstairs. This house isn't permanent; he'd never live near the Angels. He's got something going with them, some kind of split. Pretty soon the place is gonna fill up with people. They'll try to fuck up my team.

I walk out to the porch. I look at the guys.

"Let's go."

Just a little direct to Elvis, just a little "gotta go now" in my voice. Over his head. He's watching a carload of women unloading by the gate.

The Amazon is playing with the attack dogs in their cage. "Big boy. Tough boy. So vicious." The guys take it as a hinted invitation. Upstairs, a couple of Angels we know stick their heads out of windows and howl cheerful greetings to us. How the fuck we been? Jokes about watermelons to the black women walking toward the house.

If I press the guys to leave, I'm fucked. I start yelling to the guys upstairs about who's buying the beer. Not them. I collect about ten dollars from people at the front door. I swing my leg over a Schwinn and thunk thunk thunk off the porch steps on a beer run. I leave the guys there.

Out the gate, heading west to find a car to steal or a ride to hitch, whichever comes first. My friends are going to be dosed with big, cringing, paranoiac versions of every nightmare they ever dreamed. What the payback is about must have happened before I got here or maybe this is something initiated by them. The end result is the same. They'll get buried alive in the desert and no one will ever hear from them again. Tied up and thrown in a deep hole, covered over. They'll scream their heads off. They won't gag them. They'll let them talk, let them cry, let them beg, let them scream. I hear he does the digging himself. Has to do with who the baddest man in the valley is, and I guess in this case, it's the guy with the shovel. He's gonna get a ton of blow, kill two guys, and has the other one pedaling like a bastard for home. A good solider would sneak the coke out of the trunk of the car. Too close a call and I don't have the keys.

There's a party up Decker Canyon. I know this guy. I can't call him a friend, nobody can. He's just finished a movie and is hanging out spending his millions on what you can guess.

He's the most photogenic young god in Hollywood. Redford won't work with him. He carries the bad boy mystique to a point approaching realism, beyond what anyone in Hollywood has done in years. And that's saying something with all the freaks, degenerates, and homicidal maniacs that have been burning their images in the world's brains for the last fifty years or so.

Bruce Lee has been up there for about a week, hanging around and impressing the girls. Conceited little fucker. Don't tell him I said so. Anyway, you've heard about the parties and what all goes on there. He throws the lowest, most barbaric of parties, in lavish style, making it glamorous. And to go with that, he's got a lot of big wave riders around. Big waves, not to be found in California. The kind in Hawaii, over coral that no one in their right mind challenges. Except them. And they know it. Four or five of them up at the star's house. Idols and legends all high and happy. Pulling dozens of the most amazing eighteen year-olds you've ever seen. Sprinkled with these fearless women and musicians, or songwriters and actresses, or camera operators who are in their thirties and irresistible if they decide to focus a second or two on you. Everybody fucking 'til the cows come home.

Everything bigger than life and so comfortable with the servants cleaning the slop in seconds. The pool drained of puke, filled and reheated by Mexicans in uniform. Great parties, even if those fucking guys from the Eagles are always hanging around.

But the immediate problem is getting out of Oxnard. Nobody is gonna go too far out of their way, but if they happen to run across me, or if they pin me on their way to funkman's place, or if... Jesus, this is the real concern, if they see me on their way to the desert... Well fuck it... That isn't likely to happen for at least a couple of hours. Meanwhile, I'm thinking all this to avoid thinking about pedaling the Schwinn to the parking lot, which is a lot further than I thought and I'm getting real hot and tired. And I need the motivation before I say, "Fuck it" and stop off someplace and get nailed on account of being this lazy fuck, which is what I am. I can't tell you how many guys are sitting around in the slam because they took too much time doing this and that, or stopping off to get a little, or you know, just procrastinating instead of doing the right thing. The right thing is to get out of here.

Too late. Camaro grumbling toward me... or is it... No... probably not... Yep. It is.

The Camaro pulls to a stop, blocking my path. Nothing but fields around. I can outrun them if I have to.

"Fuck face." He's talking to me.

Doors on either side of the car swing open; three guys pile out. What is all this hostility about? They got on bathing suits, big baggy things about down to the knees, flower prints, big bellies on two and the other-Mr. Washboard. They must be ready to do something; they got the strut going. Why do guys strut? Jesus, like they got a hard-on down the pant leg, or just a dick so huge it has to be dragged behind them or I don't know what.

I'm sitting astride the Schwinn trying to look as confused as I can for the benefit of the tough guy walking real fast, one foot hitching and then sliding and then hitching and sliding. And because they're moving fast, they gotta hop along sideways in order to keep the strut. Looks so stupid. But they're serious, I can tell. One of them is looking over his shoulder for traffic. Highway Patrol always uses this cut off.

I lay the Schwinn down on its side. A butterfly darts in and out of the spokes. Every time something violent happens or is gonna happen, I see a butterfly flitting around. I remember being in a football game once and right down the line of scrimmage goes this little white butterfly. Made the whole scene seem stupid. Another time, I got jumped by about a million black dudes. They got out of their car, left the doors open, and with the radio blaring "My Girl," they tap danced on me and my friend's heads. A moment filled with irony, because at the time, that was my favorite song. That bass line and vocal became the soundtrack to our ass kicking. I thought it was so weird at the time. No butterflies, but a butterfly type of irony. Anyway, here they are. Back to you in a minute.

"Nice. Calling me fuck face."

His fist passes over my head. His balance is overcommitted and he's over the Schwinn. Good, shove him onto it. He gets tangled in the chain and sprocket, tries to keep his clumsy balance but fails. He's down.

"Hey, what is all this about?"

Better not wait for an answer. One guy has long hair. Why do tough guys wear their hair long? I'm swinging him around by it and the other guy can't get in. My knee hits his face, not too solid, just enough to double up his adrenaline. He's grabbing for a hand hold on the top of my pants. He's got me. Thumb hard in his eye. He lets go and grabs his face. I plant two shots on the back of his ear. Bingo. His body stiffens and he drops on his face. The third guy trying to get me down has just torn a long trail of skin off my back with his fingernails.

Fat fuck has just gotten to his feet. He's bouncing up and down with his fists prepared like a goddamn pugilist, all darty in-and-out and all showy. Pussy. I'll get him later. Mr. Washboard has a piece of wood from some farmer's fence. I see a guy coming from the Camaro with a tire iron. I am out of here.

Mr. Washboard breaks the wood over my head. Dry rot, nothing to it. But it's the thought that counts, right?

There are times when the universe works against you. When guys much like yourself are doing a job on you and you know that the sun and moon have had some kind of convergence and the planets are set up for a spinning red light and the wail of your ambulance.

But you never can tell, so you lead with a right that has your body behind it from the tips of your toes through your hips that were low to begin with and everything is lined up perfectly so that you're gonna break your fist or break a face. And then the guy contributes to the beauty of the moment. They call it "walking into a punch."

Mr. Washboard actually runs into this one. I never felt a thing, like connecting perfectly on a baseball and knowing immediately that it's out of the fucking park. So you can drop the bat and do that long look of admiration that the other team hates and watch the ball disappear. To top it off, I had a perfect view. I felt my fist caving into his nose, heard the sound like a chicken leg breaking. Down he went.

What you gotta do when you're gonna get hit like that is give them the top of your head. It'll hurt you but it will also disintegrate the guy's fist and probably break his wrist too. Mr. Washboard must have been doing sit-ups when he should have learned about taking a punch.

Still have to consider the tire iron. Fat fuck is not jumping around anymore; he's admiring my shot on Mr. Washboard, who is twitching on the ground with what looks like serious central nervous system damage. I feel so fulfilled. Time has just kind of stopped here for awhile.

I know there is an ethic against running away from a fight. And although I'm hot and bloodied from the battle and all, and I want to stay because of something stupid I have learned, I am also calculating. I deduce that the tire iron, plus the fat boxer, and maybe another guy getting off the ground are more than enough to kill my ass.

I'm already booking fifty yards across the bright yellow field. Mustard plants are snapping at my legs as I drive past, pollen from their heads exploding on me. Just jetting toward another road a half mile away, hoping to avoid a ditch here or a trench there. These guys will never catch me on foot. I hear the Camaro screeching off somewhere. I hope they don't have a way to head me off.

Just then the terrible things I do to my body begin to catch up with me. I'm gonna faint. No doubt about it. I stagger down to my hands and knees and try like hell to stay conscious. Nope, I'm gonna take a little nappy right here. The last thing I remember is rolling over on my side in a giant field of tall mustard plants. Everything settling down dark and quiet, the hum of a thousand of bees all around me.

I heard later that the Camaro guys drove around for about an hour and the last place they thought I'd be was sleeping in the field. Maybe there is a God. Think so?

Anyway, around Christmas the next year, one of the guys in the car bought me a few pitchers of beer and told me the tale. Fat fuck boxer guy was married to a woman I had been in bed with a week or so earlier. What he didn't know and should have, was that she brought me home with one of her girlfriends. I was finished in about a half hour or so, but the girls went on all night. I couldn't get any sleep at all until I moved to the couch and I still couldn't sleep with all the racket. I think I made their scene hetero or something. When she had to confess her infidelity, she left out the part about the girlfriend. To the fat guy with his hurt feelings, I looked like some rival.

In the late afternoon, the temperature in the field changed abruptly. The wind shifted bringing in the fog, which revived me.

Headache. Worse than that... Intestinal volcano.

I hitched down to the coffee shop. Invited the waitress to the party. She gave me a ride. Slept it off. The night pretty uneventful.

Next day at about three in the afternoon we're having breakfast, sitting in some kind of breakfast nook, sunlight filtering in through the windows. Antique carved table with every kind of fruit, roll, exotic breakfast thing you can think of. There's the movie star I told you about, the big time surfer I told you about, and the movie star's wife. She is trying hard to hold her family together.

They have a five month-old daughter. Mine is about a month and a half younger. His wife is pretty cool, but in what you might call denial. She thinks things are in some way alright; she thinks they have a family. It's pretty sad. The sadness carries over to me. I have a wife. I have a baby girl and I'm out doing all this shit all the time. Stuff they'll never know about, because once I get it together, I'll rescue them and we'll live the good life and I'll have this colorful past to season myself with. I'll be like a retired pirate, or like Turner in that Nicholas Roeg movie, so that I won't be some kind of weakling that kissed ass and got to be this big success at whatever it was I was fantasizing about at the time.

But right there at breakfast, things changed. I was still thinking I'd be a star somehow, since I was sitting there with one, and he wasn't any real big deal, and he liked me and probably would use me in his next action movie because I was the real deal and blah blah blah... So I rolled a few joints and listened to the stories about the movie these guys had just finished. Location in Mexico. About surfing and the dynamics of all the personalities, and the challenge, and the American values of men against nature and against the nature of themselves, and overcoming themselves to find a higher meaning for life as the sun sets on the giant waves that they surf to change their lives and learn about the beauty of the world and the stuff that Hollywood wants you to believe.

Meanwhile, behind the scenes they're doing all the drugs a pickup truck can deliver to the set and fucking anything that moves. These guys do get girls-women, wives, duchesses, singers, writers, brilliant talents and hard living, hard loving babes. This is their reality; this is how they live. The wives look the other way, not to forgive, but to blind themselves to it. Like I said, denial. Which was where I was at, since I was never gonna be any goddamn star. I was a sort of joke to myself, but I didn't want to think that anyone else could see it. You should learn it now; if you can see it in yourself, then so can everybody else. There are no secrets, only delusions.

So they started comparing the girls to dogs. The ones they had, you know, they'd think up a poodle here and Doberman there. All bringing laughs. The surfer guy commented about the Chihuahua that my movie star friend had, cause she was so little.

He looked at me, winking the sensimilla out of his eye and tapping the ash, passed me the joint. His face was real handsome for that moment, and it had a bitchin' looking killer sneer on it. It was easy to see why he was a movie star. He did a cool quick take over his shoulder to see if his wife could hear. The baby was patting the table in his lap and he looked at me real deep and knowing and said:

"More like a Mexican hairless."

Hmmm. I felt my shoulders shrug, not getting it at the moment. But then I got it. He liked them young.

I felt like making everything right again. Going back to a place that wasn't full of shit, cleaning it all up. But I knew I couldn't without destroying myself along the way. I'd have to stay this way a little longer, being in the habit of it, having what you'd call my identity a part of it.

I got up from the table and walked back home.

I lay on top of my roof, under a huge sycamore tree, with my baby girl sleeping on my chest. Wondering if I could get back what was left of my soul.

ROB
OVERTON

FROM THE BOOK

LETTERS TO ROLLINS

2/13/93
Dear Henry,

I live on a farm just outside of Iowa City and the local college radio station plays your records a lot. I have pictures of you and your tattoos all over my walls.

You know that Black Flag tattoo on the back of your neck with the four rectangles? Does each of those boxes stand for a different member of the band, and if this is so, which one stands for you? My friend Gary said that you didn't get along with Greg Ginn, so I would assume that there is at least one box between you two acting as a buffer. This is the order that I think is right:

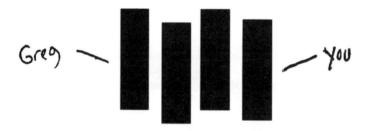

By process of elimination, I put you on the right because Greg belongs on the left, since he was left when you moved on.

Now that you're in the Rollins Band, do the boxes in the tattoo stand for the new band members? If so, could you tell me which one is your drummer, Sim Cain?

Also, I have a bet with this guy named George who says the "Search and Destroy" tattoo on your back was changed recently to "Research and Destroy" as a response to new strict rules regarding the use of Exacto-knives in public libraries. If he's wrong, he wants me to tell you to change the tattoo, because the bet was for $100.

Thanks Henry,

Jeff Peterson

Jeff Peterson
Iowa City, IA

LOCKHART & ASSOCIATES
NEW YORK · LOS ANGELES · BARSTOW

2/13/93

Henry,

As your new publicist, I hope we are off to a great relationship — I know that Jerry didn't work out that well. I just want you to know that I have both the Sesame Street incident and the altercation at Puppet Town under control, press-wise. I know how to handle these people.

I will keep you up to date on everything here in the office. You have my fax numbers, and I have your tour itinerary for Europe and the States.

Sincerely,

Larry Lockhart
Lockhart and Associates

400 N. SCHUSTER WAY STE. 900, BEVERLY HILLS, CA 90210 U.S.A.

2/13/93

Dear Henry,

Was your last call for "D-4" because that's what the
kid is calling on the cover of the game's box? Well it
was a lucky guess, and it's a hit.

2 in a row. Not bad, Henry.

My next move: F-7

SBP

Steve "Battleship" Potempkin
Austin, Texas

Carol Caldecott
25450 Warner Ave.
Irvine, CA 92745 USA

From the desk of... Carol Caldecott

2/13/93

Dear Mr. Rollins,

My 7-year old son Billy loves skateboarding, the Red Hot Chili Peppers, and the Rollins Band. But lately I've had problems getting him to wear knee pads and a helmet when skateboarding because in a recent interview in <u>Thrasher</u> magazine, you said: "Knee pads are for pussies. Helmets too. They take away from the experience."

How could you say such a thing, Henry Rollins? Have you no responsibility for the safety of your fans? How is my impressionable 7-year old son, not to mention his younger brother Timmy, supposed to discern between what's good and bad?

It can't always be <u>my</u> problem! I've already got my hands full with these kids, and I can't always be watching them.

For God's sake, use some common sense, please!

Sincerely,

Carol Caldecott

Carol Caldecott

Dear Henry,

Are you colorblind? My friend Jill says you're colorblind, and that's why you wear black.

I saw you on MTV talking about weightlifting. Do you lift weights every day? If you do, don't you get bored? Do you count reps? If you do, do you ever lose count? What do you think about when you lift weights? Do you think about losing count? Do you think about not losing count? What happens if you do lose count? Do you start over?

Jill also said that your spoken word collection <u>Boxed Life</u> is called that because you punch people. Is that true? I heard that you punched Oscar on Sesame Street. Was that part of some skit?

Can you be your own pen pal? Does that count? Are we pen pals even though you don't write back? Can I give you a pet name, even though I don't really know you? Can I call you "Smokey"? I like the sound of Smokey Rollins. You can pick a new name for me too if you want.

Your friend,

Kimberly Evans

Kimberly Evans
Raleigh, N.C.

P.S. Happy Birthday Smokey! (I hope you get this by the 13th)

Dear Henry,
your tattoos are
cool I live in
california too.
Maybe you
could come over.
your friend
Fimmy

ROB OVERTON

Dear Henry:

When you get home after months of being on the road, after grueling, never-ending weeks of people in your face — local radio porno promo people and die-hard fans tugging at your shirt, always wanting more more more of your valuable time and demanding every last second of your already waning attention until you are absolutely at your wits end and about to explode — when you are finally at home, alone, and you can shut the door behind you and rest and forget about that crazy world out there, do you ever take off your clothes and stand with your taut, muscular, naked body in front of the full-length bathroom mirror and tHink to yourself: "I am Jesus!"

A   Awestruck at first by the sheer power behind this thought, you stare at your face in the mirror and this time you say the words out loud, softly at first, with a gentleness and reverence for the   man behind them: "I am Jesus." You say the words again, and then again and again, each time a little louder than before. And for a brief second, you become lost in the moment as the words run together like a mantra: "IamJesusIamJesusIamJesusIamJesus."

But you catch yourself, and a smile appears on your face as the words suddenly change in meaning from a simple mantra into a very powerful affirmation: "I am Jesus!" You begin to speak louder and more forcefully, and the words flow from your mouth with an eloquence and ease and XXXXXXX intensity un- matched by even JamEs Earl Jones: "I am Jesus, I am Jesus, I am Jesus!" And with this moving proclamation, you feel something building up inside of you, an assurance, an awe-inspiring level of confidence that is just now awakening. It is as though you have finally arrived and are announcing something wonderful and profound to the world, something you have known all along that other people, stuck in their pre-conceived notions, might not have recognized in you.

"I am Jesus!" you vehemently declare, clenching your fist for emphasis. YOu say it again, and in the deafening silence that follows, you suddenly feel the inspirator of Charlton Heston, and you add for even more emphasis: "By God, I am Jesus!" And this new phrase now becomes the affirmation and you repeat it over and over, experimenting with different deliveries, emphasizing certain syllables over others: "By God, I am Jesus. By God, I am Jesus. By God I am Jesus!"

And then it happens. You begin to feel a warmth all over your body, a kind of tingling that you instantly recognize as a heightened sense of joy. The tears on your face are from laugh- ter as you run naked through the rooms of your home shouting "I am Jesus! I am Jesus, by God, I am Jesus! I AM THE NAZ!" YOu run back into the bathroom and begin to fill the bathtubb with water — not too full, but just deep enough that when you step into the tub you are actually walking on water. Youget out of the tub and dry off the bottom s of your feet and go into the kitchen to see what's in the fridge and all there is, is a half gallon of water. You close the refrigerator door and then quickly reopen it to find that, miraculously, the water hAs turned into Wwine. So you call over 12 of your best friends for a little XXXXXX get-together and pretty soon the party gets out of hand and someone calls the cops. When the cops arrive, you

are furious and demand to know who made the complaint. Eerily,
the fcops verify that the complaint came from a phone <u>inside</u>
your house and must have been made by one of the 12 people you
invited to your party. And as you get hauled away and the
neighbors cast nasty stone- faced glances, you wonder which of
your friendS betrayed you and if any of this was really worth
the trouble. But in your heart, you know it was well worth it,
for an event of this magnitude only comes along once every 2000
years.
        Henry , I feel your pain.

Lynn Weir

Dear Henry,

I got your form letter about how much fan mail you've been getting, and I really think it sucks that you give priority to prisoners and kids in youth homes. What am I supposed to do, hot-wire a couple of cars and do some local time just to get your attention? What about kids in hospitals? Do you write to them too? If I was a poster child, I bet you'd write.

For now, what if I just include a self-addressed stamped envelope with a blank piece of paper for you to write on? Could you just send me a letter? You at least owe me that because I have all your books and CD's.

Sincerely,

Rusty Jenkins
Janesville, Wisconsin

Rusty J.

2/13/93

"Fun flies when you're doing time"
— Henry Rollins on the set of <u>The Chase</u>.

"The fourth dimension is a waste of my space and time."
— Henry Rollins interview, <u>Thrasher</u> magazine

"Because there is no space without time, and no time like the present, then we can only assume that the future begins tomorrow."
— Henry Rollins interview, KCRW FM

Dear Henry,

I agree with your friend at Jet Propulsion Labs that the above quotes, when juxtaposed with the artwork from your album <u>LIFE TIME</u>, do shed some new light on your interpretation of the time-space continuum. At first glance, it might not seem so obvious whether you view time as a separate dimension that flows at an even rate, independent of space (classical physics), or if you subscribe to relativity theory, where time and space cannot be separated, and time is added to the three spatial coordinates as a fourth dimension.

As for the art work on the cover of <u>LIFE TIME</u>, there are two possible interpretations. Fatalistically, living life is experienced as *doing time* — life as a prison sentence — feeling at the mercy of a world shaped by someone or some *thing* greater than you. On the other hand, the more positive outlook puts you in the driver's seat, having *the time* of your life. Where life is something to live to the fullest — a free will stance with you shaping your world with your own hands (life in the moment, life in the now).

Henry, do you think it's just a coincidence that your motto is "Do It"? And by extension, doesn't this mean Do It Now? But why is it necessary to do it now, Henry? Is it because you think that there's only a certain amount of time left to live, and so why not make the best of it (time as a given--the Classic Euclidean outlook)? Or is it that time is completely relative, so why not make the best of it?

Are we confusing the map with the territory, Henry? Or does the answer lie in your other motto: "part animal/part machine"? For if you really are part animal and part machine, then YOU HENRY ROLLINS ARE A TERMINA-TOR! And that is why you SEARCH AND DESTROY. And since by definition all Terminators are Time Travelers, then you have the ability to operate outside of space and time, and therefore you have a relativistic view of time.

Albert Einstein believed there is only one absolute in a relativistic time frame; that this one "truth" is the only constant in our multidimensional world. Here now is that truth. Remember it always:

Dwarf Time is Short Ended.

Until next time, Henry.

Rob Overton

Dear Henry,

My little niece Polly just loved your appearance on Sesame Street, when you did songs from your children's record <u>NAP TIME</u>. Since I got her <u>NAP TIME</u> a month ago, she's been listening to it day-in and day-out. She especially likes "Kangaroo Tattoo", and the squealing noises on "Pigfucker". She wants to know if those are real rabbit's necks snapping in "Petshop", or just studio effects.

I wanted to congratulate you on outselling Raffi in this new market. It takes a lot of guts to change direction like you did, and I admire that. I think it's good for children to hear songs about life and death, to get them ready for the real world. God knows we're headed in a downward spiral. Sure, Erma Bombeck would say that Life isn't a bowl of cherries, that the grass is always greener over the septic tank, but I say fuck Erma Bombeck, Henry. Nobody thinks she's funny anymore. Lou Reed's painter friend Donald would say "Stick a fork in her ass and turn her over, she's done."

I'm optimistic, though. The glass isn't half empty, it's full, but full of God knows what. It's true, we may be eating shit. Well okay, that's a given. But Henry, in that shit you'll find peanuts, and in the peanuts, protein. But most of us are still saying "Hey! Waiter, there's shit in my soup!" you know? I say own up to it, you ordered it!

Take it easy,

Your pal Lyle Wilcox

Lyle

P.S. Butch "the Oreo King" told me to tell you not to worry about the club owners stiffing bands in Georgia, that the sodomy laws in that state are set up to protect you from that type of behavior.

Henry

You might not remember me, but you punched me once in
10th grade. Right in the face. In Gym. I had it coming.
Anyway, I'm not writing to bring that up, I'm writing
to tell you I was there when you punched our manager
after your performance at Puppet Town. He's really an
asshole, and he definitely had it coming.

I'm the junior assistant manager, and on days of per-
formances I double as balloon-animal wrangler. Some-
times I fill the balloons with nitrous oxide instead of
helium, just to get by (you try filling up balloons in
front of 400 screaming kids).

I haven't had this job for very long. Before this, my
brother-in-law talked me into investing the money my
Grandma left me in an ice cream truck venture. He was
going to drive the truck, but then my sister filed for
divorce and he left town. I had no choice but to take
over driving. On my first day out, I had a meltdown. My
ex-brother-in-law forgot to fix a freon gas leak in the
freezer unit, and before I knew it, I was up to my
ankles in soggy Eskimo Pies. The Mr. Freezes and the
Push-Ups were the last to melt, which is weird, because
they're usually the softest.

I guess I went kinda nuts. I turned up the volume and
blasted that stupid theme from "Love Story" out those
shitty speakers, scaring the neighbor kids and killing
a dogg as I drove 50 miles per hour down the side-
walks. I eventually hit a UPS truck. My license got
revoked for a year, but no one pressed charges. They
were okay to hire me here at PUppet Town, even if
they're idiots.

CARL PLASKE
Trenton, NJ

ROKY
ERICKSON

FROM THE BOOK

OPENERS II
THE LYRICS OF ROKY ERICKSON

ANTHEM (I PROMISE)

I promise, I promise
my green and blue eyes to you from
I promise, I promise
my green and blue eyes to you from.

For you I cool the streets with the wind at night
in the day I beat with the sun the cobblestones
and cool the wind of the Nile at night
the earth I fill with diamonds plus light
to say they never never bite.

I promise, I promise
my green and blue eyes to you from
I promise, I promise
my green and blue eyes to you from.

With you God chose me his wife
Lucifer and the mother of witches
in marriage they unite
my gremlins color purple left and light
to say they never, never bite.

I promise, I promise
my green and blue eyes to you from
I promise, I promise
my green and blue eyes to you from
I promise, I promise
my green and blue eyes to you from

I promise, I promise
my green and blue eyes to you from

May 9th, 1976
Satan came to earth view May 9th
gremlins have pictures
of the anniversary of Christ
the square root of zero
something smaller than zero
which keeps getting smaller
keep you out of sight and soul.

I promise, I promise
my green and blue eyes to you from
I promise, I promise
my green and blue eyes to you from
I promise, I promise
my green and blue eyes to you from
I promise, I promise
my green and blue eyes to you from
I promise.

BERMUDA

Are you going to Bermuda
would you go there if you could now now
if you go there plan on staying
apparently you like it
that's the way in Bermuda.

Are you, are you Bermuda bound
pulled and called like by a siren sound
it's so high and it's underground
but you never come back
or are you ever found in Bermuda.

It's just the innocent Devil's Triangle
it dares you to come there that's its angle
but the devil is innocent like mere
when the word you want is master master master in Bermuda.

Bermuda, Bermuda
does it call and haunt you
make you wonder, make you want to go
make you curious, too much burn
but you never never will return from Bermuda.

It's just the innocent Devil's Triangle
it dares you to come there that's its angle
but the devil is innocent like mirror
when the word you want is master master master in Bermuda.

Are you going to Bermuda
would you go there if you could now now
if you go there plan on staying
apparently you like it
that's the way in Bermuda.

COLD NIGHT FOR ALLIGATORS

It's a cold night for alligators
it's a cold night for dogs
the dogs choke on their barking
when they see alligator persons
in the bog and fog.

It's a cold night for alligators
when men turn into them in the night
it's a cold night for alligators
it's a cold night for their might.

It's a cold night for alligators
hiding behind the trees with moss
forever hear the swamp birds screaming
they forever a loss.

It's a cold night for alligators
in the blend
it's a cold night for alligators
a perfect monster has no end.

THE CREATURE WITH THE ATOM BRAIN

The creature with the atom brain
the creature with the atom brain
why is he acting so strange
do you think he's one of them
he threw the doll right down
ripped its guts off and threw it on the ground.

The creature with the atom brain
the creature with the atom brain.

I told you I'd come back. Remember Buchanan?
But you're not Buchanan!
I don't look like him but I am him. Don't you recognize the voice,
Jim? I promised to see you die and I will.

Hey boss, let us in! Hey boss, let us through the door! Hey boss,
let us in on it! Hey boss man, what is it?

No one stiches like that
no one stiches like that
the creature with the atom brain
the creature with the atom brain

Today's big story centers around the killing of District Attorney
McGraw, whose body was found in his garage, murdered. Doctor
Steiger is under the impression that these crimes are being
perpetrated by dead men charged with atom brains, which gives

them super-human strength and makes them impervious to bullets.
well, if you want to believe that story you can.

The creature with the atom brain
the creature with the atom brain
why is he acting so strange
do you think he's one of them
the creature with the atom brain.

DON'T SLANDER ME

Don't slander me
don't slander me, my my
never say don't I don't know why
don't slander me
just, just
for you, me and I I
don't slander me
don't slander me, my my.

False Gods will bring the devil the blues
and the blues will not themselves excuse
don't come from the blues if the blues are empty
hell is filled
don't slander me my my my
don't slander me nil.

Don't slander me
don't slander me, my my
never say don't I don't know why
don't slander me just, just
for you, me and I I
don't slander me
don't slander me, my.

Earth was built only for you
earth is a toy
here's a toy for you
perfection for a perfect you

dont' slander me, my, my, my
and don't slander you.

Don't slander me
don't slander me, my my
never say don't
I don't know why
don't slander me just, just
for you, me and I I
don't slander me
don't slander me my my.

I THINK OF DEMONS

I I I think of demons
they never kill
I I I think of demons
they never will
they don't need to
their scare is true
I think of demons
for you.

First first first I read demon
with horns with black tips
first first first I read demon
with horns with black tips
fangs in the day's moonlight
blood never touches my lips
I read demons never sips.

Lucifer Lucifer Lucifer Lucifer
who's been waiting on you
Lucifer Lucifer Lucifer Lucifer
who's been waiting on you
demon eyes and demons do
wait until you come through
to be their leader they've been waiting on you for you.

They don't need to
their scare is true
I think of demons
for you.

IF YOU HAVE GHOSTS

If you have ghosts you have everything
If you have ghosts you have everything
if you can say anything you want
then you can do anything you want
if you have ghosts then you have everything.

One never does that
one never does that
if you call it surprise there it is
the moon to the left of me is a part of my thoughts
is a part of me is me
one never does that.

In the night I am real
in the night I am real
the moon to the left of me is a part of my thoughts
is a part of me is me
forever is the wind is a part of my thoughts
is a part of me is me
in the night I am real.

I don't want my fangs too long
I don't want my fangs too long
the moon to the left of me is a part of my thoughts
Is a part of me is me
forever is the wind to the left of me is a part of my thoughts
is a part of me is me
I don't want my fangs too long
if you have ghosts, then you have everything.

LOVE

Love makes me feel so funny inside
I know your love needs my love like a body needs a high
love can make you happy love can make you cry
once it does it feels good
you never can deny yourself of love.

Love is that funny feeling
with songs that remind you of your love
brings rushing chills when it's singing
you lose interest in any other thing
talking on the phone for hours after anticipating its ring.

Loves makes me feel so funny inside
I know your love needs my love like a body needs a high
I'm always thinking 'bout you
I have to be with you to be
without you I would die.

Oh love
funny feeling love.

Love makes me feel so funny inside
everything I do is for it
I give it all it needs and desires
when someone asks you about their funny feeling
save them by telling them what they define is love.

Love is a funny feeling
a funny feeling in your stomach
you want so respectfully so much to kiss on
but it's something that needs the right permission.

NOTHING IN RETURN

I call your name in the midnight
but you don't hear me at all
I love you so nearly and dearly
but you don't love me at all
there's nothing in this big round world that worse hurts
than paying out and receiving nothing in return.

Every day and night I dial your number
but you never answer the phone
are you really not there when I call you
or did you so much chance to roam
there's nothing in this big round world that worse hurts
than paying out and receiving nothing in return.

If I only knew how to get you
but I've tried all I know
and failed you except for loving you so.

I sought you out
found out your name fast
but my name you never seemed to have called
how in this world can I date you
when you won't give me a call
there's nothing in this big round world that worse hurts
than paying out and receiving nothing in return.

If I only knew how to get you
but I've tried all I know
and failed you except for loving you so.

I call your name in the midnight
but you don't hear me at all
I love you so nearly and dearly
but you don't love me at all
there's nothing in this big round world that worse hurts
than paying out and receiving nothing in return.

PLEASE JUDGE

Please Judge don't send or keep that boy away
in society I wish you'd let him stay
(home/stay)
please don't give him time
please don't him confine
please don't say
"Send or keep that boy away!"

Please Judge give freedom to this child
it sure would make him smile
all that may do my rhyme
is deny that there is crime
please don't say
"Send or keep that boy away!"

I've been watching him for days
and most of the time he prays
that the crooked are always straight
and to know before anyone has to him
think of a pain again
if you would allow me I will say.

Please Judge don't send or keep that boy away
in society I wish you'd let him stay
please don't give him time
please don't him confine
please don't say
"Send or keep that boy away!"

Please Judge give freedom to this child
it sure would make him smile
all that may do my rhyme
is deny that there is crime
please don't say
"Send or keep that boy away!"

STARRY EYES

Starry eyes
how can I get to you
my true little
starry eyes
what can I say or do
for you my little
starry eyes, starry eyes
forever shall be mine.

Starry eyes
what can I say
to make you listen
starry eyes
what can I do
for your attention
starry eyes
starry eyes forever shall be mine.

When I'm alone
I hear and feel you
I wish that I could reach out and touch you
but knowing you're the one
to greet me and meet me
two alone in the dark
may it be.

Starry eyes
stars will fall on me

ROKY ERICKSON

starry eyes
won't you listen
that I'm here being
for you starry eyes
starry eyes forever shall be mine.

When I'm alone
I hear and feel you
I wish that I could reach right out and touch you
but knowing you're the one
to greet me and meet me
two alone in the dark
may it be.

Starry eyes
how can I get to you
my true little
starry eyes
what can I say or do for you my little
starry eyes
starry eyes forever shall be mine
starry eyes
starry eyes forever shall be mine.

WE ARE NEVER TALKING

Though we are in the same place
we surely know the beauty
of each other's face
into each other
we are not loving.

Though we know where we are coming
and the sun for light in heaven is sunning
into each other we are never running.

We can for long time
talk and talk
but no matter how long we may talk
we are not talking.

We may trip for miles
and no matter how we travel
we are never walking
we are never walking
we are never walking
we are never walking
we are never walking.

Though we are in the same place
we surely know the beauty of each other's face
into each other we are not loving.

And though we know where we are coming
and the sun for light in heaven is sunning
into each other we are never running.

We can for long time talk and talk
but no matter how long we may talk
we are talking.

We may trip for miles and miles
but no matter how we travel
we are walking
we are never walking
we are never talking
we are never walking
we are never.

YOU'RE GONNA MISS ME

You're gonna wake up one morning as the sun greets the dawn
you're gonna wake up one morning as the sun greets the dawn
you're gonna look around in your mind girl
you're gonna find that I'm gone.

You didn't realize, you didn't realize
You didn't realize, you didn't realize
You didn't realize
oh, you're gonna miss me baby
oh, you're gonna miss me baby
oh, you're gonna miss me child.

I gave you the warning but you never heeded it
how can you say missed my loving when you never needed it?

You're gonna wake up wondering and find yourself all alone
but what's gonna stop you baby
I'm not coming home
I'm not coming home
I'm not coming home.

EXENE
CERVENKA

FROM THE BOOK

VIRTUAL UNREALITY

PERFECT WORLD

THEY WERE PERFECT FOR EACH OTHER. They kept a little jar of guitar picks and rose petals next to the bed.

When they weren't feeling exactly the same, they were feeling different; and that was interesting, too. Their songs were like flowers that bloomed sober and straight from the water in a whiskey bottle vase. The clock, the moon, the sun, were all round, friendly faces that marked happiness, not time. Not the miles, not the minutes, not mortality. They were free and unopposed. There wasn't one thing she didn't like about him. He had never made a complaint against her habits. Already a month had passed, and still they loved each other.

She woke up this morning and the first thing her eyes landed on was one of his shoes. She felt funny. She didn't know why. She wondered, "Does it bother me, where it is? In the middle of the floor? Where's the other one?" And as she rose half-covered and touched it, he awoke and said, "You gonna hit me with that?" He smiled at her. She told him that it just bothered her for some reason. He said he was sorry; and he said, "I told you before I moved in that I was a slob." She set the shoe gently down on its sole.

He put his arms around her and kissed her face and neck; and as she introduced her tongue into his mouth, she knew that things weren't perfect anymore; and that his shoe was the beginning of the end. A few months later she watched him tie his laces and walk away with the moon under his arm. She cried all day to the rose petals. But they were dead, and the jar was dead, and the guitar picks were dead, and the air in her apartment was dead air, and her hair was dead, and the sun was brutally, unmercifully, alive.

Perfect worlds roll like balls through people's lives. Today, through mine; tomorrow, through yours. How lucky we can be sometimes. But how lonely and desperately sad we can be when our perfect worlds roll away.

Where are you, little star? Did you see this bitter earth roll by, a ball you shouldn't play with? It belongs to me, and I want it back!

Just like a child, I don't want my happiness to end. Just like a child, I'll get over it. And just like you, I'll find someone else to play with. I'll wait until a perfect world rolls to a stop at my feet, and when it does I'll get back on. And I'll know you when I see you, because you'll be barefoot.

CONTRADICTIONS

PART ONE * SUMMER 1992

GOING SOUTH ON HIGHWAY 5;
PLAYING WITH PLASTIC
ARMY MEN in the BACK
SEAT. SAN FRANCISCO, SAN
LEANDRO, VANDENBURG. OH,
THOSE MYSTERIOUS MEN IN
their FLYING MACHINES. I
SAW A HORNET & AN F-15
EAGLE- i SAW a TOMCAT
FLY OVER the RAINBOW.
i GUESS THAT MEANS
ARMS ARE FOR HUGGING.
WAIT, DON'T SHOOT—
i'M ONLY KIDDING. LET'S
GO TO PLEASANTON

BECAUSE I
AM FEELING
SO SAD
MY ARMY MAN
HAS FALLEN
BEHIND THE
CAR SEAT.
he was REAL —
FLESH & BLOOD, FLESH NOT
PLASTIC. NOT ALL GREEN.
i PREFER REAL SOLDIERS
OVER TOYS. NO; TOYS. NO.

IF ONLY THERE WERE NO INDIVIDUAL PREFERENCES. NO DEPTH TO OUR SADNESS; NO GRAFFITI ON OUR STREET SIGNS, NO UNDERPASSES UNDER OUR OVERPASSES — NO BLOOD ON OUR DOOR JAMBS AT 4 am 4AM FOR I am AM NOT AM TOO AM NOT.

CAR RADIO SWEET TALK K-EARTH 101 LOS ANGELES. COMMERCIALS: "DIAMONDS. BECAUSE YOU CAN'T OWN PEOPLE. WELL; NOT REALLY."

VANITY PLATES — PERSONALIZED LICENSE PLATES — EXCESSIVE FREEDOM OF EXPRESSION. "R U SNGL" YES- I AM. NO I'M NOT! YES- I AM NO I'M NOT.

LET'S turn AROUND AND
GO TO PLEASANTON. TRUCKS
STOP AND START OVER
AGAIN JUST LIKE the
TRUCKS ON TV CARRYING
FOOD & WATER TO THE DEAD.
COMPLIMENTARY SHRAPNEL FOR
YOUR DREAMS. CONTRA-
DICTORY SCREAMS.
"WATER" "FIRE" "WATER" "WATER"

IN SOMALIA TODAY... in
BOSNIA TODAY... IN IRAQ TODAY...

OH, WHAT a FEELING TO
DRIVE TOYOTA!
YOU CAN DO it in the ARMY!

FREE TRADE
AGREEMENTS.
TRADING TIME FOR
MONEY, MONEY FOR PLEASURE.
BUT THE SADDEST TRADE
OF ALL IS TO TRADE
SOMETHING BEAUTIFUL FOR
SOMETHING NECESSARY.

GARFIELD CLINGS TO A
LEXUS WINDOW NEXT TO US.
HIS FACE SO SMUG.
THE DRIVER'S, TOO.

BABY'S BIG BELLY, STICK
MOMMY. FLIES.

IS SOMALIA REAL? IS IN
—THIS PLACE REAL?
BECAUSE THEY CAN'T BOTH
BE REAL. YES THEY CAN.
NO; THEY CAN'T. YES.
THEY CAN. IS THIS the
HIGH POINT IN HISTORY?
WELL, IF IT IS; GOOD.
BECAUSE WE'VE GOT IT ON
VIDEO. AND UNDER TANKS.
MORTALLY WOUNDED. I'M
FROZEN HERE. TRAGEDY.
COMEDY. THE HEART, SLOW
MOVING BEAST THAT IT IS,
the HEART, SANDBAG in
an HOURGLASS,
REMEMBER, IT BEATS ONLY

i WANT TO GO SOMEPLACE
REAL & GIVE my HEART
away LIKE A CANDY BAR.
"SHE HAD TO LEAVE LOS
ANGELES".

KEEP GOING DOWN HWY 5
TO SAN DIEGO. MUST
BE CAREFUL — there
are 60 miles of
WARNINGS. NOT BECAUSE
OF SAN ONOFRE NUCLEAR
POWER PLANT on the BEACH,
not because of CAMP
PENDLETON where marines
PROTECT & PRESERVE
OUR NATURAL RESOURCES
FOR US — BECAUSE,

BECAUSE — it's because we are
WARNED BY FLASHING yellow
LIGHTS to "WATCH OUT FOR
PEDESTRIANS". YELLOW eNAMel
on steel; CAUTION SHAPED,
DIAMOND SHAPED SIGNS,
DEPICTING a family of 3
in BLACK SILOUHETTE; RUNNING;
their CLOTHES FLYING BEHIND
them, the LITTLE GIRL'S
PONY TAIL STRAIGHT BACK
FROM HER HEAD, ESCAPING
the IMMIGRATION VAN.

ESCAPING COMMUTERS
are coming HOME to
CREAMY STUCCO & ORANGE
TILES, SPANISH STYLe.

in advertising, living that
WAY IS CALLED "the CALIFORNIA
PROMISE". REAL FAMILIES
of 3 cars 8 lanes of
REAL SPEEDING TRAFFIC;
through the FENCES, in
SIGHT of the DEVELOPMENTS
ON the RUINED HILLSIDES
of EVERYWHERE-FOREVER.
it's DARK OUT i SEE FLASHES
of WHITE these FLASHES
OF LIGHT are PEOPLE.
when THEY GET HIT BY A
CAR OR a TRUCK
THEY BECOME a NEW
KIND OF ROAD KILL.
MEXICANS LYING DEAD ON
their SIDES ON OUR SIDE
of the ROAD. THEY DON'T

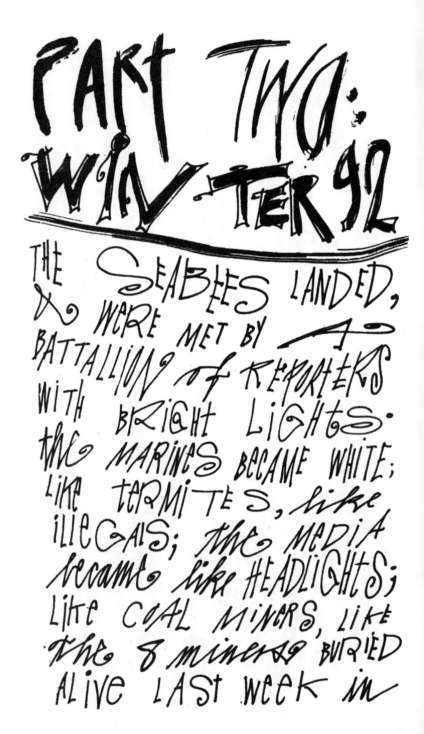

PART TWO: WINTER 92

THE SEABEES LANDED, & WERE MET BY A BATTALLION of REPORTERS WITH BRIGHT LIGHTS. the MARINES BECAME WHITE; LIKE TERMITES, like illegals; the MEDIA became like HEADLIGHTS; LIKE COAL MINERS, LIKE the 8 miners BURIED ALIVE LAST WEEK in

VIRGINIA. oh, that's
not related— that was
coal; this is FOOD.
CNN's ⚡
BERNIE asks a reporter,
who's THERE; who's
on the GROUND in
SOMALIA, what NAPOLEON
would think of all
this. the REPORTER
seems to know; BERNIE
AGREES.

WAR GRAPHICS. no,
PEACE GRAPHICS. WAR
GRAPHICS. no. PEACE GRAPHICS.
PEACH & PLUM COLORED
BATTLE GRAPHICS.

SLOW MOTION SADNESS
BORDERED FAUX TRADITIONAL
TRIBAL DESIGNS; trying
to be an REM COVER;
I CAN RELATE TO CNN
ART— it's BEEN TAKEN FROM
MY VERY OWN SUB-CULTURE.

the TOYOTA PICK-UPS
WITH MOUNTED GUNS &
TEENAGERS ARE, the
newspapers tell us,
" SIMILIAR to the VEHICLES
in 'MAD MAX' & 'ROAD
WARRIOR', MOVIES that
STARRED ACTOR MEL GIBSON."
in case we WANt to

KNOW WHAT it's REALLY
LIKE HERE; ON the
GROUND, IN SOMALIA.

ROADBLOCKS. THE
DIRECTOR OF AFRICA
WATCH, RAKIYA OMAAR,
SAID that food is getting
to the people. the
UN SAYS 80% of ALL
Relief SHIPMENTS ARE
BEING stolen. OMAAR
SAYS THAT'S NOT TRUE.
What if the marined start
SHOOTING? what if
that puts the Relief
WORKERS at GREATER,

RISK—what about the U.N.
TROOPS; there, BUT never
DEPLOYED, NO BLUE HELMETS,
NO GUNS, PLAYING
CHESS since APRIL.
SHE SAID, "the U.N.
PROGRAM is incompetently
RUN.".

SHE went on CROSSFIRE.
the LONE DISSENTER.
A SOMALIAN. OMAAR was
FIRED for CONTRADICTING
in PUBLIC.

POST COLD WAR LOGISTICS.
it's a DESERT STORM
G.I. JOE CHRISTMAS.

OUR TOYS ARE EXISTENTIAL;
RIDICULOUS. OUR TOYS
ARE US.

THEY'VE STOPPED SHOWING
the STARVING. NOW THAT
they HAVE our SYMPATHY
& SUPPORT, they CAN
STICK to IMAGES of our
HAPPY—GO-LUCKY media,
our OWN TEENAGERS
with MOUNTED GUNS,
SMILING KIDS & their
CANDY BARS.

is the PRICE of FRENCH
wine GOING UP OR NOT?

JOE
COLE

FROM THE BOOK

PLANET JOE

6.4.86 Salt Lake City, UT: Yesterday we drove all day from
Spokane, Washington across Idaho and into Utah. It was a long ass
haul, but Rollins, Ratman and I had fun doing it. We stopped and
swam in the Snake River in Idaho. We also stopped with others at an
amazing spot off the road past a suspension bridge where the river
ran about 500 feet below us. We hung out near the cliff of the gorge
throwing rocks over the side and chasing snakes. I caught a small
snake and Rollins knew everything about it. He was an encyclope-
dia, it blew my mind. Then Ratman caught a different snake and
Rollins knew all about that one too. He used to collect snakes and
also worked in a pet store so I guess he should know a lot about
them.

I'm feeling like I don't belong on this tour anymore. Sometimes
I wonder what the hell I'm doing here, killing time while I sit here
watching my life pass before my eyes.

I'm in the loft outside the club called the Monastery. The last
couple of days went fine, I started to feel less depressed and actually
began to feel sort of happy. Then yesterday morning something
weird happened. Greg Ginn laid into me about being negative. I'm
sleeping in my sleeping bag on the floor and I open my eyes and he's
sitting over me staring down at me and said "Don't even move. Don't
even get up unless you can think one positive thought. Try to think
one positive thought today." I thought he was kidding, but he was
dead serious. It was very strange to have him say things like that to
me. He hardly ever says a word to me. Later that afternoon at a gas
stop he starts up again, like he's real upset with me. I said maybe I
should smoke some pot and then I'd be positive and he goes, "Hey,
I'll smoke you out with some killer bud. Come on, right now." I must
have really annoyed him for him to go off like that on me. Ratman
told me this morning that Greg asked him what my problem is. I
didn't think I had a problem, but now I'm starting to wonder. If I
didn't have so much respect for Greg, I wouldn't think twice about it.
Lots of people probably think I'm a jerk and I could care less, but it
bothers me to have Greg think I'm an asshole. After all it if wasn't
for him my favorite band wouldn't exist and none of us would even

be on this tour. We'll see what happens, but right now I sure don't feel like being here. This is grinding me down and I'll be glad when it's over.

Gone's inside playing now. Another night, another show. Same old thing. Followed by another long drive tomorrow. I hate to be so down, but this just bores me. The best thing about the whole tour for me is driving. That's when I get to see the country and also have the chance to think. The shows are pretty much the same everywhere but the drives are what make it interesting for me. Also seeing Carlsbad Caverns and the Grand Canyon were memorable. The days off are always cool for me. It'll be finished soon. "Somebody" is today. Where did my dreams go?

I guess I have to find complete happiness in myself because I can't seem to find it any other way. I've tried and tried but I end up disappointed. I'm the only one who won't let me down. I'm all I've got. I'm into myself, I feel close to myself and that's about it. I've got me and that's all I really need. Gone's on their last song, so now it's time for me to go inside and set up the lights for Painted Willie. How exciting!

Back in the loft now, Painted Willie is inside doing their thing. They're about 3/4's done. I can't even watch them anymore. I don't want to go in there anymore even though I have to. I need money so I can be free from the things I do for it. I'll probably never be wealthy. I don't have the ambition for it. I'm glad to be alive and healthy, that's the main thing. What if nothing becomes of me? If I never make anything out of myself and I just keep floating along from day to day not ever really connecting with anything. What then? I don't know. It probably doesn't matter. What the fuck, I'll probably wind up fine even though I don't know what I want to do. Teach tennis, wait for my dad to die, marry into money are the only things I have a feeling I might do. I'm a pretty unspectacular dude when it comes down to it. I know what I am. I'm not going to try to fool myself. I'm still alive and together enough to know the value of that. I'm going to keep living day to day, moment to moment and let fate do the rest. I'm not like most people, I can't live the way other people do. Sometimes I think I'm really fucked up because of the way I am, and other times I feel really special to be me. The truth lies somewhere in the middle. I never did that well in school. I never tried to. I could have done well if I wanted, but I didn't care. I don't care about most things. I'm sort of like an oddball. I never hang onto anything long enough to see it through. I lose interest very quickly. In fact, I'm losing interest in writing this, so I'll stop.

The cops came in and closed the show down at the end of Painted Willie so Black Flag didn't even get to play. The cops were real assholes about it too, ordering people about and threatening violence if they didn't comply. Fuck the cops. We loaded out and Ratman gave me hit of acid for tomorrow's long drive to Denver, Colorado. Some skinhead from San Francisco gave him five hits of blotter with a green and red rainbow on it. Should be great.

6.6.86 Denver, CO: Yesterday was one of the heaviest days of my life. We took off from Utah for Denver at 10:00 a.m. Ratman was driving the Rat Truck, and I rode shotgun. We started out in a convoy with Davo leading in the Flag van, followed by the Willie van and then us. On the freeway I dropped the hit of rainbow blotter Ratman gave me the night before and came on to it pretty quickly. The Willie's got pulled over by the cops for some reason and we stopped and waited by the side of the road for them. That's when I started really frying. The dirt on the ground was greenish brown and shimmering like a heat wave. I just sat there staring at it and that made me even higher. That's the last I remember seeing the Willies or Davo. We got separated from them and the rest of the drive was just me and Ratman. As we drove up the highway, I got higher and higher and the sky had turned green and the road was red. I couldn't believe it and started laughing, telling Ratman that this was the most amazing acid I'd ever had and that he should take a hit of it too. We switched places and he climbed out of the passenger side window of the cab onto the roof and into the loft through the ventilation window while we drove 60 miles an hour down the road. He climbed back into the cab and dropped a hit of acid and them climbed out and into the loft again to get the ghetto blaster so we could listen to some tunes. It was like a stunt from a James Bond movie. Half an hour later he was just as high as I was and put Metallica's "Master of Puppets" tape in the blaster. He adjusted the speed control so that it played about twice as fast as normal and that made us even higher. We laughed so hard it made my stomach hurt. Next we listed to Hendrix's "Axis Bold as Love" at double speed and by the time that ended I thought I was going to burst through the roof of the cab and jet into outer space. I began talking and took over. I told Ratman we were driving straight down and the road began to look vertical like we were falling down the road on a roller coaster. Then I said I was going to make the truck fly and then it seemed like we were flying through the green clouds. I felt totally in control and had Ratman locked into whatever I was saying. Anything I described he could see as well as me. I started talking about how I knew he didn't respect me very much and didn't think I was very smart because I wasn't mechanically or electrically inclined like he was. I said that he thought he was funny by playing with firecrackers and bottle rockets, but that I could take that mountain over by the side of the road and blow it into smithereens just by pointing my finger at it. I told him I was only ten years old in his world but that in my world I could do anything. I live in cartoon land like the Flintstones and in my world there are no cops because dinosaurs eat cops. They pull them right off their motorcycles, chew them up and spit their heads out onto the ground with their helmets still on and they roll away. As I described all this we could both see it happening clearly and I started feeling incredibly powerful and all my resentment of Ratman's attitude towards me came out along with my hatred of cops. I talked about how the cops keep shutting down all the shows lately and how they should all be put to death. I looked over at Ratman and could tell that I had overpowered him and that made me feel even stronger, I felt like I could do anything, I said that I could take the Earth in the palm of my hand and crush it like it was a dirt clod. When I closed my fist we could both see it happening. That's when I lost it. I yelled, "I fucking hate cops!" and smashed the windshield as hard as I could with my right fist. I've never had a greater feeling of power before in my life than the moment I punched the window. I didn't think about what I was doing and didn't feel any pain at all, I just released all my energy into that window. The window cracked in all directions all the way across and the cracks filled with green and red light. Ratman's face was swimming with green and red and his voice changed into something I've never heard before and he looked at me and said, "You are evil!" I didn't know what was going on or what to do next, so I apologized for losing control and then he said, "I am that cop that you want to kill." Then he told me that my energy was caught inside him and that I had to get out of him because I was killing him. He said I was very powerful and he didn't want to fight me but he would if he had to. He kept saying that I was evil and full of bad thoughts. He said that the green and red colors swimming around in the cab and in the cracks of the window was energy that I had released by smashing the windshield. He kept talking in this weird voice that sounded old and alien. He pointed out the green around his body and said it was his aura and that I had penetrated his aura and I had to get out of it. It was like the Twilight Zone for real. I felt connected with his brain and everytime I would think a thought he could tell it if was positive or negative, but I couldn't stop thinking evil thoughts and he kept telling me, "No evil" every time he picked up on it. He said I was a destroyer and he was a builder and right now I was like Hitler and he was a Jew but he would fight me even though he didn't want to. I didn't want to be evil so I kept apologizing. I started crying and couldn't drive anymore so we switched and kept driving down the road. He wanted to tape our conversation on the ghetto blaster, but I said no because it seemed too weird and I was scared of what was happening. We started communicating on three different levels: one normal with words, one without using words like we could read each other's mind and then one that was beyond both of us where we could see into the past to when the Earth formed and when dinosaurs lived and when Romans fought battles and when Nazis marched down the streets of Germany. It was like seeing the struggle of life throughout all time and space. We tapped into things that we had no knowledge of and after awhile I didn't think we should know a lot of what we were seeing. We looked at each other and Ratman just said, "Some acid trip" and all I could say was, "Yeah. Some acid trip." What was going on was more than an acid trip. We crossed over into some realm that is beyond LSD. It was like knowing too much too soon and it was overwhelming me. I started it by losing control and punching the windshield, and now I didn't know what was happening or what to do with it. On the road we passed a tourist attraction that was a life size town called Flintstone Land. It was Bedrock, straight out of the Flintsones cartoon. Then shortly after that we passed another tourist attraction that was dinosaur fossils in the side of the mountain. Shortly after that we got pulled over by the cops. It was like everything I said before I hit the window coming back at me. Flintstones, dinosaurs and cops. As we pulled to the side of the road, Ratman said in the voice, "We are being pulled over by everyday police officers. We are now going to be taken to jail." I said that we could get out of it, and he said, "The fight has just begun." One of the cops came up to the truck and asked Ratman to step back to the police car with him, and it was like he already knew what was going on. I sat there watching in the side mirror as the cops questioned him. I couldn't believe what I was seeing. Ratman was sitting on the hood of the cop car with his jacket half on, losing his cool, slobbering like a madman and pointing at the truck telling the cops that I was evil and to get me away from him. He looked insane but the cops were just standing there quietly listening to him and nodding their heads. They didn't seem surprised at all by the way he was acting, and I sat there thinking this is it, I'm busted for being evil. Finally, the main cop walked up to the window where I was sitting and stared at me. He had black hair, a thin mustache and mirrored shades, and he stood there staring at me for a long time before he talked to me. The first thing he asked, "Your friend says you're evil, is that true?" "No sir, I'm not evil." "When is the last time you got some sleep?" he asked. "About eight hours ago." "Well, your friend says he hasn't slept in eighteen hours" he said. "He must just be really tired, we're on this nationwide tour with a few bands and we've been traveling a lot and he must just be tired." "Are you on drugs?" he asked. "No sir." "Do you have any drugs in the vehicle?" he asked. "No sir." "Have you two been fighting?" he asked. "No sir, everything's fine." Then he points at the cracked windshield and asked, "Who did that?" "I did. Umm, I just got mad and hit it... but it's ok now, I just lost control for a second." He took his glasses off and nodded at me. Then he picked up a packet of birth control pills that Ratman's girlfriend left on the dashboard. Rollins had drawn swastikas on the pills and wrote, "Fuck Kill Fuck Kill" all over the packet. He looked at it for a few seconds and then asked, "What is this?" "Those are his girlfriend's birth control pills, she left them there." It was like I was on trial and he was trying to determine whether or not I was evil. Then I said, "Look officer, we're really good people. I'm not evil. We just want to get to the next show. I'll drive and everything will be fine. Please." He looked at me and I knew he knew exactly what was happening. It was as though he was a spiritual police officer there to make a judgment on me. He told me to wait there and went back to the cop car to talk to Ratman. Then the other cop came up from the other side and started talking to me. He was younger with blond hair and looked like an all American jock. He acted friendly and said that everything is all right and that we would be on our way as soon as his partner finished talking to my friend. Shortly after that they let us go and even let Ratman keep driving. We drove on talking about good and evil, building and destroying and Ratman was telling me how the energy I rely on is negative and that I must change. He kept saying how he was a builder and I was a destroyer. He was right. I am totally into destruction. I have an evil mind, but my heart is pure. As we drove on through the Rocky Mountains it did not wear off but kept getting weirder. I could feel our minds melding into one brain that was locked in conflict. Every time I thought a bad thought he would turn to me and say, "No evil," and I would try to stop the thought. The problem was that I couldn't stop thinking bad thoughts no matter how hard I tried and it was wearing me out trying to stop it. Ratman said that he saw a red baby demon face on my face that would turn and laugh at him every time

I thought an evil thought. To me his faced looked like it was shrouded in green gas. That along with the energy swimming around inside the cab of the truck made it all seem like a dream. Further down the road we got pulled over by another cop who wanted to know if we had a permit to haul equipment in the truck, which we didn't, but somehow Ratman talked his way out of it and we pushed on. By the time it got dark we were deep in the Rockies feeling drained and exhausted. I was driving and the lights on the truck started going dim like they were losing power and then the engine began sputtering like it was breaking down or out of gas. If we would have broken down there in the middle of nowhere at night who knows what would have happened. Neither of us wanted that to happen. Ratman told me that I could make the truck work and that I had to think hard and do it. The truck was almost stalling out and the lights were going dark, but then I put my mind to it and the lights got bright again and the engine started running normally again. It gained power and ran well, but every time I let my mind wander it would start breaking down again until I concentrated on it. It was wearing my brain out, but I kept it up until we reached a gas station about twenty miles away. The gas tank was completely empty. We had been running on fumes or else I was making the truck work on willpower alone. We got into Denver around midnight after driving and tripping 14 hours not knowing where we were or where the other guys were. Ratman looked wiped out and he said I could get us to where we were supposed to be. I drove around the city thinking of where the others were, but I kept getting lost. A carload of kids saw the Black Flag bars on the back of the truck and started following us around asking us where we were going and where Black Flag was. Finally we got rid of them and kept looking. I thought about the early 70's, when I was about ten or eleven years old growing up in Hollywood and remembering how sleazy it was. Then I drove down a street called Colfax and it started looking a lot like the sleazy parts of Hollywood in the 70's with prostitutes, pimps, strip bars and porno theaters on the streets. It was like everything I was thinking was transforming itself into reality and I had taken a street that took me back in time to what I was thinking about. Then the name of the street hit me. Colfax. Like the facts of Cole's life. Ratman seemed to know what I was doing and went along hoping I could get us to where we were supposed to be. Colfax led to a dead end in a bad part of town. It was like I was dragging Ratman on a tour of my mind. He kept saying, "Joe, you've got to get us there." I was trying, but I couldn't do it. Then I started thinking about when I was 14 years old living in Canoga Park and raced motocross. We saw a Denny's and Ratman asked if I wanted to stop and get something to eat. Denny's are like an oasis, I said yeah let's eat, thinking that it would give me time to get my head together enough to find our destination. When we walked in, I noticed a sticker on the door. It was a sticker from Flying Machine Factory, a motorcycle parts company that was from the Valley where I lived when I was racing motocross bikes in '75. That company went out of business over 8 years ago. Why would this sticker be here on the door of this Denny's in Denver, Colorado? It was like it was put here for my benefit as an omen. We went to the counter and sat down and a waitress gave us menus. I was still controlling the trip and Ratman was reacting to whatever I thought. I was thinking about how it's not good to eat animal flesh, and he picked up on it and started talking about how he was going to stop eating meat and said we should order pasta. Then the waitress came to take our order and it was like she knew what was going on just like the cop did and she was there to help us on our way. We ordered pasta, and I was thinking of drinking milk and she suggested that we get milk without me even saying anything. As we sat there waiting for our orders, I began thinking of '83 when I was in the mental hospital after trying to kill myself and remembering all the freaks that were there with me. Then I looked around the restaurant at the other people sitting at the counter and saw sitting to my left a mentally ill old woman crying and rubbing her face with her hands. Then I looked to my right, and down the counter from me, staring off into space was a younger guy in filthy clothes who was obviously a drug casualty. It scared the shit out of me. Then the waitress came with our food and looked at me like she had read my mind and gave me a look as if to say don't think about those things anymore. She began treating us like children because I was thinking like one and it reassured me. We finished our meal and when she came with the check she took my money and counted it out for me because I couldn't deal with it. She then wished us luck and sent us on our way. I felt better but also felt that I was holding Ratman hostage with my juvenile mind. There was nothing he could do. I was in control. I felt like that kid on the Twilight Zone who could wish people into the corn field if they weren't nice to him. We drove around some more and Ratman wanted me to make a decision about where we were going to stop so I finally chose a place called Denver 8 Lodge because I liked the sign out front. I went in and got us a room and we went in and tried to get some sleep. It was about 3:00 a.m. and we should of been able to sleep, but we were still frying on acid and our minds were still tangled. I lay there on the bed looking at the wall melting green in front of me, and I could never recall a single moment of my life when I had not been on acid. It was like I was born on acid, lived my whole life on acid and would always be on acid. I thought I was never going to be normal again and it scared me. I could still feel Ratman's thoughts in my head, and I knew he was afraid to go to sleep because he thought I would take his mind away from him while he slept. I got out of bed and took a shower and started crying and praying to God to make this go away and return me to my normal state. I said I would never take drugs again if only this would wear off. I tried going back to sleep but couldn't. After a sleepless night we got up and went to have breakfast in the hotel dining room. Ratman kept spinning his knife on the table and it kept pointing to me when it stopped. The drugs were wearing off but our minds were still connected. After breakfast we got back in the truck and began searching for the club. It was called the Rainbow Music Hall and we didn't know where it was but found it somehow. Ratman looked totally burned out like he hadn't slept in a week. When we got there none of the others had arrived yet so we parked and tried to get some sleep while we waited. Ratman fell asleep on the ground next to the truck, and I was laying on the roof trying to sleep when I heard Greg, Sim and Andrew walk by. They looked at Ratman and I heard Andrew say, "What's wrong with him?" and then I heard Sim say, "What happened to the window?" I just lay on the roof not saying anything, feeling like a criminal. I didn't want to face anyone or try to explain what had happened. When it came time to load in we opened the truck and there was dust all over the equipment like we had gone through a dust storm. We never went through any kind of dust storm and I don't know how everything got covered with it. It was just another weird phenomenon.

When I talked to Dave Markey he said that after they got pulled over by the cops they caught up with Davo and had a great drive. He said that they drove through a double rainbow and were inside it as they drove down the road. He said it was raining while they were driving, but we never saw any rain or any rainbows. It makes me think that we were on different drives even though we were on the same highway. The whole thing was bizarre. I'm glad it's over and I'm still alive. It's one of the heaviest experiences of my life.

Tonight's show should be a good one. This club is big, clean and professional. Everyone seems to be in a good mood now. I feel a little fucked up, but I guess that's to be expected after frying on acid for 24 hours straight.

The show went real well. Big crowd. The bands all played good and I'm feeling better. There were a few skinhead type idiots in the crowd giving Gone a bunch of shit during their set, but they were just a few fuckheads in an otherwise cool crowd. After the show Rollins came up to me with a couple of bright yellow and orange Painted Willie "Mind Blowing" tour shirts for us to wear. Mine says "Personality" and his says "Style" on the back written in magic marker to honor their epic set closing finale, "Personality and Style." We decided a few weeks ago to wear these shirts for the rest of the tour without taking them off or washing them as a tribute of sorts to the Painted Willie experience. Rollins bought them off Mitch Bury and now we're sporting them with pride. After load out, Ratman and I were talking to the others about what happened to us and I said to Greg that he was probably trying to warn me the other day when he went off on me about being negative, like he knew something was going to happen. He just said that he could tell me lots of things and left it at that. Greg seems like a very intensely aware person to me. Sometimes I think he is a genius.

JOE
CARDUCCI

FROM THE BOOK

ROCK & THE POP NARCOTIC

THE BAND WAGON'S ODOMETER

IT'S TOUGH TO BE PART OF A BAND. Every band is ultimately doomed to fail. There are emotionally-charged situations constantly cropping up that invite ridicule or shame, usually in a three against one scenario. A band demands of its members relationships more akin to family than to co-worker, however the lifelong experience at accommodation developed in family relationships is lacking. On top of the vagaries of the musician's life itself, the work involved in writing, arranging, practicing, recording and performing music with others is more apt to bend egos than conventional jobs. Each individual player's ego is on the line to some extent at every little artistic decision. Generally, there is one dominant personality in the band, so even the required accommodations are not equally distributed. Ideally, the dominant personality is not an absolute control freak and the others are not frustrated leaders. Still, they should be more than simply hired guns and find stimulation and satisfaction in the mass of work necessary to write, arrange, record, and perform a band's music.

It's more common for the music or the money to keep a band together than the camaraderie. **Dinosaur Jr.**'s now ex-drummer Murph explained to Erik Davis that he had reservations, as something of a partyin' dude, about playing with such weird high school nobodies as Mascis and Barlow: "But musically something just clicked. Instantly this bizarre dynamic was formed. It's an awkward situation to sit down with somebody and realize that musically you're really close but socially you're miles apart. We all saw it as a challenge. We were kind of awed by it." (*Spin*, 6/93)

Even when friends form a band the relationship tends to be quickly overwhelmed by the sheer quantity of time and tension involved, particularly in touring. When you see band members smile to each other on stage or play around together while performing, you are seeing them dramatize the band ideal for the benefit of their audience of believers. The same stage pals may not even be able to bring themselves to speak to each other off stage. Or perhaps at a single gig in the middle of an endless tour in Missouri or Cleveland or Dresden they might just be so on that they face each other and sync up so completely that for a few bars or a few tunes they're back in their first cramped practice pad playing for no one... but burning to be in fact where they are.

The sad truth is that not only is life on stage false, so is life off stage for the musician-certainly in the midst of touring. Performing is dangerous enough for the ego; performing within a band is a bizarre adventure indeed.

Greg Ginn, (**Black Flag, Gone**) who spent upwards of a decade in the rock band psych wards (let's hope he returns there soon) attributed the difficulty of keeping a band together to the fact that it must be a commune of sorts and most Americans aren't culturally prepared for this reality. Greg's legion of ex-bandmates might say they'd have gladly settled for a communal set up, but then neither point quite accounts for the fact that Ginn as catalyst did make the whole thing go. It is interesting to speculate on the extent to which these tensions are desirable and necessary, though of course everyone has his breaking point. The hatred that developed between Lennon and McCartney, ex of the **Beatles**, has been traced by the band's many historians, but the interesting thing to me is that neither did a damn thing worth listening to in rock terms (Lennon's **Plastic Ono Band** existed contiguous to the **Beatles**). As I said, "Doomed." When you think about it, those double-insulated carpet covered practice studios bands use look quite a bit like rubber rooms.

Black Flag's personnel problems over the years were exacerbated by the intensity by which they were a band in the face of so little return. Still, the band's fundamental tension arose from the fact that guitarist Greg Ginn and bassist Chuck Dukowski were, in Greg's mind, musically incompatible. Greg felt this from the beginning. (He knew Chuck's style well because Chuck's band **Wurm** dated back to 1970.) And yet Chuck was the obvious choice for bassist given the times, and came to be crucial both musically and operationally to the band they did become. Once it was all going, his removal was bound to be traumatic; Greg's reluctance to either face up to his musical judgment or forget it just made it worse for Chuck.

Saint Vitus lost their first singer Scott Reaghers when his girlfriend, now wife, insisted that he bail on the band mid-tour. He did, and though guitarist Dave Chandler had to suddenly sing while playing, which he hadn't done since the band's prehistory, Scott managed to stay on good terms with the band. His replacement, however, Scott Weinrich, left after one of their German tours went safely back home but did not ever call the band to let them know officially. He instead let them find out that he'd reformed his pre-**Vitus** band, the **Obsessed**. This lack of a phone call, totally understandable when you consider the typical musician's aversion to nasty detail-work, led to bad blood. Instead of a call, Wyno wrote a song for his bold bandmates which appeared on the Lunar Womb album:

> No Blame
> No blame—I'm gonna live to live,
> live for something to die for.
> No Shame—got somethin to give,
> gonna give it a try for.
> No blame—I'm gonna live to live
> No game—If you're lookin to lose,
> this is the place for,
> No shame, I'm gonna shine my shoes on your face for
> The name of Rock 'n' Roll.
>
> ©1991 The Obsessed

Oh well, Dave, at least it's a great tune.

Husker Du was another tension-filled rollercoaster ride of death disguised as a rock band. When I first ran into them, bassist Greg Norton did their business. Then there was a mysterious but distinct coup whereby guitarist Bob Mould assumed control of business, and Greg's songwriting and therefore singing ceased. One of Greg's last songs had been a little number called "Drug Party" and they apparently hoisted him on this pretard though his crime was merely preferring cocaine to speed. (Remember that cocaine in 1981 had no street credibility, unlike now.) As it turned out, Bob did the business very well—certainly **Husker Du** were the easiest of the bands to stay current with and plan for from my position at SST—but the band's internal tensions came to allow for tours no longer than three weeks, and cut their practice regimen down to that needed to learn the new songs before recording. Thus after *Zen Arcade* it was more that there were either Bob songs or Grant songs. The idea that a rock band called **Husker Du** transformed song material was falling by the wayside. Depending on speed and psychodrama for what should be a musical transformation is not a long term strategy. Still, these boys had strong stomachs and stuck with it longer than I'd have thought; I heard about that last tour!

In the aftermath Grant Hart left the drums to lead his next band, **Nova Mob**, from the position of guitarist/vocalist. He'd hung on to a fifty/fifty quota of songwriting/singing from the weaker position of the drumstool up until the end of **Husker Du**, but was about to get aced on what would've been the third Warners LP (ninth over all). After **Husker Du**, Bob did a session player solo record, then used his touring all-star type band to record the second "solo" record which was much more the rock record. But he junked that band for the mercenary pros they were, and formed his current band, **Sugar**. Great band, Bob. (Do you think he read my book, or Nirvana's sales figures?)

Back in the van.

The variables in good rock bands' stylistic character may be innumerable, but invariably the art of rock music is found at that superheated nexus in performance where each musician, while playing his part in the material, hears and feels and anticipates the greater whole as it is being reincarnated. This whole—a multidimensional simultaneity—is at once solid and evanescent: solid enough for a good band to wail on and improvise from, and evanescent enough for a lousy band to never reach no matter how much they may study the work of their inspirations. It is conjured up by three or four players like some phantom. It rises in their midst and at least a few people will pay to witness it. Any real musician chases that phantom in communion with other players until he dies or the marketplace convinces him he's been a chump. Do not confuse musicians with the far more numerous pseud-musicians who are out chasing psychological compensations and simple adrenaline rushes.

The task of the serious listener is to develop an ear for this difference. In another's words: "'Rock' and 'roll,' the two kinds of syncopation arising from the fundamental rhythm, one discontinuous, the other continuous, merge in an eerie, oscillating stillness for which swing is a wonderfully accurate term. In effect the completion of our kinesthetic response to rhythm has been strategically deferred, channeled upward along lines of unrelieved rhythmic tension until lit can occur simultaneously with our apprehension of the musical idea. Thus one can never know exactly whether swing is a nervous phenomenon or a musical one: we seem to have accepted the music bodily into ourselves at the same moment that the perfect repose of contemplation has fallen over it." (Robert Cantwell, *Bluegrass Breakdown*.) In two out of every three **Meat Puppets**' words: "Curt: It's a matter of believing in the music itself. We make changes from record to record and we never consciously tried to maintain a particular style. Derrick: In that our style is not necessarily in the music. It's not so much an attitude, either. Curt: Even our attitude doesn't affect the styles we play. An ideal is a better word for it. Yes, and that ideal can be completely surpassed by the group playing. You can have an ideal of perfection in your head, and practice can go way beyond that idea." (*Bam* 5/24/85.)

In rock music, songwriting may be a significant aid in the conjuring, but it's still essentially a pretext for the art itself. Better songwriting and arrangement provide a more fertile base for performance. But the tonal coloring of the music's chords and notes and the way they ride the rhythm is frequently more telling than the tune itself. When the masters took away the slaves' drums and left them with guitars, banjos, and violins, what resulted was a rough physical approach to string instruments that was also a restless approach as the now African-American players probed and bent the notes, searching for phantom African tonalities and textures within the

European scale. The southern white's appetite for roughed-up tonalities may have originated in the drivingly flat keening of Scottish/Irish marches and ballads, but the basic one-five blues move is common to all musical traditions. However, as European music evolved melodically and harmonically, these more primal maneuvers were discouraged or even ruled out by church authorities. (The one-five evokes a solid resonating dramatic foundation, and was common in medieval European music but avoided as crude later on. The diminished chord or the Devil's tri-tone is unresolved and implies transition; they banned this sucker immediately—it's the **Voivod** sound.)

But rock's use of song is similar to jazz's in that it is not the replication of a song that matters but what jam/spirit can be invoked in the musical use of the tune. A song that in its structure recalls previous rock experiences may better or more easily set up both the musicians and the audience for the performance, but as bands pursue their own musical paths the songwriting sometimes moves beyond such traditionally resonating dynamics. In such cases a band's audience may fall off to just those most intensively interested in music and its construction. (There are actually alot of such people but the media does such a poor job alerting them to *music* that most people find out about the good stuff only after the bands have broken up.)

But there is a need for any kind of American music to retain its ties to the Western tradition of over-arching melodic arrangement. That is, the changes from song-part to song-part should both refer back to earlier parts and forward to a final resolution of the melodic tease. This is a European inheritance but America has its own spin on this too. Melancholy ballads are common to all European cultures, but there they tend to cast a more passive mood. American melancholia may be reflective, but any implied stasis is more an active transfixion as if awed at the scale of our tragedy/heroism. (My favorite recent hits of American melancholia is John Anderson's "Seminole Wind.")

When you hear a band that lacks this melodic facility, then you're dealing with fans who formed a band, not musicians. These bands' rhythm sections ought to split to find a musical guitarist. The new metal underground is especially swamped with bands so cut off from blues and pop tradition that they have no melodic skills whatsoever. Comics and horror movies are no paradigm for music. And riffs mean nothing if they are just unresolved pummeling of the air; they must serve a greater melodic structure. **Metallica**, **Saint Vitus**, **Motorhead** and **Black Sabbath** are all highly skilled melodically, though when a bum tune slips out of them it's always for lack of melodic conception; it's not that they suddenly forgot how to play. Early **Metallica** and **Motorhead** suffered this more often, but I would name "Sweet Leaf" as one of **Sabbath**'s duffs; forget how much you like it as a pot anthem and listen to the arrangement's featurelessness. **Saint Vitus**' tunes are frequently simple to the point of minimalism and yet their melodic sense rarely fails them. "The Troll" is **Vitus** at its bone simplest, but the riff actually covers alot of ground as it winds its way along the permutations of its nearly seven minute arrangement (and dig on that production).

Melodic anemia is a common disease of R&B as well. The funk, like the riff, works best in a strong melodic context. The African-American musician's need for a facility with their Western melodic inheritance-by-force may never wash politically, but musically it damn well better. C&W's problem is usually melody overload in a treacly attempt at Tin Pan Alley class (let Frank be Frank, Gomer; You just be Gomer). Irving Berlin and Sammy Cahn might not have recognized what I'm calling a melody here, but contrast **Black Sabbath**'s "Supernaut" with "Sweat Leaf" and if you don't hear what I mean go get your money back on this book.

If there are lyrics to rock performance, their delivery by the vocalist may be a part of this process or apart from it. Like the guitarist does over the rhythm section or the bassist does over the drummer, the vocalist must place his phrasing into both the rhythmic and melodic structures.

There is always some amount of tension between a band's players and its singer. It's usually in part a product of envy, but it's also rooted in musical issues. However, when the sex groupies and the mind groupies both line up after gigs in front of the singer, it tends to turn off the players who may have written the music and in any case played it. When musicians let their payoffs slip from musical ones to those supplied by the audience, they are in trouble.

These issues vary depending on whether the singer writes, plays an instrument, is the only vocalist, etc. Mike Watt of the **Minutemen** once mentioned that that band could never have survived with a vocalist that only sang, given the high-strung nature of that trio's relationship. Meaning that in the politics of a band a singer without an instrument is essentially unarmed and outnumbered, and must turn his back to the players at the precise moment their resentments are made concrete by the live audience.

Many a guitarist has insisted on singing so as to seal his control of the band (rare is the bassist or drummer that can contest him). Jimi Hendrix, Ted Nugent, Tom Verlaine, Greg Sage; each could conceivably have improved their music's overall sound by looking for a more qualified singer. Nugent and Verlaine each had one (Derek St. Holmes and Richard Hell, respectively) and threw him over. In frustration, even such tuneless wonders as Robin Trower and Greg Ginn have committed attempted warbling. But part of rock's appeal is its collision of blued and roughed up tonalities with jacked up rhythms, and I don't mean to suggest that odd or even failed (on some TPA level) singing can't add to distinctive rock achievement.

Joy Division apparently had some kind of blood oath that if any of the four left the band the others would not continue. (How new romantic!) When singer Ian Curtis left town for good the others cheated a bit and changed their name to **New Order**, and more tellingly made a switch from rock (art) to pop (craft). The name change, reference-wise, switched from victim identification to perpetrator identification. Never has this switch been made and executed by a band so clearly. On successive releases, **Joy Division** had been pushing keyboards forward and guitars back in the mix—sweetening the sound—but they had still been playing a highly refined, yet Stooges-derived rock music. But rock rhythm was traded for an electro-disco one and **New Order** went down the sophisto-dance path emphasizing techno tricks and textures and eliminating guitars altogether. Curtis' lyrics had been straight and had emotional content; the remaining members could only substitute a canny, hip vacuousness in their place. The curious thing is that they made the same such musical substitute though no players changed. **Joy Division**'s vocalist was certainly part of their rock nexus. **Blind Idiot God**, a powerful instrumental guitar/bass/drums trio, explained why it did not have a vocalist in the press bio of its debut album release (SST): "Because nobody can scream loud enough to get over the sound we make, and even if they could, they would undoubtedly sound like they were really angry or in some sort of severe psychic pain. And we don't want to sound like we're angry or angst-riddled, because we're not. There's a lot of very good music out there that gets screwed up by all these overbearing, dogmatic exhibitionists who call themselves vocalists; the music usually ends up being relegated to mere backdrop status..."

Jeff Beck explained to Don McLeese that in choosing to play without a vocalist: "You're never gonna get the girly contingent or the all around happy family rock crowd (because) you've got no front singer who can put the message across. But the great thing with instrumental music is you're totally unlimited. You're not dealing with the limitations of the singer or the moods they go through or the songs they write. It's just expression in sound, which is total freedom." (*Chicago Sun-Times* 11/5/89.)

Instrumental rock helps make clear the essence of the rock process because the grip an instrumental performance can have on the listener is quite different and deeper. A vocalist invites the audience to focus on him and switch attention to the players only during their solos. A band without vocalist presents three or more equal foci of attention. In watching and listening to the players play without the literal distraction of words and visual distraction of being addressed by a singer, the audience more properly become listeners. Bands in which one of the key instrumentalists also sings, such as **Eleventh Dream Day** and **Television**, affect an audience somewhere in between the likely temper any tension between the singer and the others.

In defense of singers, I should make the point that it's basical-
ly impossible for them to put in the same time at the practice pad as
the others. The others will hold this against him just because they
can; in the marketplace of psychic guilt you grab while the grabbing's
good. But realistically, the human voice shouldn't be spent in a prac-
tice space with an inadequate P.A. drowning in dead amp volume. If
the band starts jamming on a theme they are wasting the vocalist's
time. A vocalist needs to stay current with the players but this can
probably be done once or twice a week if the band practices daily, less
if less. The vocalist needs tapes of practices so he can control the vol-
ume and not shred his voice to no point. This unavoidably works
against him in real politic terms, of course.

Henry Rollins put up with constant low-level backbiting in
Black Flag, and the high turnover in the rest of the band amplified
this as new members cemented their bonds with each other outside
of Henry's presence, at least until the touring began. The point I wish
to emphasize here, though, is that the intensity and type of work
Henry was in fact doing away from the practice pad has served him
and his bands well. Eight years past **Black Flag,** the quality and
quantity of Rollins' work speaks for itself.

The rise in the number of largely or totally instrumental bands
after 1985 (**Pell Mell, Gone, Alter Natives, Blind Idiot God, Black
Sun Ensemble, Left Insane,** Ronnie Montrose, **Universal
Congress of, Tolls of Ignorance, Gore, Joe Satriani,** and the many
Dead-style jamming bands) was not a response to market demand
except insofar as there was virtually none for any decent contempo-
rary band. Musicians decided that as they couldn't make any money
anyway, it would be better to have no singer than to keep a problem
child for nonexistent commercial considerations.

Remember that instrumental rock by the **Mahavishnu
Orchestra,** the **Edgar Winter Group** and **Jeff Beck** received consid-
erable commercial airplay as late as '75. But once out of favor and
format the "genre" died as that generation of musician either com-
plied with the pop and rock markets' demands for vocals, or retired
into that space/folk/jazz hybrid-to-be new age. Virtually alone in the

late 1970s/1980s, the **Dixie Dregs** were tooling in the chop shop, but they soon added a vocalist, switched vocalists, broke up and then reformed sans vocalist. Even as commercially peripheral a market as the blues no longer accepts instrumental music. Guitar great **Albert Collins** has explained he reluctantly began singing on order to keep gigging (he's actually a good singer and lyricist).

It seems that as the music audience (and Americans as a whole) have become less literate and more dependent on the electronic media, their involvement with music has also become more passive. Instrumental music, other than new age or muzak, requires more involvement and a higher, more abstract involvement at that. A vocalist is perhaps most effective as the audience's vicarious stand-in, guiding its response to the music. His clear signs indicating how the music is to be taken aren't present in instrumental music. Thus the less musically "literate" the listener, the more likely he is to require that a singer determine his response to the music. (I'm of course exempting highly musical persons who may be entirely illiterate because they do not make up the bulk of the rock or pop audiences.) And again, a vocalist can indeed be a party of a band's musical process; it's just that too often he isn't.

A L A N
VEGA

FROM THE BOOK

CRIPPLE NATION

SLAZ DRAIN

YA DRAINS
YA FUCKIN' DISEASES
FUCKIN' LUCK
IT AIN'T THERE
IT AIN'T THERE

YA MEATS
SWEET SLAZ
YA HEAD JOBS
FUCKIN' WORSE
HEY LETHALS
TAKE VEINS
DROWN
IN THA 2 CRAP SIGNS
AN LOOK
AT YA AGONY

FREE YA FRENZYS
SHADOW IT
NAZI GAMES
THA FUCKIN' ABUSES
DUMB GANGLAND BAG RIP SWEETHEARTS
FREE MOTHA ALREADY
AN DIE DAZZLER
CUT YA SLAVES
AN DIE DAZZLER
WITH YA FUCKING' DAMN PIECE

SWEEZY
THE LEAD DREAD HASELF
PHILLY SMOOTHY
FAVORS... FA THA RIGHT PRICE

DOIN' SHITS
FUCKIN' BLASTS
SUDDEN DEATHS
FA RIGHTEOUS CHRISTS
SHE GET YA BLIND
HERO
SHE GOT A BLADE UP HER ASS
GUARANTEED FAITH
FOR INFINITIES

HEY SISTA
IT'S 7 CENTURIES
TRILLIONS
FUCKIN' MINDS
MELLADRONS
MONGOLORDS
HYPNOTIZERS
PRAY
PRAY
PRAY RICH
PRAY RICH, YA BASTARDS
GET YA DAMN TICKETS
FA YA UNIFORMS
YA VOODOO'S

FATS
SWANKIN'
SHINE'N
POOR WHACK FUCK
SHE'S BESERKO
GIVE UP
SHUT UP
HOOK THEM ANIMALS

PARTY, PARTY
PORNO COP
BEFORE YA GET YA BRAINS BLOWED OUT
SHE'S A FACE
DUMPIN' YA

JINX YA JINX
FUCKED
TRY GALAXY ASSHOLE
GET YA BIRTH
CRACKIN'
PUZZLER

CHEAP INDIANS
CHEEK KIDS
A PUKE'N SHITS
THA CHAMP LIVES FOREVER

THA DEAD SEES
THA DEAD SEES

YA KNOW
SHE'S
THA FUCKIN' MESIAH
BANGED
WAITIN'
THRU THA FUCKIN' DOOR
WASTED
HEY
THA FUCKIN' SKULL

DON'T WANNA KNOW 'BOUT IT
LITE YA HIDEOUS BEDS

PAY THA WAMBEE
EVERY DAY
EVERY DAY
ASSHOLES
BONZOS
DREAMOS
SPIDER QUICKS
DON'T DON'T
SLEEP YA SWEATS
YA FUCKIN' DOG GANGS
YA LOUSY FENCES
GOTTA LIVE

CAN'T REMEMBER FRIENDS
GOTTA SMOKE
SWEARIN' TA BELLY

OUTTA HERE
OUTTA HERE

TAKE YA FUCKIN' PISS ROADS
AN SUFFER
YA MURDER FREE
DO
ANYTHING
LIKE
LATE MAYBE'S
DOPED

FINISHED
WADAYA KNOWS
JUDGES
HEY
UGLY GIRL
DON'T STOP
FA A CHANCE

DAGGIT
DAGGIT
FAT DRAX
SAY SAY KOOLA
NEED YA GRIEF
RAG SOUL
HEY
WHO'S KILLIN' THEM BEAT UP WHORES

SAY YOU
SCUM ASS
IT'S YOU BLUE

SCUZ CHRIST'S
FUCKED OUT
YA MONEY'S STICKIN'
OUTTA YA JOINT, MAN
YA IN FA POP CITY, MAN

DON'T SHOW
THA BIG NEWS
YA COULD BE DEAD, STUPID

IT EATS
YOUR HARD
THA CHEAPLORD
FAST FEVER
FIXIN'
SO'S YA COULD PLAY FA REAL
THA GOOD FUCK
IN YA FUCKIN CAGE
WITH THEM STUY BAPS
AN' THEM WARSAW BULLETS
GO REASON
GO REASON
TA SWEET HEAVEN

I REMEMBER YA
THA WRONG HAIR
FLIES IN THA EYES
THA FORGET ITS
ACCUSED OF NOTHINGS

TOO AFRAID
TO SAY
FA DECADES
THA MISERABLE MOTOR GOES
IT AIN'T
SCIENCE FICTION BABY
IT FUCKIN' DRIPS
LETHAL ORGANS
FOOD CLOUDS

THA FUCKIN' BONGO ROOM'S READY MAN
YEA YA KNOW THA BIG BUM BUY, RIGHT
YA KNOW
YA KNOW
THA SKY D'S
YA KNOW, YA FUCKIN' KNOW 'EM
THEM LUNOS AUTOMATIC
WIPES
AUTOMATICS
ON HAZE
AUTOMATICS
CUT TA RIBBONS
YA KNOW MAN
THEM DRILL KILLS

HEY DON'T LOOK AT ME
FA PROTECTION
TELL ME
TA GT MY FUCKIN' HANDS OFF OF YA
FUCK YOU
CRACK YA FUCKIN' SKULL

GET YASELF SOME LIFETIMES
IN SOME SHIT ROOM EXECUTION
RIGHT KING LEE
YA GOT THA STUFF KING LEE

LOOK AT YA
NO CHANCE
ON YA LIES... KING LEE
BANG YA FUCKIN' WRISTS, BABY
YEA DON'T FEEL BAD
DREAM YA NOWHERES TA GO, KING LEE
YEA, WITH YA BUSTED HEAD, KING LEE
TA GO YOU'LL BE WOLFIN'
KING LEE

RAISE HELL DEATH ROW
DUMP PAIN

SINISTER SWEARS
TWIST YA EYES
CRACKED MONGOL
TASTE
CRAZY GRAVES
TASTE
BRAIN THINGS

YA FUCKIN' DISEASE CHILDS
BONED TA DEATH
YEA...
IN SHOW MOUTH

FUCK HELL DEATH ROW
SMELL
THA DAMN FUCKIN' WAR

HEY CRACKERJACKERS
THA TWILIGHTS
OUTTA CONTROLS
THEM'S MUTILATIONS
FUCKIN' THERE, BABY

WAIT
WAITIN'
FA THA COPS

BREATHE
BREATHE
BREATHE
HAND CHAINS

FUCK AROUND MAN
LOOK FA SLOPS
FIRSTS

ONE OF THOSE EMPTY'S
IS DREAM DAD
CRAWLIN'
FA PEARLS

HEY YOU, MAKE IT ENDLESS
IT DON'T MATTER

THA SCAZ SCUMS DONE
BETTER THAN GOD
TALK NOSE TA THA BITCHES
RULE YA TOILETS

FRANKIE TEARDROP

Frankie Teardrop
20 year old Frankie
He's married, he's got a kid
& he's workin' in a factory
He's working' from 7 to 5
Just tryin' to survive
Let's hear it for Frankie
Frankie, Frankie
Frankie can't make it
Cuz things are just too hard
Frankie can't make enough money
Frankie can't buy enough food
Frankie's gettin' evicted
Let's hear it for Frankie
Frankie, Frankie
Oh Frankie, Frankie
Frankie is so desperate
He's gonna kill his wife and kid
Frankie's gonna kill his kid
Frankie picked up a gun
Pointed it at the six month old kid in the crib
Oh Frankie
Frankie looked at his wife
Shot her
What have I done
Let's hear it for Frankie
Frankie Teardrop
Frankie put the gun to his head

Frankie's dead
Frankie's lyin' in hell
We're all Frankies
We're all lyin' in hell

HOLY SKIPS

Hey what the really been away living like some crazed dog skin of my teeth in my ugly shoes hey bacho ya want to fight about it now you got the blade c'mon let's do it hey I don't want to slice the guy's face taking some garbage food hey that's what I'm about doing anything to stay alive I don't know why holy skips jumps at you hey does this shit mean staying alive maybe it does hey who the hell am I kidding slop with the blue girls hey who's useless in the hole in the hole holy skips dealing the baji boys all kinds of crap hey death what's my name I mean hard on times smashed in some tank I mean hard time holy skips hey hey released in two right holy skips jumps at you it's it holy skips jumps at you it's it can't even look the other way losing all my friends to the dead hell it's hopeless there's no way out yea try something else so what happens you get dragged back 'cause if ya fuckin' poor holy skips you're goddamned nothing holy skips nobody wants to know you you're last in line hey so what there's nothing left for you anyway hey I'm back in hell doing the hell business back into the hole it's the only way to stay around holy skips deal illegal 'cause it's fucked anyway hey take that to your girl hey I ain't no champion like who needs emergency rooms I'm getting tired of the punch outs hey fast go holy skips jumps at you it's it hey I'm tired of all kinds of assholes taking all kids of shit when was the last time for a life hey hey don't you even look at me 'cause I'll do you man real fast man don't you even fuckin' look at me cuz that't me look holy skips holy skips I'm going to put some fast shit on you so fast you don't stand a breath I mean it 'cause that's me the only one I know holy skips jumps at you it's it.

Other books from 2.13.61:

HENRY ROLLINS / Solipsist
HENRY ROLLINS / The First Five
HENRY ROLLINS / Black Coffee Blues
HENRY ROLLINS / See A Grown Man Cry-Now Watch Him Die
HENRY ROLLINS / Get In The Van
HENRY ROLLINS / Eye Scream
HENRY ROLLINS / Do I Come Here Often?
JOE COLE / Planet Joe
DON BAJEMA / Reach
DON BAJEMA / Boy In The Air
BILL SHIELDS / Human Shrapnel
BILL SHIELDS / The Southeast Asian Book Of The Dead
BILL SHIELDS / Lifetaker
BILL SHIELDS / Rosey the Baby Killer
EXENE CERVENKA / Virtual Unreality
EXENE CERVENKA & KEN JARECKE / Just Another War
IAN SHOALES / Not Wet Yet
IGGY POP / I Need More
TRICIA WARDEN / Brainlift
TRICIA WARDEN / Attack God Inside
MICHAEL GIRA / The Consumer
ROB OVERTON / Letters to Rollins
NICK CAVE / King Ink
NICK CAVE / King Ink II
NICK CAVE & THE BAD SEEDS / Fish In A Barrel
ALAN VEGA / Cripple Nation
ROSS HALFIN/ Fragile: Human Organs
ROSS HALFIN / Metallica: The Photographs of Ross Halfin
STEPHANIE CHERNIKOWSKI / Dream Baby Dream
THE PHOTOGRAPHER'S LED ZEPPELIN
ROKY ERICKSON / Openers II
JOE CARDUCCI / Rock & The Pop Narcotic
NICK ZEDD / Totem Of The Depraved
HENRY MILLER / Dear Dear Brenda
ART FEIN / The L.A. Musical History Tour
ELLYN MAYBE / The Cowardice of Amnesia
JEFFREY LEE PIERCE / Go Tell The Mountain